To Eloise

CONTENTS

ACKNOWLEDGMENTS

A CENTURY AGO JOHN HUMPHREY NOYES ASKED, "HAS ANY ATTEMPT at close association ever succeeded, which took marriage into it substantially as it exists in ordinary society?" This question challenged me to examine the literature and records of the major utopian communities of the nineteenth century in America in an effort to determine if communal societies could indeed exist over an extended period while maintaining the nuclear family. I am deeply indebted to Dr. Russell B. Nye, Professor of English at Michigan State University, for his encouragement to pursue an answer to Noyes' long neglected query.

Dr. Joseph C. Kiger, Chairman of the Department of History at the University of Mississippi, has been extremely cooperative in giving me suggestions in pursuit of evidence and in offering advice on matters of style.

Miss Shirley Birdsall and her library staff at Harding College are to be commended for their many hours of labor in ferreting out obscure materials. Dr. James D. Bales allowed me access to his vast library of materials on Mormonism and the Shakers. Mr. Fred Bailey was most helpful in securing documents from the University of Tennessee Library. Miss Barbara Oliver, my secretary, patiently attended to many mechanical jobs which were time-consuming but essential to any research project.

My wife, Eloise, proofread the manuscript and made several valuable suggestions from which I greatly profited. I have appreciated her willingness to play the role of a "researcher's widow" during the long and arduous months of compiling material for this volume.

Sex and Marriage

in Utopian Communities

Prologue

NEARLY TWO THOUSAND COMMUNES LOCATED IN THIRTY-FOUR STATES now flourish in remote mountain regions, rundown farmhouses, and cluttered city apartments in America. The average commune consists of fifteen or so persons, usually in their late teens or early twenties, who are allegedly seeking an escape from the traditional life style of the nuclear family. Dissatisfied with society as it now is in the artificial, impersonal, suburban environment, they have embarked on a path which they hope will lead to things as they should be. But this path was traveled a century ago by utopian idealists who somehow never managed to arrive at their destination.

Modern communes vary in their purposes, ideals, and functions, much like those of a century ago in America. Groups of unrelated persons committed to living together and mutually sharing their resources come in various shapes and sizes. Some are political in orientation, others are non-political, vegetarians and non-vegetarians, free sex and celibate, authoritarian and leaderless. Most are just collections of establishment drop-outs. Whether they call themselves a commune, cooperative, colony, or affinity group, they have rejected the traditional life style that is based on the concept that only those who are bound by blood or legal ties can live together as a family.

Agricultural communes attempt to support themselves by growing their own produce and selling surpluses to wholesale and retail establishments. In reaction to a polluted environment, some cooperatives have been formed to bring their members close to raw nature and to preserve a small part of the world in its natural beauty. They often support themselves by collecting cans and bottles for recycling. Several arts and crafts colonies have been organized to afford their members an opportunity to ply their creative talents both for monetary profit and inner satisfaction. Political ideologists, feeling out of sorts with the present political order of modern America, have formed communities wherein they share their ideologies in rap sessions but rarely carry their revolutionary ideas beyond the pale of their unique domiciles. Religious communes, not altogether unlike the Perfectionists, Harmonists, and Inspirationists of the nineteenth century, have been formed within the last decade to permit their brotherhoods an escape from a materialistic society with its attendant frustrations. Modern spiritualists have culled the teachings and rituals of oriental religions and dwell together in remote areas, where they attempt to draw near to their newly found deities as well as to one another. Some communes have no permanent address but are always on the move in vehicles gayly decorated with flowers, peace symbols, and slogans.

The commune is definitely becoming a way of life for more and more Americans. Realtors, eager to capitalize on the movement, have begun to mark out plots specifically for the communal life style. The inner cities of San Francisco, Chicago, Boston, New York, and St. Louis are prize pickings for those who wish to secure large apartments cheaply, knock down walls and make accommodations for colonies of fifteen or twenty people. Most large universities are ringed with boarding houses where both male and female students live together as families. "Mother Jones," "Fishermen Collective," "Committee on Public Safety," and other such exotic titles mark the living quarters of those in pursuit of an alternate life style. This is a new social frontier in which people have forsaken the uptight society fostered by the Protestant ethic and have laid claim to new human relationships.

Utopian communities established in America during the nineteenth century also provided unique laboratories for the testing of social ideas. The new nation was particularly suited to those who wished to take leave of the present evil society in order to pursue an idealistic course. There was room in America for almost any kind of experiment. The seemingly endless frontier afforded an escape from the Old World variables which would interfere with the laboratory-like conditions essential for an experiment in group living. Freedom to "pursue happiness" was a theoretical principle which had been expounded by the founders of the republic and which received an annual reaffirmation in public assemblies on the Fourth of July. Under these conditions, religious and social dreamers were eager to try their particular social panaceas.

Three basically different types of utopian community were founded in the nineteenth century in America: (1) the sectarian communities, inspired by a common desire for the good life on earth, but particularly for eternal life; (2) the reform communities, which attempted to lead the world to a perfect order through the application of reform principles on a small scale, and which trusted others, and eventually the whole world, to follow their example; and (3) the purely economic cooperatives, which sought to alleviate the distresses of their members by combining their resources apart from the harsh competition of capitalism.

Chronologically, despite some overlapping, the three types of utopian community fell into the following periods: (1) the sectarian communities, some of which had their origin in the preceding century, were at their zenith during the first half of the century; (2) the reform communities were popular during the three decades preceding the Civil War; and (3) the economic cooperatives came into vogue during the last quarter of the century.

The economic bases of utopian communities ranged all the way from pure communism to laissez-faire capitalism. The majority, however, attempted some form of socialism. The Fourieristic phalanxes were joint-stock companies and many of the stockholders were not citizens of the communities in which they held stock. Appeals were made in their literature for capitalists to invest in their enterprises with the promise of sizable returns for their investments.[1] The sectarian communal experiments practiced some form of collective economy and were generally noted for their industry and relative prosperity. They were usually drawn from the lower socio-economic classes and blindly followed their charismatic leaders.[2] They were required to subscribe to a particular religious creed from which the slightest deviation was not tolerated. Their communistic communities existed for the purpose of isolating their membership from the evil influences of the world.[3] Mutual sharing of property also assured them of the necessities of life on an often alien and hostile frontier.

Millennialism, or belief in the imminent advent of Jesus Christ and his thousand-year reign on earth, was another factor which figured prominently in most sectarian utopian communities. The communal arrangement was perfectly suited to a proper preparation for the millennium, wherein only the righteous would inhabit the earth. The amassing of private fortunes held little incentive to those who sincerely expected to hear the last trumpet of God at any moment. Sectarian communal experiments increased their membership during times of intense revivalism. Society's sins were given a thorough exposure in pulpits until it was little wonder that those with tender consciences sought an escape in idyllic communities. The Catholic church had monasteries for those who wished such an escape. The celibate Shaker, Rappite, and Zoarite communities were, for all practical purposes, Protestant monasteries. Whether celibate or monogamous, the sectarian communities had one thing in common: the withdrawal of a chosen few from the contamination of human wickedness.

The Perfectionists of New England were also communal architects. The Calvinists had long regarded man as totally depraved, but Jacksonian Americans revolted against this somber assessment. Signs of discontent began to be manifested in the very citadel of Calvinist New England, during the early years of the nineteenth century. Calvinistic ministers were charged with having lost touch with reality as they engaged in "spinning cob-web systems between the worm-eaten rafters, quite oblivious to the common sense world on the outside." [4] John Quincy Adams sensed the change and confided to his Diary that "since the establishment of the theological school at Andover, the Calvinists and Unitarians have been battling with each other upon the atonement, the divinity of Jesus Christ and the Trinity. This has now very much subsided; but other wandering of mind takes the place of that, and equally lets the wolf into the fold." [5] Human perfectibility through self-reliance, apart from the agency of the sedentary clergy, was the wolf that Adams feared. It opened up a completely new world for those who dared to dream and gave impetus to dozens of new religious sects during the turbulent thirties and forties. Utopians of this era believed that man was not naturally depraved but virtuous, and that a favorable environment was needed to bring him to perfection. Man was not only good, but far better than many of his inherited institutions. True perfectibility could come only with a complete withdrawal from society. John Humphrey Noyes believed that he had created that ideal environment at the Putney and the Oneida communities.

The Perfectionists represented a transitional stage between the sectarian communities and the social reform communities of the 1840s. To be sure, Robert Owen's New Harmony experiment of the 1820s had spawned several reform communities, but the real epidemic of utopias broke out two decades later with the appearance of at least fifty communities. Ralph Waldo Emerson wrote to Thomas Carlyle in the autumn of 1840: "We are a little wild here with numberless projects of social reform. Not a reading man but has a draft of a new community in his waistcoat pocket." [6]

The panic of 1837 and its aftermath created a reform sentiment the like of which America had never experienced. Every institution was called before the bar of human reason and asked to give account. Laissez-faire industrialism was regarded as the real culprit in creating the disparity between the "haves" and the "have nots" in the considered judgment of men like Horace Greeley, William E. Channing, Charles Dana, and Albert Brisbane. The latter had recently returned from France, where he had sat at the feet of Charles Fourier and had become enamored of his utopian scheme to rid the world of capitalistic abuses. Fourier himself had drunk deeply of the philosophies of Rousseau and Morelly, and concluded that man's depravity was due to bad institutions and not inherent by nature. If the institutions under which he was living were improved, his natural virtue would reassert itself. Fourier's plan called for the establishment of phalanxes in which sixteen hundred to two thousand men, women, and children were "scientifically organized" to form the basic social unit of a regenerated world.[7]

The pictures of Fourier's new world, not wholly unlike those painted by Robert Owen, presented a sharp contrast to the living conditions in an industrial village. Orestes Brownson described a New England factory town in the 1840s in terms calculated to elicit a sympathetic response from social reformers. Brownson wrote in the *Boston Quarterly Review:*

> We know no sadder sight on earth than one of our factory villages presents when the bell, at break of day, or at the hour of breakfast or dinner, calls out its hundreds or thousands of operatives. We stand and look at these hard-working men and women hurrying in all directions and ask ourselves where go the proceeds of their labors? The man who employs them for whom they are toiling as so many

> slaves. . . . He shouts for liberty, stickles for equality, is horrified at the Southern planter who keeps slaves.[8]

Such observations as these inspired George Ripley, Horace Greeley, and Albert Brisbane to seek a solution for the working people in America by establishing cooperative communities in which the environment would be changed to suit man's nature rather than to pervert the natural man to suit an unnatural and ill-conceived, competitive society. Theirs was an effort to turn the clock back, to reject competitive capitalism in favor of a medieval type of guild harmony and order in which each man had his place. However, the retreat into a pastoral Brook Farm or an idyllic Fruitlands did not appear to them to be reactionary. They were men's redeemers. They were attempting to peg progress at a given point by establishing a few communities in which men could live happily and attract the attention of outsiders and thereby inspire them to join the ever-increasing band who marched toward a better world. Etienne Cabet, for one, claimed that the world was but fifty years away from a perfect natural order.[9]

The majority of the transcendentalists, although they gave encouragement, refused to join in the ventures of the associationists. They regarded collectivism as a threat to the individualism which they prized as essential to human happiness. Emerson claimed that he had not conquered his own house and he did not wish to remove from his "present prison to a prison a little larger." [10] He regarded the plans to bring the good and the like-minded into a community arrangement as folly, and argued that it was "better that they should disperse and so leaven the whole lump of society." [11] Henry David Thoreau preferred Walden Pond to a crowded phalanx. The transcendentalist William H. Channing, on the other hand, saw "cooperative individualism" as man's only hope and was an ardent supporter of Brook Farm.

The reformist utopians differed from the sectarian utopians in the main on two counts: spiritual salvation was not the aim of the reform communities, as they were concerned about the regeneration of man in his daily life; and, although the appeal of the reformists was in the behalf of the poverty-stricken wage earners, they, unlike the peasant religious communes, were almost to a man from the upper or middle classes. One thing they both, however, had in common: they implicitly believed in a millennium. The reformists' millennium was to be a heaven on earth without the literal reign of Jesus Christ and possibly exceeding the thousand-year limit. In a lecture delivered by Charles Dana before the New England Fourier Society in Boston, March 7, 1844, he announced: "Our ulterior aim is nothing less than Heaven on Earth,—the conversion of this globe, now exhaling pestilential vapors and possessed by unnatural climates, into the abode of beauty and health, and the restitution to Humanity of the Divine Image, now so long lost and forgotten." [12]

The Civil War dampened the spirit of the social utopians. Oneida and several of the sectarian communities managed to survive but no new ones were begun. The urge toward communal panaceas was also neutralized by the rise of Marxism. Karl Marx was highly critical of the utopians for their limited views and oversimplifications of complex problems.[13] The Marxian thesis did not fully take hold in America, as most Americans preferred an increase in wages, shorter working hours, and a few social benefits to world revolution. Communism began to take on sinister connotations. Josiah Warren might be tolerated when he preached anarchy at Modern Times on Long Island, but the subject had little appeal to the post-Civil-War American. Individual freedom was a reality, at least to the majority of the people, and there was little point in becoming a socialist in a land where opportunities for getting richer abounded. America was yet a young nation and her potentials were still unexplored. To destroy the system at this point would be suicidal. Capitalism as an ideology became more palatable as a new crop of millionaires, many of whom had risen from the depths of poverty, had proved that in America every man had the opportunity to pull himself up by his own bootstraps and improve his station in life.

The same inequities and injustices which drew the wrath of the utopian reformers in the antebellum period persisted, but other channels of dealing with these problems were opened which were more direct and realistic than that of utopian communities. Industrial workers combined their efforts in labor unions in order that their discontent might be heard in a single and powerful voice. Political parties, realizing the need for votes, promised legislation to alleviate the distresses of the working people. Marxists had attempted to purge socialism of its utopian elements, but the community idea, although dormant for nearly twenty-five years, was not altogether dead. Stripped of its pastoral and idyllic features, the community could accept industrialism as a fact of modern life.

Economic cooperatives appeared the answer, particularly to those who were caught in the daily treadmill of a northern industrial village. J. A. Wayland, who published a socialist paper, *The Coming Nation*, in Greensburg, Indiana, was the arch proponent of the cooperative community idea and was largely responsible for the founding of the Ruskin Cooperative, ten miles from Dixson, Tennessee. For a small capital investment a worker could join the community with his family and share in the benefits of scientific socialism. Here he could ply his skill in an enterprise whose profits would revert to the community at large and not settle in the hands of greedy entrepreneurs. In addition to economic advantages, cooperatives promised social and educational opportunities often denied the industrial workers.

Such were the utopian communities of the nineteenth century. The American spirit was one of optimism, since only the truly optimistic dare to attempt impossible dreams. When the concept of the unlimited perfectibility of mankind was added to this optimism, the golden age which would put every other civilization in the shadows was believed to be ready to dawn in America. But the utopians were or became disillusioned. They found the task of trying to perfect imperfect human beings impossible. The communities of the social reformists lasted no more than five or six years at the most, and the economic cooperatives fared little better. A few cooperatives continued into the twentieth century but were torn asunder by internal strife, which usually ended in litigation.

Some 500 communities existed in nineteenth-century America. I have limited my study to those which appear to be original and unique in their approach to sex and marriage.

I

Germs of New Institutions and New Modes of Action

UTOPIAN COMMUNITIES IN NINETEENTH-CENTURY AMERICA WERE BEST remembered for their experiments in the unique and the untried, but they also had to wrestle with the problem of what to do with the ordinary and commonly accepted institutions of the society from which they withdrew. Rousseau, from whom many American utopians received inspiration, pointed out that the present social system, founded on convention, was an artificial arrangement which must be altered.[1] The North American Phalanx pled in its propaganda for all who were imbued with the communal spirit to join them in planting "the germs of new institutions," and in adopting "new modes of action." [2]

Usually a written credo or constitution, framed by the founders and subscribed to by the members, laid down the order of the community and the choice of institutions was not left to the discretion of the members. Some communities were at the arbitrary will of their leaders in these matters, who claimed divine inspiration or whose wisdom none dared to counter. Often institutions were added, dismissed, or altered as trial and error warranted. An amendment or a new constitution was an admission of error and indicated a determination to admit to the realities of group living. New Harmony, under the Owenites, had a total of seven constitutions in less than three years. The new constitution of Brook Farm in 1844 admitted that after nearly three years' existence, "the misfortunes and mistakes incident to an undertaking so new and so little understood . . ." had led them to take a new direction in their experiment.[3]

If the community were intensely religious, a special "revelation" from God was all that was needed for a change in institutions. Joseph Smith is reported to have received a revelation authorizing the adoption of polygyny[4] at Nauvoo, Illinois, in 1843.[5] The same God, however, was claimed to have revealed to Ann Lee, the founder of the Shaker society, the necessity for the adoption of celibacy.[6]

In determining the institutions of a utopian community, one basic factor had to be observed: those which threatened the communal spirit by causing one to seek his own interest, or the interest of a particular group within the community, above the interest of the community at large, would have to be greatly modified or excluded. The one institution which more than any other caused concern among the communitarians was that of the individual or private family based upon monogamy, the most ancient of all social arrangements.

Utopians have wrestled through the centuries with the problem of what to do with the family. Plato, in his *Republic*, solved the problem quite handily on paper: he forbade marriage, established a community of wives, and put the children under the supervision of the state, where they were reared completely oblivious of their parents' identity. The Essenes of ancient Palestine, who practiced communal living, abolished the family and chose to live in the state of celibacy.[7] Sir Thomas More did not attempt to grapple with this thorny problem but assumed that the family could co-exist in the communal arrangement without any major harm coming to either institution. He did propose that if one family had an excess of children they should be distributed among the households which had too few.[8]

Marriage and the family were regarded as the basic foundations of the society and the state in nineteenth-century America. To attack these institutions was to undermine the political and social order. All of a woman's experience and training before marriage were designed to prepare her for the role of a future wife and mother. Margaret Fuller aptly described the American woman in that era:

> As a little girl she is to learn the lighter family duties, while she acquires that limited acquaintance with the realm of literature and science that will enable her to superintend the instruction of children in their earliest years. It is not generally proposed that she should be sufficiently instructed and developed to understand the pursuits or aims of her future husband; she is not to be a help-meet to him in the way of companionship and counsel, except in the care of his house and children.[9]

The family exists, however, for the benefit of the wife and mother. The long duration of human infancy and childhood necessitates an arrangement where the mother and child are assured sustenance and protection. The family also exists for the socialization of the child. It is his microcosm of society, which is fashioned according to society's accepted patterns of living, and in which the child learns to adjust to the larger social arrangement outside of the home. The monogamous marriage has come to be regarded in Western civilization as the most feasible domestic institution for the socialization of children. Organized religion has heartily endorsed monogamy and has declared all other relations between the sexes sinful. The state concurs and declares any deviation from monogamy to be illegal.

The utopians of the nineteenth century encountered difficulty with monogamous marriages and the family on the threshold of their experiments. The communal arrangement, particularly where all lived in unitary housing, ate at a common table, and the sexes came into daily contact with each other, was totally different from the typically isolated family in America. John Hyde Preston, who lived in a commune in North Carolina in the 1930s, identified this problem when he wrote of his experiences:

> The initial shock was staggering. After some years of quiet householding in the Connecticut countryside we suddenly found ourselves forced to sit down to three meals a day with eighty-five to a hundred people, ranging in age from seven to seventy; we had to live, eat, sleep, and work in the midst of all those people and we even had to be polite to them before breakfast. The result was that we lost our appetites, slept badly, and did no work at all. The baby caught our jitters like a disease and filled with her screams the only

> hours we had alone. By the end of the first week we had decided that the whole business was intolerable. We stayed only because we were too broke to move. Every morning we walked up the mountain—the only escape from the people who seemed to have no understanding of two unregenerate individualists—and desperately discussed a way out of this mess. . . . Something very subtle happens to the average marriage. Perhaps the first thing that happens is that it is gravely endangered.[10]

The Jewish Kibbutzim, not unlike the communistic experiments of the nineteenth century in America, have had their problems with those who chose to place the interests of their families above that of the community. Henrik Infield, who has written a history of the modern Jewish communities, observes:

> The most crucial kind of internal trouble arises . . . from some basic attitudes of the women. . . . She may feel neglected when he [her husband] gives all of his time to the community, and she may go so far even as to sabotage the formation of a Neighbor Group for fear that, 'with so much intimacy,' her husband may get himself entangled with another woman. Yet, on the whole, she does her share. It is only when there are children she may balk. She will resent nothing more than seeing them neglected by their father and she may confront him with a choice between his home and the community. Conflicts of this kind, as we know from the early history of the Kvutza, are apt to destroy many a struggling group.[11]

The current communal movement in the United States, which finds its origin in the hippie tribalism of the 1950s, is experimenting in a wide range of group relations in search of a viable counter culture. Although most of the modern utopians prefer the traditional family arrangement while they enjoy the benefits of a collective economy, there are several who have abandoned the nuclear family as being inconsistent with the ideals of communal life and have adopted group marriage. The concept of group marriage differs widely among present-day communitarians. On a continuum from left to right they range from the practice of uninhibited sexual permissiveness, to the mutual sharing of husbands, wives and lovers within defined limits, to living under the same roof but stoutly condemning marital infidelity.[12] The Moorehouse communes in the San Francisco Bay area, and Lama, near Taos, New Mexico, represent the position on the far left. There are no restrictions in these communes as to who sleeps with whom. The members must relinquish all claims to private property, change their names, and completely submerge their identity into the group.[13] One observer, who with his wife lived in one such commune in the Pacific Northwest, recently claimed: "What we were doing with each other, it turned out, was 'coupling' (images of dogs or railroad cars, and those were exactly the overtones)." [14]

The fatality rate of these types of communes is extremely high, conservatively estimated to be about 50 percent within a year or two.[15] Many members in search of approved sexual license join these communes and leave within a few weeks. Unless the members are committed to a higher cause than mere sexual gratification, group marriages have failed to afford satisfying and lasting relationships. The system demands a self-discipline which the average utopian-minded individual is rarely able to acquire because of his freedom-loving nature. The attitudes and skills of group living are not quickly developed. It is difficult enough for two people to live together for more than a few months without getting on one another's nerves. The problem is compounded many times over when fifteen or more people share the same love nest.

The homophile liberation movement has given rise to a type of community unlike any of those of the nineteenth-century utopian experiments: the homosexual commune. The purpose of these communes is to provide an asylum for the gay set and to permit them to share a life style denied them in ordinary society. Admission requirements are strict and only homophiles are permitted to join.[16]

John Humphrey Noyes perceived the problem that the separate family in communal life would create. In 1870 he queried: "Has any attempt at close association ever succeeded which took marriage into it substantially as it exists in ordinary society?" [17] Noyes did not believe it would be possible and opposed the members of his Oneida community maintaining the monogamous relationship. Robert Owen, in setting forth the goals of the New Harmony experiment, stated that they were "to change from the individual to the social system; from single families with separate interests to communities of families with one interest." [18] Owen regarded the family as the main bulwark in the defense of private property and divisive individualism, which he believed undermined the bases of communal living.

Charles Lane, who was associated for a time with Bronson Alcott and Fruitlands, attempted to come to grips with the issue of marriage and the family in communal living in one of his articles in the transcendentalist magazine, *The Dial.* In the essay, written in January 1844, Lane asserted that monogamous marriage and the family form the chief cornerstone of present society and that:

> The question of Association and of marriage are one. If, as we have been properly led to believe, the individual or separate family is in the true order of Providence, then the Associative life is a false effort. If the Associative life is true, then is the separate family a false arrangement. By the maternal feeling, it appears to be decided that the coexistence of both is incompatible, it is impossible. . . . The monasteries and convents, which have existed in all ages, have been maintained solely by the annihilation of that peculiar affection on which the separate family is based.[19]

Emerson agreed with Lane on this point and regarded communal living as having failed because the women associated with the movement were not by nature adapted to the rigorous demands which were made in sacrificing the privacy of home life. He concluded that "It was to them like the brassy and lacquered life in hotels. The common school was well enough, but to the common nursery they had grave objections. Eggs might be hatched in ovens, but the hen on her own account much preferred the old way. A hen without her chickens was but half a hen." [20]

In attempting to create a new social order in which the family no longer occupied the central position, utopians were generally concerned about the new role of women. Practically all of them attempted to demonstrate how their program of economic reform would bring about the liberation of womanhood. If women no longer depended on their husbands for a livelihood and were regarded as equal in all matters, their status would be measurably altered. Some of the leading feminists of the nineteenth century were directly or indirectly associated with the utopian communities. Frances Wright, founder of the Nashoba community near Memphis, Tennessee, was actively involved in the Owenite community at New Harmony, Indiana, and became an early spokesman for equal rights for women in America. Margaret Fuller was identified with the Brook Farm community, and, although not a member of the colony, she found the utopians there receptive to her ideas regarding the liberation of her sex. Robert Dale Owen, son of the founder of New Harmony, became the leading proponent of women's property rights in the Indiana State Constitutional Convention in 1850. The Shakers led the way in granting equal rights to women. The Fourierist and Owenite, as well as the transcendentalist, communities were noted for their feminism. Since the success of their endeavors depended on the cooperation and companionship of the women, they shared in the decision-making process in community affairs.

The removal of the family from its central position in society brought additional responsibilities to the utopian communities. New institutions and new modes of action were devised to fill the vacuum created by the abdication of parental care and education. The communities took on the responsibility for the education, feeding, and clothing of the children of the members. In some instances, the children were removed from their parents at an early age and housed in nurseries, where parents were not allowed to communicate with their offspring.

Utopians proceeded with unflagging optimism toward a solution to the problem of what to do with the monogamous family. New institutions were created and old ones were modified; not all communities followed the same pattern. Some insisted that the family must co-exist with the communal arrangement. The Icarians went so far as to make marriage mandatory for all adult members. Some, like the Shakers and the Rappites, could not envision success unless the husband and wife severed the marital bond and agreed to live a celibate life. The Mormons, in order to turn attention away from individual to social well-being in their communities, adopted polygyny. The perfectionists at Putney, Oneida, and Wallingford adopted the unique system of "complex marriage," where every man was theoretically married to every woman in the community and vice versa. Free love was practiced at Josiah Warren's Modern Times on Long Island, and in several of the economic cooperative communities of the latter part of the nineteenth century.

The purpose of this volume is to show how the utopian communities of the nineteenth century dealt with sex and marriage: what institutions and what modes of action were developed in order to ameliorate the difficulty posed by the separate family within the communal arrangement.

II

They Neither Marry Nor Are Given in Marriage

FAMILY LIFE BASED ON MONOGAMY CONSTITUTED A STUMBLING BLOCK to communitarians in the nineteenth century, particularly when all things were shared in common. Advocates of communism proposed to abolish, alter, or regulate the institution of marriage. Some religious communities, taking their cue from the monastic orders and from the New Testament Scriptures, found celibacy the simplest and best answer to this problem. If one vowed to live a life of virgin purity he could seek what was in the best interest of both God and the community, rather than what was best for a wife and children. Celibate communities made frequent references in their literature to the statement of the Apostle Paul, who said, "He that is unmarried careth for the things that belong to the Lord, how he may please the Lord: but he that is married careth for the things of the world, how he may please his wife." [1]

Strong theological underpinnings and clearly defined regulations were needed to insure proper social intercourse of men and women who lived in daily contact with one another. Theological arguments in favor of separation of the sexes usually followed the same line of reasoning: Adam and Eve were untainted with sin until they lusted for one another and allowed their animal passions to dominate them.

To return to the pure, original Adamic state one must conquer his flesh and live above its desires. The only way to insure this was to live the celibate life. The community served to isolate the righteous few from the corruption of worldly influences. While in the community one must rigidly control himself in all of his fleshly appetites. In order to assist him in conquering the flesh, a set of rules having the force of law was given him. If he found temptation too much to resist patiently, the religious communities, like the monastic orders, had a method of confession to a superior which assured him a complete catharsis and encouragement to rise above the temptations of the flesh.

Foremost among the early American utopian communities which practiced celibacy was the United Society of Believers, more popularly known as the Shakers. Celibacy was not adopted by the Shakers because their experiences in communal living called for such a drastic move to prevent marriage and propagation. Unlike most celibate communities, the Shakers had incorporated celibacy into their doctrine before any attempt was made at communal life. Prohibition of sexual relations was the result of the personal attitudes toward sex of the founder of the order, Ann Lee.

Ann Lee developed her theory about sex while in England before immigrating to America. She had married a blacksmith, Abraham Stanley, in 1762 and her marriage was anything but happy, mainly because of her deep-seated aversion to the conjugal act. She gave birth to four children, all of whom died in infancy. The birth of her last child was particularly difficult and Ann Lee nearly lost her life. She later regarded her own agony and the death of her children as God's punishment for her concupiscence.[2]

Ann Lee joined a society of Quakers in Manchester, England, in 1758 and because of the group's unusual and violent manifestations of religious fervor, they were known as the Shaking Quakers. Shaking Quakers were accused of a variety of "crimes," and were frequently haled into court in Manchester. Ann Lee was among the number accused of Sabbath breaking in 1770. While she was in jail she received her alleged vision of the fall of man in which Jesus appeared to her and showed her that the foundation of human depravity was the sexual relations of Adam and Eve in the Garden of Eden.[3] The Shaking Quakers of Manchester accepted Ann's inspiration and her leadership, and from that time forward referred to her affectionately as Mother Ann.

Ann Lee was afraid of her own sexual impulses, which may have been extremely powerful,[4] and was ashamed that her body possessed such a craving for sex. Complete abstinence from the sex act gave her a sense of triumph. Her husband once complained to the cathedral authorities in Manchester of his wife's refusal to share his bed.[5] She separated from her husband and resumed her maiden name. Ann Lee was eager to share her sexual liberation ideas with others, even when they were not welcome. Her father became distressed when she scolded her own mother for her "carnal acts of indulgence" in the marriage bed.[6]

In order to institutionalize celibacy among the Shakers, Ann Lee developed an intricate system of theology, beginning with the nature of God and progressing through the history of man to the present. God was regarded as both male and female, fully capable of reproducing himself. Man was made in the image of God, also a dual-sexed creature.[7] God commanded man to "be fruitful and multiply and replenish the earth," but only within "the times and seasons appointed by the Creator and established in the law of nature."[8] But man disobeyed God and lusted for his companion in the Garden of Eden. The temptation appealed to man's animal nature and he relinquished the "governing power of his soul . . . and gave loose to his animal desires and under this excitement yielded to the temptation. This occasioned his fall; and hence the loss which ensued." [9] The woman, who before was on an equality with man, was guilty of tempting man and thus was made subservient to man after the fall.

The history of man, according to Shaker theology, is divided into four separate eras in which the institutions of one era were not to be carried over into the next. The first era was one of unbridled passion, where "every thought and imagination of man was only evil." [10] This era ended with the flood, in which Noah and his family were said to be the only survivors. The second era was one in which the Mosaic Law regulated and restrained sexual relations. However, this law also sanctioned war, revenge, private property, marriage, reproduction, and many other Judaical practices. The Shakers conceded that these were proper under Judaism, "but very wrong, impossible for Christians to practice." [11] The third era was inaugurated by the coming of the male messiah, Jesus Christ, who exemplified purity in his fleshly body by remaining celibate. His church was founded on five leading principles: (1) common property; (2) a life of celibacy; (3) non-resistance; (4) a separate and distinct government; and (5) power over physical disease. The church apostatized, owing to the influence of the anti-Christ, and degenerated to its nadir during the Dark Ages, as exemplified by the shockingly immoral lives of many of the clergy. The fourth era was ushered in by the second coming of Christ, this time in female form in the person of Mother Ann Lee. Her mystic experiences confirmed an affinity between herself and Christ as she announced, "I Converse with Christ. . . . I feel him present with me, as sensibly as I feel my hands together. . . . I am married to the Lord Jesus Christ. He is my head and my husband, and I have no other." [12] With the coming of the female messiah, woman regained her equality with man and Eden was restored.

Perfectionism was a cardinal point of Shaker theology. Once man mastered his fleshly lusts he could be as the angels of heaven. James Whitaker boasted that he had so completely subdued the flesh that he had "no more lust than an infant . . . or a child unborn." [13] Perfection could only be attained by an admission into the Inner or Gospel Order of Shakers. The Outer Order consisted of the unregenerated. Here the law of nature prevailed. It was not necessarily the order of the eternally damned, for here one might have opportunity to undergo purification in the next world. Marriage was not condemned in the Outer Order, nor was private property or any of the other institutions of society as long as the law of nature was not violated. In the official *Roll and Book* the Outer Order was admonished "that all such as desire to live in nature propagating their own species, keep the law of nature unviolated, as I [God] have commanded from the beginning." [14] The Outer Order was also admonished to use discretion and common sense in propagation. Nature, the Shakers maintained, did not require that the reproductive organs be used simply because they existed. The celibate life, while one was yet in the Outer Order, was the sensible way to begin the task of conquering the physical nature in preparation for admission into the Inner Order. But if one were unable to part with every gratification of the flesh, marriage was condoned in the Outer Order. Ann Lee once admonished David Moseley:

> . . . unless you are able to take up a full cross, and part with every gratification of the flesh, for the Kingdom of God, I would counsel you, and all such, to take wives in a lawful manner, and cleave to

> them only; and raise up a lawful posterity, and be perpetual servants to your families; for of all lustful gratifications that is the least sin.[15]

The propagation of the human species was not regarded as sinful; but only the lust which attended sexual intercourse. Therefore if one were convinced that he had full control of his passions, and if he were "able to lay the propensities of lust entirely aside, and enter upon that work without the influence of any other motive than solely that of obeying the will of God, in the propagation of a legitimate offspring," the sexual act was not regarded sinful.[16]

To enter the Inner or Gospel Order under the law of grace and to live as do the angels was the goal of every sincere Shaker convert. In the beginning, before communal life began, most of the converts were young men and women in their early twenties who were willing to sublimate their normal sexual desires for the joys of a novel and ecstatic religion. "The first and chief requirement, on admission," wrote Elder Albert Thomas, "is that the neophyte shall make a complete and open confession of his sins of his whole past life to two elders of his or her own sex; and the completeness of his confession is rigidly demanded." [17] If a candidate for the Inner Order was married to an unbeliever, he was not admitted until a separation was mutually agreed on by both husband and wife, or a legal separation was effected under the civil law. If the husband were the convert, he had to give his wife her share of his possessions.[18] If there were children, they were to be provided for and placed either within the society or with others who would care for them properly. Married couples were admitted to the Inner Order but from the moment of their admission they were to live as brother and sister in separate quarters. The wife relinquished her husband's name and resumed her maiden name in order to eradicate, as much as possible, all traces of the marriage. Once in the Inner Order one was admonished to "keep the law of Grace where the dominion of Christ is established in souls, and where the law of Grace reigns, and the law of nature is superseded." [19] In this Order and this Order alone was perfection to be found. The Inner Order was also regarded as the Resurrection Order, since Jesus had said, "For in the resurrection, they neither marry, nor are given in marriage, but are as the angels of God in heaven." [20] But even angels have reportedly fallen, and the Shaker was cautioned to cleanse himself frequently with confession and prayer and to be on constant alert against the temptations of the flesh. Although he was *in* the world, he was reminded that he was not *of* the world.

The Shakers, while yet in England and for ten years after their arrival in America, did not practice communal living. A. J. Macdonald claimed that Mother Ann Lee received a revelation while in England which directed her to come to America and to separate her followers from the world in communes.[21] There is no evidence to support this in any of the Shaker writings. Communal living appears to have been adopted by the Shakers more out of expediency than revelation. Upon coming to America in 1774 most of the Shakers went into the back country of New York state in search of farm employment, while a remnant, including Ann Lee, remained in New York City. Mother Ann nursed her alcoholic husband, with whom she had reunited, but not as a wife, until he eloped with another woman. It was mainly through the efforts of James Whitaker and Joseph Meacham that the Shakers were gathered into communistic communities. The latter complained that his preaching was making little progress, especially as regards the doctrine of celibacy, and urged that the Shakers gather in communes for survival.[22] Ann Lee died on September 8, 1784, before a Shaker community could be organized. Whitaker and Meacham hastened to establish the first Shaker village at Watervliet, New York, in 1787.

The Rappites were also noted for their celibacy, but unlike the Shakers, their doctrine on the subject was not developed until after they had experienced three years of communal life in America. George Rapp was the founder of the Harmonist Society in Württemberg, Germany, in 1787 and came to America in 1803 in order to gather his flock of some three hundred families into an experiment of communal life in a land he hoped would be more tolerant than his native country. The Harmonists settled in three successive colonies in America: Harmony, Pennsylvania in 1804; Harmony, Indiana in 1814; and Economy, Pennsylvania in 1824. Prosperity and piety were the earmarks of each community. The Harmonists were almost entirely from the peasant class and implicitly accepted Rapp's leadership. D. E. Nevin, who visited the Harmonists at Economy, Pennsylvania, thirty years after the death of George Rapp, noted the reverence with which they continued to speak his name. " 'Father Rapp says it,' " Nevin wrote, "was enough to settle all questions of duty, sacred or secular, and quiet the controversy." [23] George Rapp's dictatorial powers over his followers were based on his alleged divine inspiration. The German pietists regarded him as God's medium and to refuse to obey him was to refuse to obey God. Robert Dale Owen, whose father purchased the Rappite community at Harmony, Indiana, claimed the Harmonists had bought their security and prosperity

> by unquestioning submission to an autocrat who had been commissioned—perhaps as he really believed, certainly as he alleged—by God himself. He bade them do this and that, and they did it; required them to say, as the disciples in Jerusalem said, that none of the things they possess were their own, and they said it; commanded them to forego wedded life and all its incidents, and to this also they assented.[24]

The Rappites, like the Shakers, envisioned the community idea as the most feasible arrangement for protecting the saints from the evil influences of the world. The economic value of such an enterprise was also attractive to the German peasants, who were unable individually to purchase even the cheapest of lands in America. Collectively they succeeded in amassing a sizable fortune. Much of their success must be attributed to George Rapp's adopted son, Frederick, who acted as business manager for the three communities. William Faux reported from Harmony, Indiana, in 1819:

> They keep no accounts, and all business is done and everything is possessed in Frederick Rapp's name. They have been in this Harmony five years only; they bought a huge territory of the richest land, which is all paid for, and keep an immense quantity in high cultivation, and continue to buy out bordering settlers, and thus ever enlarging their boundaries.[25]

Thomas Hulme, who visited Harmony, Indiana, in 1818, claimed: "This congregation of far-seeing, ingenious, crafty, and bold, and ignorant, simple, superstitious, and obedient Germans, has shown what may be done."[26] Morris Birbeck, who had come from England and settled in Illinois near Harmony on the Wabash river, found he could leave his thirty thousand acres untended and buy produce cheaper from the Rappites than he could raise it himself.[27] Robert Dale Owen called the Harmonist venture in Indiana a tremendous financial success, since when they came to Indiana their worth averaged about twenty-five dollars per person. But by 1825, Owen estimated they had increased their wealth to two thousand dollars for each man, woman, and child, or about ten times the average wealth in America.[28]

While Frederick Rapp's responsibility was to make the Harmonists prosperous, it was George Rapp's intention to keep them righteous. Wealth, when allowed to go unchecked, was a detriment to communal living. Members of a community, after fulfilling the goal of establishing a firm economic base, often lost their zeal for communism. George Rapp was fully aware of this pitfall and made plans for the removal of the community to a new location when he sensed complacency among the members. The clearing of land and building of houses brought new vitality to the Harmonists and gave them little time for leisure and bickering.

Celibacy was not at first a feature of Harmonist theology but grew out of economic necessity on the American frontier. The first three years in Pennsylvania were ones of extreme hardship and deprivation. The stubborn primeval forest had not provided sufficient food for the community of nearly two hundred families. Children had to be fed and clothed, as well as tended to, and this left fewer people to do the productive work. With material deprivations came a deepening of spirituality among the Harmonists and the year 1807 witnessed a true religious revival. As the young men and women were attracted to Ann Lee and her theology of sexual abstinence, it was the youth who approached George Rapp and asked him to declare celibacy the rule.[29] Celibacy was not only more economical for the community, in that it lessened the number of non-productive citizens, but it also enabled the members to be more spiritually minded. Lord Byron regarded the Rappites' adoption of celibacy as purely an economic one and wrote in "Don Juan:"

> When Rapp the Harmonist embargo'd marriage
> In his harmonious settlement—(which flourishes
> Strangely enough as yet without miscarriage,
> Because it breeds no more mouths than it nourishes,
>
> Without those sad expenses which disparage
> What Nature naturally most encourages)—
> Why called he "Harmony" a state sans wedlock?
> Now here I've got the preacher at a deadlock,
>
> Because he either meant to sneer at Harmony
> Or Marriage, by divorcing them oddly.

But whether reverend Rapp learn'd this in Germany
Or not, 'tis said his sect is rich and godly.[30]

Until this time, marriage had been an accepted institution among the Harmonists. Father Rapp had personally solemnized the marriage of his only son, John, after their arrival in Pennsylvania. The "Record of Marriages" of the Society lists six marriages in 1804, three in 1805, and two in 1806.[31] To suddenly separate husband, wife, and children in the midst of a fever of revivalism might be accomplished with some degree of ease, but George Rapp knew that the fever would abate and the natural ardor would return. He warned his disciples to proceed with caution.

George Rapp needed time to formalize a creed regarding marriage and a theology sufficiently convincing so that there would be complete unanimity among his followers. He did not go to the extreme of denouncing all sexual relations as evil, as did Mother Ann Lee. However, he did develop the same theme regarding the dual sexuality of God and of Adam. Had Adam been content to remain as God, in his image, had created him, Rapp contended, he would have replenished the earth without the help of a female. But Adam saw the animals mating around him and desired to be more like the animals and less like God.[32] God separated the female part from Adam's body when he removed one of his ribs, and gave Eve to him that he might satisfy his animal-like desire. This constituted man's fall from his original state. Afterward, Adam and his partner found that they had physical sex organs of which they were ashamed and tried to hide them with fig leaves. The original man was reproduced by God in the form of Jesus Christ. Rapp believed that Jesus was perfect and did not possess a physical sex organ. In an effort to be Christ-like, men were counseled to strive for that perfection which was in God's only begotten son. By living a celibate life upon a "rebirth" into the kingdom of God, men could return to that blessed estate of Eden and their sexual organs would again disappear.

Once Rapp worked out a theology to give celibacy divine sanction, he proceeded to encourage the Harmonists to adopt the rule. R. L. Baker told Nevin:

> Father Rapp suggested the measure at one of our meetings, during the height of religious excitement. The immolation of endeared family ties on the altar of religion which the step would require, at first startled our adult members, but as we looked on our venerated leader

and saw, as we thought, the light of holy inspiration on his face, we felt reassured and resolved almost unanimously to take up the cross.[33]

George Rapp and his son, John, set the pattern for the community and announced they would from that time forward have no marital relations. Those married couples who were convinced of the righteousness of the move signed a covenant to treat their mates as a brother or a sister. Unlike the Shakers, husbands and wives continued to live in the same houses and, if they preferred, to share the same beds.

No specific measures were taken to insure that the covenant of celibacy would be enforced. Celibacy was never incorporated into the constitution or bylaws of the Harmonists. Two factors were relied on to provide some guarantee that celibacy would remain a feature of the society: the strength of religious conviction and the society's censure of violators. One Harmonist wrote fifty years after the adoption of celibacy by the community: "Convinced of the truth and holiness of our purpose, we voluntarily and unanimously adopted celibacy, altogether from religious motives, or in order to withdraw our love entirely from the lusts of the flesh." [34] Nordhoff asked in Economy, Pennsylvania, what kind of watch or safeguard was kept over the intercourse of the sexes and was told: "None at all; it would be of no use. If you have to watch people, you had better give them up. We have always depended upon the strength of our religious convictions and upon prayer and a Christian spirit." [35]

Marriage and cohabitation were not formally outlawed. Adlard Welby, upon visiting Harmony, Indiana, in 1819, observed, "the interdict [of celibacy] has been since removed and plenty of children were to be seen as proof of it." [36] Richard Fowler, who also visited Harmony that year and who five years afterward arranged the sale of the village to Robert Owen, observed in a letter to a friend that the Harmonists did not forbid marriage.[37] Frederick Rapp, in an article which appeared in *The Harrisburg* (Pennsylvania) *Morgenrothe*, October 9, 1819, denied the charges of a rumor that marriage or children were forbidden at Harmony, and pointed out that their school at that time had from eighty to one hundred pupils in attendance, who ranged from six to twelve years of age. The relatively large number of children may be accounted for, in part, by the recent admission of families to the community. John Wood observed in 1821 that an American widower with ten children had joined the community shortly before his visit.[38] Thomas Hulme claimed there was not a single child in the place when he attended worship services there on July 1, 1818.[39] There must have been some special reason for the children's absence that day, for normally the children took their places alongside the adults in church. William Faux attended a religious service on November 21, 1819, and was particularly impressed by the number of Rappite children who were present.[40]

Several marriages were performed and recorded in the Harmonite communities after the adoption of celibacy in 1807.[41] Weddings were not occasions of joy but evidence of falling from grace. If a husband and wife broke their covenant with the society and had sexual intercourse, they could be forgiven for this temporary lapse from holiness. The Schwartzes, the Vogts, and the Killingers violated the Harmonite covenant of celibacy and produced several children. One Martin Roll is reported to have asked Rapp's permission to add a room to his house, which the patriarch permitted and allowed him to use the community's lumber, but forbade others in the community to assist him. Father Rapp rebuked Roll and told him that if he would cease adding to his family he would not have to add to his house.[42] Despite Rapp's insistence on celibacy, between 1814 and 1824 there were sixty-nine children born at Harmony, Indiana.

Thomas Hulme claimed Rapp used the celibate covenant as a chancery lawyer would use a restraining clause in order to control population. When the number of citizens in the community was reduced to where the society's existence was jeopardized, Hulme claimed Rapp would give the order and couples would copulate and children would be born, "all within the same month, perhaps, like a farmer's lambs." [43] Gilbert Vale, who settled in the Harmony village after it had been purchased by Robert Owen, gave a different version. He asserted that "The contracting couple [those who signed the celibacy covenant] lived together one year and then parted for six. The arrangement was such that there was never more than one family member at a time who was completely dependent." [44] It is doubtful, however, that George Rapp deliberately encouraged mating seasons, as Hulme and Vale reported. It was entirely out of line with the theological system which Rapp developed in support of the institution of celibacy. One would hardly lose his physical sex apparatus and return to the pure and original Adamic state, as Rapp's theology taught, if he were periodically called upon to use it for propagation purposes. But more importantly, the Rappites were millennialists. They believed the second coming of Jesus was near, and fully expected it to occur in the year 1829.[45] Propagation would serve no useful purpose as there was no fear that the society would die out before that date. When the year 1829 passed, the Harmonists were disappointed but in nowise lost faith in the millennium. R. L. Baker admitted to D. E. Nevin that "with the millennium, as we thought, just before us, it was morally impossible . . . for us to have rebelled against the [celibacy] measure." [46] Rapp was perfectly content to let the population level remain as it was. No concerted effort was ever made by the Rappites to increase their ranks by converting others to their religious views, as was made by the Shakers. One Chester Chadwick wished to join the society at Economy and was told by Frederick Rapp: "We have not admitted any person this long time, having been so often deceived by people who lived here one or two years, and finding the path to follow Jesus too narrow, they break off and calumniate us, then all our trouble spent to make them do better was lost." [47] The Rappites were not as interested in saving the world as they were in preparing their own faithful few for the millennium.

The Separatist Society of Zoar, which settled in 1817 in Tuscarawas County, Ohio, about midway between Cleveland and Pittsburgh, practiced celibacy in the initial stages of their communal life. Upon coming to America, these German pietists did not practice communism; each family attempted to establish its own economic independence in the new world. But the Zoarites were extremely poor and had it not been for a few philanthropic English Quakers in Philadelphia, who provided eighteen dollars for each Separatist who arrived, they would have starved before making it to Ohio. Once they settled in Ohio, communism was adopted by the Zoarites out of economic necessity. There were several aged members among them who were unable to work and pay for their land and it appeared their enterprise would fail unless a move were taken to pool their resources and share all things in common. In 1819 a resolution was made to establish a community of goods which was signed by 157 members of the community. Concurrent with this resolution was the resolve to forgo the marriage relation. Celibacy was adopted for two reasons: their poverty demanded that no more children be brought into their community; and to sublimate individual interests to the interests of the community.

Unlike the Shakers and Rappites, celibacy was not a major part of Separatist theology. *The Zanesville* (Ohio) *Gazette* reported: "At their first organization marriage was strictly forbidden, not from any religious scruples as to its propriety, but as an indispensable matter of economy. They were too poor to rear children." [48] The Zoarites did not have an Ann Lee or a George Rapp with sufficient ability to work out a theological justification for celibacy. Joseph Michael Baumler was chosen as their leader, and although a good speaker and powerful persuader, he did not develop an extensive theological basis for his position. It is easy to understand, therefore, why they chose to abandon the practice in 1830 after they became affluent and settled their debts.

Baumler took the lead in the readoption of marriage. A young girl had been assigned by the community to wait on the aging Baumler, whom he found irresistible, and they were married and raised a rather large family. Celibacy, however, was still regarded as the ideal and many Zoarites continued the practice. Several restrictions were placed on marriage, once the institution was readopted. One could not remain a member of the community upon marrying an outsider. Since the Zoarites rejected the usual type of ceremony and had no priests or preachers, marriages were contracted by mutual consent before witnesses, but without the customary vows.

Before a marriage could take place at Zoar, the couple had first to receive the consent of the leaders of the society. If approval were given, a simple paper was drawn up and the couple signed their names. All conjugal relations were regarded as sinful, except when necessary to perpetuate the species. The community provided quarters and furniture for the newlyweds and this was often a factor which prevented the approval of requests for marriage, particularly when the economy was suffering. All children, upon reaching three years of age, were to be separated from their parents and placed in large houses, the boys in one, the girls in another. From that time forward they would never again live with their parents. The Zoarites signed the following covenant:

> . . . we promise and bind ourselves to obey all the commands and orders of the Trustees and their subordinates . . . without opposition and grumbling . . . . Also we consign in a similar manner our chil-

> dren, so long as they are minors, to the charge of the Trustees, giving them the same rights and powers over them as though they had been formally indentured to them under the laws of the state.[49]

These restrictions were sufficient to keep the number of marriages and births to an absolute minimum. After fifty years of communal life there were but seventy-five additions to their number, and most of these by admission of outsiders. *The Zanesville* (Ohio) *Gazette* reported that "for years their little town presented the anomaly, of a village without a single child to be seen or heard within its limits." [50]

Several of the restrictions on marriage were lifted after 1845. The seventy-four-year-old Jacob Ackermann, who was interviewed by Alfred Hinds, regretted the return to unrestricted marriages in the community and regarded it a backward step in the direction of familism.[51] One factor which probably accounted for the resumption of family life in Zoar was their economic success. They had pooled their resources and were able to repay their debts. A windfall came in 1833 when work was begun on the Ohio canal in their vicinity. Their young men went to work digging the canal, while the community supplied the contractors with lumber, food, and accommodations. This enabled them to retire their debts and thus the circumstances which had occasioned the adoption of both communism and celibacy were removed. Only those who were thoroughly indoctrinated with their hard-times ideology persisted in the belief that communism and celibacy were the best of all possible social arrangements.

The Ephrata community, founded by Conrad Beizel in 1732, eight miles from Lancaster, Pennsylvania, simultaneously practiced celibacy and monogamy. Like the Rappites and the Zoarites, they emigrated from Germany. Beizel fled the Palatinate with his disciples in order to escape religious persecution. Upon settling in Pennsylvania, two orders were established among the members: the Cloistered Order and the Outdoor Order. The latter, fewer in number than the Cloistered Order, was made up of monogamous families who lived in their own separate houses. The Outdoor Order did not practice communism and conducted their affairs as if they were a part of ordinary frontier society, without sacrificing their membership in the Ephrata community.

Life in the Cloistered Order was quite different from that in the

Outdoor Order. All goods were held in common, and except for the presence of both sexes, the cloistered order gave every appearance of a medieval monastery. The women lived in a Sister House and were organized into two groups: the Roses of Sharon and the Spiritual Virgins. The men, tonsured and bearded, lived in the Brother House. Both sexes wore the same style of attire, which resembled that of a Capuchin, "with a surplice extending to the feet, and an apron in front and a veil behind, entirely indistinguishable as to sex." [52] In both the Brother and the Sister Houses scriptural texts were to be found around the wall which pointed up the blessedness of celibacy: "They that are of the flesh do mind the things of the flesh"; "He that is unmarried careth for the things that belong to the Lord." [53] However, their hymns were filled with such erotic verses as:

Sweet are the kisses of thy mouth
Come, O dove, come, my love,
Let me give you a thousand kisses.
Mouth to mouth and heart to heart.[54]

It was not an unusual occurrence, after the death of Beizel in 1786, for the members of the Cloistered Order to renounce their vow of celibacy and join the Outdoor Order. None of the successors of Beizel had the charisma to inspire the members to continue a life of asceticism. Nearly all who left the cloisters and married settled nearby and sent their children to the brothers and sisters of the Cloistered Order for their education. Ephrata continued as a community into the twentieth century, although after its incorporation in 1812 the membership dwindled until there were but seventeen aged members at its demise in 1905.

The Bishop Hill community, established in Henry County, Illinois, had a stormy history, during which the leaders attempted to impose celibacy on two different occasions and each time were met with stubborn resistance. The community had its beginning in 1830 when Eric Janson preached a return to the New Testament in the region of Helsingland, Sweden. In addition to instruction in piety, Janson taught his disciples the virtues of equality of conditions and community of property. Upon their refusal to attend the services of the state church and to submit to its teachings, they were frequently fined and incarcerated. When they found no toleration in Sweden for their unorthodoxy, Olaf Olson was sent to seek a new home for the Jansonists in America. In 1848 more than 800 disciples settled on the site purchased by Olson in Illinois, and soon their ranks swelled to over 1,100 people. At first, each family had its own one-room tenement, but all ate at a common table and secured their clothes and other provisions from a common store.

Like the Zoarites, the colony at Bishop Hill consisted of many aged and infirm members during its initial stages, and Janson, like Baumler, called for the adoption of celibacy for reasons of economy and to augment the community spirit. Several left the colony rather than separate from their spouses. Janson sensed the possible collapse of the communal enterprise and changed his plans about making Bishop Hill celibate. Instead, he ordered: "All to whom God has given a desire to marry should forthwith be joined together or else be condemned to hell!" [55] There was no balking at Janson's word this time and young couples paired off, some without the usual period of courtship. One Sunday afternoon twenty-five couples were united in marriage in the midst of a grove. About two-thirds of the members were women, so several women had to remain single. Janson, himself, surprised the community by announcing his intention to marry just four days after the death of his wife. Fredrika Bremer, who visited the colony in the autumn of 1851, reported : "Eric Jansen [*sic*] stood up during divine service in the church, and declared that 'the Spirit had commanded him to take a new wife!' And a woman present stood up also and said, that 'the Spirit had made known to her that she must become his wife!' " [56] The woman of whom Fredrika Bremer wrote was Sophia Gabrielson, on whom Janson evidently had his eye before either of them had their "revelations." Sophia, who had served as Janson's secretary, had been married three times. Her first husband went to sea and never returned. Her second husband refused to join her at Bishop Hill when she became a Jansonist and soon afterward died. Her third husband died of cholera in the colony. Janson had been accused of illicit sexual relations on several occasions with various women of the community. Only once did he admit it. The wily Janson then blamed the woman, Karen Erson, for "having used her evil charms and wiles" to cause him to err.[57]

Eric Janson persistently meddled in the private affairs of the members of the Bishop Hill colony and eventually lost his life because of it. He had given permission for his cousin to marry a Mexican War veteran, John Root, on the condition that if Root ever decided to leave the community, he could not take his wife. Root, who was anything but a good Jansonist, grew restless in the colony and decided to leave and to take his wife with him. His wife, however, refused to follow him. Root returned and kidnapped her and Janson pursued the couple, recaptured her and brought her back to the colony. Root swore out a warrant for Janson's arrest and marched into the community a second time and kidnapped his wife, but she managed to escape his clutches and to return to Bishop Hill. Root proceeded to round up a motley crew of sympathetic Mexican War veterans and laid siege to the community. Janson's neighbors intervened and managed to drive the band of ruffians away. In the meantime, Janson, fearing the worst, managed to escape to St. Louis and when the danger passed he returned to Bishop Hill. He was arraigned by the Henry County Circuit Court to answer Root's charges on May 13, 1850. During a recess of the trial, Root entered the courtroom, saw Janson standing near his counsel's table and shot him. Janson died instantly.

Jonas Olson, who had selected the site of the community, succeeded Janson as leader. Nils Hedin had visited several Shaker communities in 1854 and had identified their affluence with their practice of celibacy. Hedin convinced Olson of the merits of celibacy and for the second time an attempt was made at Bishop Hill to impose it on the community. Olson appealed to the New Testament scriptures in support of celibacy. Anders Shogan reported that the leading preachers of the colony began to set forth "as a doctrine of the Bible that [the] marriage relation was unchristian; that the relation belonged only to those who belonged under the law of Moses and to the heathens, but was condemnatory to true Christians." [58] In their anxiety to purify the community, there were to be no more marriages, and those already married were commanded to cease the conjugal relation. Those who refused to acquiesce were dealt with according to Article Three of the bylaws, which forbade anyone to preach or disseminate a religious doctrine contrary to that of the Bible upon pain of expulsion.[59] Several chose to leave the community and some were compelled to depart. Olson afterward found the group more pliant and it appeared the ideal celibate community had been at last created. But three years later, in 1857, Bishop Hill fell on hard times. The nationwide economic depression that year disrupted the colony's finances and adherents soon quarreled among themselves. The second imposition of celibacy had driven away many of the young and industrious members. Those who remained did not have the strength to weather the financial storm and within five years the venture collapsed, never to be revived.

Jemima Wilkinson, who founded the New Jerusalem community near Seneca Lake in western New York in 1788, also preached communism, equality of the sexes, and celibacy. Her followers, dubbed "Jemimakins," believed that she was divinely inspired and at first they followed her implicitly. Jemima allegedly died and was permitted to return to life with divine instructions to establish a church. She claimed that she possessed the power of Jesus Christ and would retain that power until his return to the earth.[60] The first converts were mainly Quakers, or Friends, and Jemima Wilkinson, as the leader of the cult, was affectionately called "The Universal Friend."

Unlike George Rapp and Ann Lee, Jemima Wilkinson did not develop an intricate theology to support her contention that men and women should forgo the marriage relation. She relied on a few well-chosen passages of New Testament scriptures to supplement her preaching on this point. Not all of her followers were chosen to become celibates; but when a pregnancy was discovered, the expecting parents could count on a thorough tongue lashing from the Universal Friend. On one occasion she suggested that the baby be named "Abomination."[61] The non-celibate households at New Jerusalem were never regarded as a part of the inner group of devout believers.

Jemima Wilkinson died in 1819. At her death there were seventy-five families living at New Jerusalem in addition to about 100 women, many of whom had taken the vow of celibacy. The Jemimakins were as sheep without a shepherd and dispersed the year after the death of the Universal Friend.

Late in the nineteenth century Cyrus R. Teed, known as "Koresh" or the reincarnation of the messiah, established a utopian community at Estero, Florida. Teed's sect originated in Illinois, and searched America for a suitable location to build a New Jerusalem. They found it on a narrow strip of land jutting out into the Gulf of Mexico, south of Fort Myers. Here, in 1894, Teed gathered his followers and erected a large temple. He preached celibacy as superior to marriage for those who desired a closer relationship with God. Not all of his followers chose to separate from their families; some elected to live in cottages surrounding the temple.[62] The colony continued into the twentieth century and was not dissolved until the beginning of World War II.

Nearly all of the religious communities of the nineteenth century were founded by Protestant sects. However, two were founded by Catholics in which celibacy was a feature. In 1854 a group of more than 100 Catholic emigrants from Germany settled at St. Nazianz in Manitowa County, Iowa, under the leadership of Father Ambrose Oschwald. The colony, which practiced a modified form of communism, grew to 400 members within fourteen years of its founding. As at Ephrata, there were a Brother's House and a Sister's House. There were eighty men, in 1868, who had chosen to live celibate lives and 150 women. One hundred and seventy lived as families in separate houses within the village. In 1874 the Catholic Church took over the community and it ceased as a utopian enterprise.

The New York Tribune reported the existence of a German Catholic utopian community near Lake Michigan in Wisconsin in the middle of the nineteenth century. The neighboring farmers called it "The Bavarian Cloister." Celibacy was voluntary and no lifetime vows were taken by the members. Each person was at liberty to leave the community at his own pleasure. The *Tribune* article compared the venture to that of Etienne Cabet's Icaria in Illinois, except for the religious feature of the Wisconsin commune.[63]

One of the most unusual communities which adopted celibacy was that of the Women's Commonwealth. A ladies' Bible class at Belton, Texas, in 1876, developed some positive ideas about religion, economics, and sex. Martha MacWhirter, leader of the group, persuaded the ladies to leave their husbands and to form a communistic community. There were twenty-four women who began the enterprise and resolved never again to marry. Men were not excluded from the movement by any specific bylaw. One man did join for a time, but found the independent feminists not to his liking and withdrew.[64] The community was materially successful, but came under steady harassment by neighborhood rowdies. In 1898 the women sold their community property at Belton and moved to Mount Pleasant in the District of Columbia. Here they could not attract any new members and the women grew tired of each other's company. The project was abandoned in 1906.

Not all celibate communities adopted the practice for the same reasons, but one factor appears paramount in each: celibacy served to reorder the priorities of the members and thus aided the effective establishment of communistic societies. The interest of the community took precedence over selfish interests of the individual. At Zoar and at Bishop Hill, when celibacy was abolished and familism reestablished, the communistic principle was threatened and the communities not only declined but were shortly abandoned. The Shakers, Rappites, and Ephrataites, who each retained celibacy, enjoyed a much longer life, despite the fact that they were always but a generation away from extinction unless they adopted children or made new converts.

III

It Is Good for a Man Not to Touch a Woman

THE SUPPRESSION OF SEXUAL URGES OVER AN EXTENDED PERIOD OF TIME in communities where both sexes were in daily contact with one another provided a problem for those communities which adopted celibacy. Saint Paul's caution that "it is good for a man not to touch a woman," was taken in downright earnest! [1] Various safeguards were employed with different degrees of rigor. It was hoped that a thorough conversion to the spiritual intentions of the community would serve as a deterrent to fleshly desires.

A candidate for admission into the Shaker colonies underwent an exhaustive course of instruction and afterward served a period of probation in order to test his sincerity. The Shaker hymns were not only for the praising of God, but to teach and admonish one another to live a pure and virtuous life. The theme of celibacy filled the Shaker hymnals. One song, which was sung with gusto, was entitled "Victory over the Man of Sin," and ran:

By a poisonous fleshly nature
  This dark world has long been led;
There can be no passion greater—
  This must be the serpent's head:
Our coast he would be cruising,

If by truth he were not bound:
But his head has had a bruising,
And he's got a deadly wound.

And his wounds cannot be healed,
Light and truth do not forbid,
Since the Gospel has revealed
Where his filthy head was hid:
With a fig-leaf it was cover'd
Till we brought his deeds to light;
By his works he is discover'd
And his head is plain in sight.[2]

Every effort was made to inculcate in children reared by the Shakers the rigorous principles which would make them choose the spirit over the flesh. However, only about one-tenth of them remained in the communities upon reaching maturity. Children were taught the value of confession of their sins upon entering the society. One young lad related that when he first arrived

> they required the boys to confess all their sins. If the boys pleaded they had no sins, it was hinted to them what they were expected to confess and this was sometimes disgusting. They were often impeached with some offense and it was no use to plead innocence. They were compelled to shake their heads until willing to confess—and if they stopped shaking their heads they were cained [*sic*], or cowhided, so that many of the boys, to get the character of being faithful, and avoiding punishments, confessed to have done things of which they were really innocent.[3]

The Shakers claimed their society was built on four basic pillars: Virgin Purity, Christian Communism, Separation from the World, and Confession of Sins.[4] Confession of sins was a safeguard for virgin purity, and they were to undergo a complete catharsis before the Elders or Eldresses when they entertained the slightest amorous feeling toward a member of the opposite sex.[5]

The Rappites were certain that if all members were to "crucify the flesh, with the affections and lusts," there would be a union of the spirits of all and the celibate community could survive indefinitely.[6] They trusted that their members had been so indoctrinated that a husband and wife could share the same bed and not be tempted to have conjugal relations.[7] Adlard Welby noted on his visit to Harmony, Indiana, in 1819, that "Nothing short of a pure religious principle . . . could keep such a community in harmony."[8]

In the Cloistered Order of the Ephrata community indoctrination in the virtues of celibacy was part of their daily routine. Everywhere they looked in the Brother and Sister Houses there were subtle reminders that God blessed the pure in both heart and body. Little time was given to leisure so that their minds would not be filled with desires for the members of the opposite sex. What time did remain after the countless menial tasks were performed was devoted to prayers and Bible reading.

The Zoarites and Jansonists did not fare as well as the Shakers, Rappites, and Ephrataites. One possible reason for this failure may be attributed to the causes for which celibacy was adopted in these communities. The leaders at Zoar and Bishop Hill preached celibacy out of economy and expediency in order to insure the success of their communal experiments. Neither of them developed a system of theology which made celibacy mandatory for their eternal salvation. Only those communities which made celibacy an essential part of their theology were able to maintain the institution throughout the length of their existence.

Indoctrination alone did not guarantee that all fleshly desires would be sublimated indefinitely. Both sexes working, eating, worshiping, and playing side by side in utopian communities had their moments when the flesh was weaker than the spirit. In order to reduce temptations as much as possible, social intercourse and dress were carefully regulated in the celibate communities. Ephrata was the strictest Protestant utopian community regarding the daily relations of the sexes and their dress. The sexes lived in separate houses and dined separately. At worship services, when the celibate and Outdoor Orders came together, the men sat on one side of the meetinghouse and the women on the other. Footwashing was a ritual in which the Ephrataites engaged preparatory to the Lord's Supper. But the men washed only the feet of their brothers, and the women performed the same task for their sisters.[9]

The dress of the Cloistered Order of Ephrata was designed to conceal the form of the human body, that it might not excite lust in the members of the opposite sex. Beizel believed that the body was seductive when dressed in the fashions of the world. A Brother Lamech observed: "It was resolved to muffle the mortal body in such a style and in such a garment as would fit it for its immediate transportation to the skies and the eternal hereafter." [10] Howard Pyle remarked, upon observing the women at Ephrata, that "an air of almost saintly simplicity is given by the clear-starched cap, the handkerchief crossed on the breast, the white apron, and the plain gray or drab stuff of the dresses." [11]

The Shakers exercised extreme caution in the social relations of the sexes in order to prevent the growth of personal affections. This was the more difficult since, unlike the Ephrataites, both sexes lived under the same roof and frequently husband and wife were occupants of the same house. The Shakers were divided into "families," consisting of thirty to ninety people. There were between two to eight families in each Shaker village. Each family was cared for by an eldership and a deaconship. The eldership consisted of one head elder and a brother, or one head eldress and a sister. These cared for the spiritual welfare of the Shaker family. The deaconship consisted of one head deacon and a brother, and one head deaconess and a sister. These cared for the operation of the household and superintended all labor in the village.[12] A Shaker family lived in one large house, usually of three stories. The kitchen, dining, and laundry facilities were on the ground floor, as were also sitting and guest rooms. The Shaker family ate in a common dining hall, but the men were placed at separate tables from the women. There were numerous serving dishes in order to reduce the passing of food and conversation during mealtime. William Hepworth Dixon observed: "Not a word is spoken, unless a brother need something from a brother, a sister from a sister. A whisper serves." [13] There was also to be no "winking or blinking" at the table.

Sleeping quarters were located in the upper stories of a Shaker dwelling. Both sexes occupied the same floors, but usually entered by separate staircases, always with the women on the right and the men on the left. In case there was but a single set of stairs, there was a rule that no member should pass one of the opposite sex on the steps. A husband and wife visiting a Shaker community were not allowed to occupy the same guest room. Charles Nordhoff, on his visit to the Canterbury community, noted the following printed placard in the dining hall: "Married persons tarrying with us overnight are respectfully notified that each sex occupy separate sleeping apartments while they remain." [14]

There was absolutely no privacy in a Shaker house as each dormitory room contained from four to six beds. The women's side of the upper floor was separated by an unusually wide corridor to prevent bodily contact with the males when passing. The women did not open their doors until "the second trump" was sounded in order to give the men an opportunity to leave their rooms with their chamber pots, which might be suggestive of sex. Each male Shaker was assigned to a woman who took care of his clothes, washed and repaired them, and told him when he needed to replace a garment. In a sisterly way, she reproved him when he was disorderly. The women made up all the beds and were careful when they entered the male quarters that they received permission. The sexes did not unite their labor in the fields or workshops and they were not allowed to visit the work area of the members of the opposite sex except on special business and with the permission of their superior. And then they had to be accompanied by a member of their own sex.

Children, who either entered the community with parents or who were adopted as orphans, were housed separately according to their sex and put under the supervision of a master of their own sex. The children were also divided by sexes in the schools. Usually the boys attended classes in the winter months, as they were needed in the fields during the summer, and the girls received their formal education in the summer months.

The sexes were not allowed to converse with one another at any time except in the presence of a third party who was above the age of ten years. If a visiting member of the opposite sex were to offer to shake hands, a Shaker must oblige; but before a subsequent religious service he was required to confess the matter to his superior in order that he "with clean hands" might enter the worship.

As in most celibate communities, the Shakers sat on opposite sides of the meeting house for religious services. This rule also applied to visitors, as Charles Robinson was informed that he and his wife could not sit together when they visited the services at the Canterbury community in 1854.[15] They entered by separate doors, always the men on the left and the women on the right. Once inside, they sat facing each other. During their famous dance they formed separate lines by sexes and, although the maneuvers were often ecstatic in nature, there was never to be any bodily contact between the men and the women. The Shaker dance provided an outlet for pent-up feelings. During the normal activities through the week there was to be no show of emotion. Women were commanded to move about "on the toes, left arm folded across the stomach, right hand at the side, tips of the fingers touching the thumb." [16] However, at the dance these somber people let themselves go in lively movements. B. J. Lossing, who witnessed the dance at the Lebanon Springs community, observed: "The women, clad in white, and moving gracefully, appeared ethereal . . . all appeared happy." [17]

Although the Shaker ministry took every precaution to keep the sexes apart in daily life, pressures for social intercourse became too great to suppress indefinitely. The ministry acquiesced and set aside the "Union Hour" in order to allow the brothers and sisters to enjoy one another's company. Hervey Elkins, who spent sixteen years among the Shakers, described these meetings as follows:

> For the union meetings the brethren remain in their rooms, and the sisters, six, eight or ten in number, enter and sit in a rank opposite to that of the brethren's, and converse simply, often facetiously, but rarely profoundly. In fact, to say 'agreeable things about nothing,' when conversant with the other sex, is as common there as elsewhere. . . . An hour passes away very agreeably and even rapturously with those who there chance to meet with a special favorite; succeeded soon, however, when soft words, and kind, concentrated looks become obvious to the jealous eye of a female espionage, by the agonies of separation. For the tidings of such reciprocity, whether true or surmised, is sure before the lapse of many hours to reach the ears of the elders; in which case, the one or the other party would be subsequently summoned to another circle of colloquy and union.
>
> No one is permitted to make mention of anything said or done in any of these sittings to those who attend another, for party spirit might be the result.[18]

Shakers were never allowed to give or to receive presents among themselves, for this could easily reveal a personal liking for a member of the opposite sex and might obligate one to return the show of affection. "Sparking," as the Shakers called amorous attachments, occasionally occurred, despite the careful scrutiny of the elders and the surveillance of spies. Couples sometimes "fleshed off," or eloped, as a result of the Union Hour contacts.

The Shakers, like the Ephrataites, were careful in their dress that no occasion be given for lust. Thomas Hamilton, who visited the Canterbury community in 1831, remarked that the women "were the veriest scarecrows I had ever seen in the female form." [19] Not all observers were as uncomplimentary as Hamilton. William Hepworth Dixon, who was rather caustic in his evaluation of Americans, wrote, after visiting the Mount Lebanon village: "The women are habited in a small muslin cap, a white kerchief wrapped around the chest and shoulders, and a sack or skirt dropping in a straight line from the waist to the ankle, white socks and shoes; but apart from a costume neither rich in color nor comely in make, the sisters have an air of sweetness and repose." [20] There was general uniformity in the Shaker dress, but there was no uniform as such. The drab colors, numerous folds and pleats, and lack of any ornaments whatsoever hardly enhanced the attractiveness of the women.

The Rappites attempted to control the social intercourse of the sexes, but not as rigidly as did the Ephrataites and the Shakers. This was mainly due to their allowance for a moderate degree of familism in their communities. Fathers, who retained their positions as heads of households, were responsible for seeing to it that the rules of the society regarding the relation of the sexes were not violated by the members of their own families. The unmarried men and women, however, lived in separate dormitories and were carefully regulated. A watchman roamed the streets at night and every hour announced: "Again a day is past, and a step made nearer to our end; our time runs away, and the joys of heaven are our reward." [21]

There was privacy in the Rappite villages. The families who so chose lived in their separate houses and had their own little gardens, a cow, some pigs and chickens. All else they procured from the common store, which was supplied by common labor. Father Rapp, in order "to keep his line of communication with God clear," demanded a fine brick house apart from the disturbances of community life.[22]

Unlike the Shakers, the Rappite women worked alongside the men in the fields. However, as in other celibate communities, the sexes did not sit together when they attended religious services. The Rappite church building at Harmony, Indiana, was designed in the shape of a Maltese cross. The women entered at the tower door, located at the front of the building, and the men entered at the side doors.

The Harmonists were careful about their dress and refused to adopt the fashions of the world. John Wood observed that the women's clothes were "uncommonly plain, mostly of their own manufacturing. . . . The women wear a kind of jacket and petticoat, with a particular kind of skull cap, and a straw hat made peculiarly flat." [23] William Faux claimed the Rappite women "are intentionally disfigured and made as ugly as it is possible for art to make them."[24] Adlard Welby figured the way the Harmonist women looked they had no worry that the men would be sexually tempted when in their presence. He observed: "The women, to use the phrase of a polite man, are the *least handsome* I ever beheld: the Colony therefore may possibly not be much disturbed by female intrigues, and thus be free from one other great cause of embroilment among mankind."[25]

During the time celibacy was the rule at Zoar, there were few attempts to regulate the social activities between the sexes. Several families occupied a large house and did their work together, much as did the Shaker families. But there were no rules such as one finds among the Shakers. Since celibacy was adopted for economic and social expediency, and was not a permanent principle, when affluence came to the community the rule gave way and each family found separate living quarters and governed its own affairs. However, one practice did remain upon a return to familism: at church services, the women and the men continued to enter by separate doors and sit on opposite sides of the meetinghouse.

As regards dress among the Separatists at Zoar, there was no deliberate effort to make the women any less sexually appealing. Although they were conservative in their German fashions, one observer remarked that they were "not uncomely in their nut brown bare arms, short kirtles, and very broad brimmed, low crowned hats."[26]

The Jansonists at Bishop Hill, during their two attempts to follow the rule of celibacy, had a limited number of restrictions on the social intercourse of the sexes. Families occupied separate living quarters and were under the oversight of their respective fathers, who answered for the conduct of those under their care. Single persons lived together in separate houses according to sex. There were few or no precautions regarding the mingling of the sexes at mealtime. All ate in common dining halls which were located in a large brick building on the northwest corner of the public square. There were two dining areas, one for both men and women, and another for the children. In the adult dining hall, women ate at separate tables from the men.

The Jansonist women worked alongside the men. Two-thirds of the community's population were women and they filled practically all of the unskilled trades, including that of carrying bricks. The Jansonists did not wear a uniform and were quite undistinguishable from their neighbors in Illinois. The women usually wore blue drilling on workdays, but on special occasions they dressed in gingham and calico.[27]

The celibate communities were forced to deal with mortals whose desires of the flesh could not always be curtailed. Violations of the rules and scandals occurred in practically all of the communities, but certainly to a far less degree than in ordinary society. European visitors on the American frontier generally remarked about the contrast between the mode of life and the sincerity of purpose which they found in the celibate communities and what they observed in ordinary society.

Communal celibates were not always to be depended upon to carry their faith and morals with them when they went beyond the confines of their respective communities. The Shakers were extremely cautious about permitting their members to go outside their villages, even to visit sister communities. Hervey Elkins reported: "All visiting . . . is under the immediate superintendence of the ministry, who prescribe the number, select the persons, appoint the time, define the length of their stay, and routes by which they may go and come." [28]

The saintly Jemima Wilkinson of New Jerusalem occasioned some gossip when she, along with her sister, Marcy, and William Aldrich, went to England on a preaching tour. While there she met an officer in the British army and allegedly had a whirlwind romance with him. Some of the members later left the colony at New Jerusalem over the incident and charged that the Universal Friend had been jilted by her lover and had even given birth to his child.[29]

Olaf Johnson, a leader in the Bishop Hill colony, was known to have made frequent trips to Chicago on "community business." The police allegedly broke into his hotel room one night during one of his visits and found him with a prostitute. The rumor spread that he had offered the police "fabulous sums" to keep silent about the episode.[30]

Even the God-fearing Rappites did not escape scandalous charges. George Rapp's only son, John, died under mysterious circumstances at Harmony, Pennsylvania, five years after the community adopted the rule of celibacy. A rumor spread that John had died as the result of an infection which had set in after his father castrated him as punishment for his carnality. John Duss, a Harmonist writing in 1866, claimed John Rapp strained himself while working at the community's store lifting grain. Duss affirmed that an autopsy was performed after he had died of a chest injury; water was found in his chest and one lung had been destroyed.[31] Karl Arndt called the castration rumor "malicious slander." He admitted, however, that there were serious differences between George Rapp and his son, and that John had begun legal proceedings against his father for some unknown reason.[32] It is strange that the grave of John Rapp is the only one marked with a tombstone to be found in any of the three Rappite cemeteries, since George Rapp had always forbidden graves to be marked.

The Harmonist Jacob Sheaffer once proposed marriage to one of the community women at Economy, Pennsylvania. Father Rapp learned of the proposal and summoned Sheaffer to appear before him and answer for his flagrant disregard of the celibate vow. A witness reported that Rapp told Sheaffer

> that if ever he should talk to the girl again he would have to take his bundle and go, and that he [Rapp] then, as the priest of the society, would heap all the sins he had committed upon him, for which he would be damned for millions of years. He then told him he would give him grace and pardon once more, but if he should get to hear that he had any conversation with the girl, he would let his power of violence loose against him, and would mash him up to a hundred pieces himself and tramp on him with his feet.[33]

However, George Rapp himself was not past casting an eye at a pretty girl. Hildegard Mutschler was very close to Father Rapp and he showered her with attention. Hildegard also received the attention of one Jacob Klein. Rapp became jealous, ordered Klein to leave Economy, and gave him a hundred dollars. Afterward, Hildegard had an affair with Conrad Feucht and eloped with him. In a lengthy letter, dated September 2, 1829, Frederick Rapp took his father to task for his familiarities with Hildegard and for his mourning over her departure, and for his numerous attempts to get in touch with her, unbeknown to her husband. Frederick wrote that he was glad that she was gone, since she was a detriment to the spiritual welfare of the community.[34]

George Kurtz also had an illicit affair with a woman at Economy. She became pregnant and Kurtz offered her a hundred dollars if she would, in writing, release him from further obligation. She accepted, but the paper she signed was declared worthless by a judge. He thereupon took the woman to Madison, Indiana, but could find no peace of mind. He pleaded with Father Rapp to again receive him into the society.[35]

The relatively docile Harmonists managed to weather the storms of a few isolated incidents of impropriety during their experience as communal celibates, but in 1831 an unexpected gale nearly wrecked their community at Economy. Bernhard Muller, who had assumed the title of Count Maximilian de Leon, paid a visit to the Pennsylvania commune and the ignorant peasants welcomed him with all the courtesy due his exalted position. Muller announced that he was a fellow believer, and convinced some of the Rappites that he was John the Baptist incarnate.[36] Once he attained a foothold in the community, he began to undercut the rule of Father Rapp. The tempting morsels which Muller held out to the Harmonists were those of the joys of matrimony, a less somber life, and a few temporal benefits. Had not George Rapp acted quickly and called for a vote of confidence, Muller would probably have taken full control of the colony and celibacy as a principle would have been abandoned. As it was, 500 Harmonists voted to remain with George Rapp and to retain their cherished institutions, while 250 chose to stand by Muller. The Mullerites established a community ten miles away at Phillipsburgh, Pennsylvania. They retained the communistic principle but overthrew the rule of celibacy. Muller soon forsook the community at Phillipsburgh and attempted to establish a community near Alexandria, Louisiana, on the Red River. A victim of cholera, he died before the new enterprise had an opportunity to flourish. The ex-Rappites at Phillipsburgh dispersed. Some followed William Keil to the Bethel community in Shelby County, Missouri, and later moved to Oregon when the colony of Aurora was established on the Pacific coast.

The Shakers were able to maintain order in their communities with relatively few violations of their stringent rules. A. J. Macdonald claimed:

> I have heard individuals who have lived with them for periods varying from thirty years to a few months, all declare, that there was no such immorality among the Shakers, as had been attributed to them. . . . I have never met with one individual who was a witness to or could prove a case of immoral conduct between the sexes in any of the Shaker communities.[37]

However, an air of mystery surrounded the Shaker communities, and the public was eager to learn more about them. When one left the order under duress he was tempted to "tell all" and to garnish his tale with a few falsehoods, for this is what many people wished to read. David Lamsen, Thomas Brown, Colonel James Smith, and William Haskett were among those whose accounts of their experiences must be accepted with caution. It was Thomas Brown who first related the oft-told story of two young Shaker girls who were caught by an eldress watching two flies copulate. The girls were allegedly commanded to strip their clothes and whip one another.[38] David Lamsen claimed that his wife was a confidante to some young Shaker women who told her of their clandestine romances on the first floor of the Shaker House while everyone else was asleep upstairs.[39]

The Shakers never officially denied that at times amorous attachments took place between the sexes in their villages. When they did occur, the couple was put on a six-month probationary period in hopes that they, through confession and obedience, would be reconciled to the Shaker way of life. If after the period they were still in the mood to marry, they were given a sack of flour, a horse, and a hundred dollars and told to go their way.[40] A few Shaker girls developed a liking for the neighborhood boys outside the village. James Flint, upon visiting the Union Village commune in Ohio, vowed that several of the young ladies had been carried off from the settlement by the young men of the neighborhood.[41]

For a people who avoided every semblance of sex, it is ironic that the Shakers had no aversion to the copulation of their animals for eugenic purposes. They used the latest principles in scientific breeding of animals, and through experimentation they were able to make their stock among the most sought after in America. Union Village alone sold $8,420 worth of blooded Durham cattle in the year 1853.[42] But the Shakers kept no pet animals, except cats, and those for the purpose of controlling the rat population. It was feared that the maternal instinct would manifest itself if there were pets around on whom the girls could lavish affection.[43]

Perpetuation was a perennial problem for celibate communities. It was obvious that if no new members were added, when the present generation died the community would cease. The Rappites were not overly concerned about "dying out," except in the latter years of their experiment, when it became obvious that this was taking place. They did not believe in evangelism but did adopt a few children now and then. About the time of Father Rapp's death, in 1847, their number began a gradual decline. Their last settlement at Economy, Pennsylvania, after Muller had carried away several members, dwindled from 522 in 1827 to 385 in 1844. Twenty years later only about 200 remained. One by one these passed on, but the Harmonists never gave up the hope that Jesus would appear in their lifetime and they would reign with him on earth.

The Zoarites realized their efforts would gradually go the way of the cemetery if they did not introduce new people into their society to replace the ones who died. People, however, were not overly eager to get into Zoar. The aging Zoarite, Jacob Ackermann, whom William Hinds interviewed in the 1870s, claimed: "The change from celibacy to marriage was made more than forty years ago, and a principal argument in favor of the change was that we might raise our own members. We supposed children born in the Society would become natural Communists." [44] The first generation Zoarites were mistaken about their children's willingness to perpetuate their communistic society. When the depression of the late 1850s hit the colony, they were among the first to go, as they were unwilling to make the sacrifices their parents had earlier made in order to get the community on a solid economic footing.

The Shakers relied on both evangelism and the adoption of children to increase their membership and to keep the society from dying out. Shaker preachers always made it to the big religious camp meetings on the frontier in an effort to convince those who were under religious "conviction" to forsake the world and to follow Christ. But celibacy was a selective agent and proved a stumbling block. It was during the great revivals of the 1840s that the Shakers reached their peak enrollment of 6,000 members. By 1874 they could no longer count on "awakenings" and were forced to advertise in newspapers for members, promising a comfortable home for life to those who would accept their principles.

Every Shaker village had several children whom the society had adopted. The increase of the Shaker enrollment, however, was not the only purpose for the adoption of children. There were few homes for orphans during the nineteenth century and the Shakers cared for the homeless for humanitarian reasons. They also supplied the few orphanages that did exist with food and clothing. Each year the Watervliet community sent a wagonload of produce to the Orphan Home at Albany, New York.[45]

Experience taught the Shakers that indiscriminate adoption of children was not wise. Nordhoff asked at the Harvard Society near Boston, "Do you like to take children?" An eldress replied, "Yes, we like to take children—but we don't like to take monkeys . . . blood will tell." [46] In later years the Shakers began the practice of investigating the children's background before they accepted them. At the age of twenty-one the adopted children were given the choice of remaining with the society or departing. In the late nineteenth century only one in ten chose to remain. The loss of evangelical zeal and the large percentage of dropouts had their effects on the Shaker population. The principle of celibacy was maintained to the very end, however, and by the beginning of the twentieth century less than 600 Shakers could be counted.[47]

Celibate communities were objects of curiosity in the nineteenth century and hardly a day passed that visitors did not pour into the villages to get a first-hand impression of what the inhabitants were like. European visitors on the frontier usually scheduled their tours to include as many utopian communities as possible. All were interested in the effects prolonged sexual abstinence had on the citizens of celibate communites where the two sexes were in daily social contact. Thomas Hulme noted that the citizens of Harmony, Indiana, were happier there than anywhere else on the frontier.[48] Donald Macdonald reported that at the same community "Several of both the males & females were good looking, strong and healthy, and a very general contentment seemed to prevail among them." [49] Charles Nordhoff, in 1874, found that at Economy, Pennsylvania, most of the Rappites lived to a ripe old age and were "almost without exception stout, well-built, hearty people, the women as well as the men." [50] The Shaker elder, Frederick W. Evans, was enthusiastic about the healthful aspects of celibacy when questioned by Nordhoff. He affirmed: "We look for a testimony against disease . . . and even now I hold that no man who lives as we do has a right to be ill before he is sixty. . . . The joys of the celibate life are far greater than I can make you know. They are indescribable." [51]

The sublimation of the biological urge to propagate needed strong reinforcement in celibate communities. This reinforcement was accomplished by religious conviction based on a credible theology, the dictatorial rule of leaders whose wisdom none dared to counter, stringent rules regarding the social intercourse of the sexes, simple dress, and a system of catharsis where the tempted could regain the posture of virgin purity both in mind and in body. In the communities where these reinforcements were minimized or non-existent, celibacy as a principle was constantly threatened.

IV

Separate Firesides: The Owenites

UTOPIAN SOCIAL THEORISTS SPECULATED IN THE NINETEENTH CENTURY whether the separate fireside was compatible with the associative life in communities. The nuclear family was generally regarded as a divine institution and the chief cornerstone of ordinary society. The father was the head of the household, the mother bore the responsibility of giving birth to and nurturing the children to maturity, and the children were expected to respect, honor, and obey their parents. Each family was a sovereign unit, subject only to the rules of society at large, which permitted broad latitude in each man's choosing what he regarded to be in the best interest of himself and of his family. The separate family was a sanctuary, protected by the laws of the state and sanctioned by institutional religion. If society was to be reordered, as the reform utopians anticipated, the sovereign family stood in jeopardy. The celibate communities, recognizing this problem, chose to strike a blow at the cornerstone of ordinary society by prohibiting future marriages, and either destroying or greatly modifying the family as an institution. Thus separate loyalties and divided affections were reconciled with a single-mindedness considered essential for a community's success.

Several utopian theorists thought communal living could be carried out without the abolition of marriage by the maintenance of separate families. Most of them, however, agreed that marriage would have to undergo certain modifications in order to bring the institution more in line with the overall idea of the society, particularly where women's liberation was concerned. The problem was compounded when the society attempted to house all of their members in a single dwelling. The father's position as head of the household suffered as he was no longer the sole provider for his family. Children were cared for as common property of the society and the role of the mother was reduced to that of mere propagation. The familiarity between members of both sexes who lived in close association threatened the monogamous relation.

Owenite, Fourieristic, independent, and religious communities, as well as a few socialistic cooperatives, attempted to retain monogamy and the separate family in their utopian communities, each with a limited degree of success. Charles Lane, a utopian idealist, doubted that the individual family could be maintained within socialistic communities. He wrote:

> This is the grand problem now remaining to be solved, for at least, the enlightening, if not for the vital elevation of humanity. That the affections can be divided or bent with equal ardor on two objects, so opposed as universal and individual love, may at least be rationally doubted. History has not yet exhibited such a phenomena [*sic*] in an associative body, and scarcely perhaps in any individual.[1]

Some communitarians, undaunted by prospects of failure, proceeded in an attempt to retain separate families and the monogamous relation within their utopian experiments, as if to test Lane's thesis.

Robert Owen, one of the most famous social theorists of the nineteenth century, formulated plans for a perfect society which he trusted would become a reality at New Harmony, Indiana, in 1824. Earlier, in 1812, Owen turned his cotton mills at New Lanark, Scotland, into a showplace of social welfare and education for his employees. He invited other industrialists to come to New Lanark and to observe what could be done to elevate society, if they would but follow his lead. Those who came complimented his project but showed little inclination to experiment with their own employees. Owen realized that unless all industrialists were willing to cooperate in the improvement of the lives and fortunes of the workingmen, his own efforts would be of little lasting effect. In his attempt to reorder society, Owen had been particularly harsh in his denunciation of such basic institutions as the family and the church, which caused many who were otherwise disposed to listen to him to withdraw their interest.

Owen did not regard evil as inherent in human nature; it was due to the vices of the social system. If man were to be good, his environment must be altered. This included the established institutions which perpetuated the miseries and the vices of men. In a speech delivered at New Lanark at the opening of the Institution for the Formation of Character, January 1, 1816, Owen claimed that "all the assumed fundamental principles on which society has hitherto been founded are erroneous, and may be demonstrated to be contrary to fact." [2] He proceeded to lay before his audience a panacea which he called "The New System," which, he said, "is founded on principles which will enable mankind to *prevent*, in the rising generation, almost all, if not all of the evils and miseries which we and our forefathers have experienced." [3] Owen soon came to regard the effects of hundreds of years of tradition in Europe as too much for him to cope with, and he made plans to establish a community on the frontier in America where such factors were minimal and where the air of freedom was more conducive to experimentation.

George Rapp had been financially successful in his experiment with the Harmony community on the Wabash river in Indiana, but his success carried with it a threat to his power and leadership of his people. A new beginning would enable him to regain his former posture as spiritual and temporal leader of the Harmonists. On the pretext that the climate in Indiana was unhealthy, Rapp put Harmony up for sale.[4] Richard Fowler, whose daughter, Sarah, wrote the hymn, "Nearer My God to Thee," was offered a $5,000 commission if he would find a buyer for Harmony. Fowler, a reformist of sorts, went to New Lanark and proposed that Robert Owen purchase the location for an experiment in his social ideas. Owen bought the community in 1824 for $150,000, far less than the village and the 20,000 acres surrounding it were worth. He christened the town "New Harmony," and began his famous social experiment in the New World.[5]

New Harmony had all of the ingredients Owen regarded as essential for an experiment in sociology. The village had been carefully laid out, dwellings and meeting places were available, also a sizable stone house for storing common goods, transportation by boat up the Wabash, not far from the Ohio river, as well as good roads, which made the community accessible. The surrounding countryside was drained and fertile. The one ingredient needed was people. A call went out for all who were in sympathy with Owen's ideas on the founding of a new society, free from the institutions which mutilate and irritate the natural forces of men, to join him at New Harmony. About 900 people "from every state in the Union, with the exception of the two most southern, and almost every country in the north of Europe," accepted the invitation.[6] Applications for admission exceeded the capacity of the town to contain them.[7] Owen, himself, did not arrive at New Harmony until January 18, 1826. He brought with him the best minds he could persuade in Europe and America, including the Pestalozzian educator, William Maclure; Thomas Say, later regarded as "The Father of American Zoology"; the naturalist, Charles Alexander Lesueur, the first to classify the fish of the Great Lakes; and Gerard Troost, the Dutch geologist. Associated with Owen for a time at New Harmony were other utopian architects, including Josiah Warren, founder of Modern Times on Long Island, and Frances Wright, founder of the Nashoba community near Memphis, Tennessee.

The New Harmony Gazette began publication on October 1, 1825, and announced: "If we can not reconcile all opinions, let us unite all hearts." There was to be complete freedom on "all subjects of knowledge and opinion." [8] All members of the community were asked to subscribe to a constitution and to agree to "never, under any provocation whatever, act unkindly or unjustly toward, nor to speak in any unfriendly manner of, any one either in or out of the society." [9] Tolerance, sympathy, and understanding were the initial watchwords in all their social relations. Owen, a thoroughly opinionated individual, was the epitome of tolerance at New Harmony. Although he had denounced established religion as a detriment to society, he allowed those who were so disposed to conduct religious services at the old Rappite church building with but one restriction: speakers were to avoid saying anything that might cause ill feelings or assault the religious prejudices of those present.[10]

Owen was also tolerant of conventional marriage and the nuclear family at New Harmony, in spite of his severe criticism of these institutions as they appeared in ordinary society, and his lectures and writings before his arrival in America. He was not opposed to two people uniting in marriage, but he strenuously objected to what he termed "marriages of the priesthood," in which a couple vowed to remain together until one or the other died. In his objections to such a rash promise, Owen also struck a blow at the family. Families, according to Owen, were not to be indissoluble entities. When love was no longer felt between husband and wife, the sooner they were parted the better.

In ordinary society, two factors interfered with divorce and family breakup. First, the wife, under existing laws, was unable to lay claim to her property and thus would be left without means of support. Second, since the family existed for the welfare of the children, its dissolution put them at the mercy of relatives or neighbors. Owen realized that only through a thorough change of the existing social structure could these problems be removed. Women must be given equality in all matters pertaining to livelihood and children must become the charges of society. When this had been effected, a mother and father who no longer contributed to one another's happiness could dissolve the marriage relation.[11] It was only when a separation of parents imperiled the education of the children that Owen advised against divorce.[12]

Robert Owen did not regard New Harmony as perfect, but as a "half-way house" on the road to a just and equitable society.[13] He believed that through education of the citizens of New Harmony, through experimentation with new institutions, and through the deletion of practices which he calculated to be detrimental to human happiness, the environment at New Harmony could be altered to improve men. He affirmed that he did not believe that men were forever doomed to be victims of their circumstances, and "incapable of altering and improving their general character, but . . . that men collectively create most of the circumstances favorable and adverse to their own happiness." [14]

After his arrival at New Harmony, Robert Owen chose the following Fourth of July, 1826, as the occasion on which he would announce his ideas on a variety of subjects, including private property, religion, and marriage. He prepared an address, which he fittingly entitled, "A Declaration of Mental Independence," and which he delivered on the fiftieth anniversary of American independence. Owen vowed that he had discovered an era in man's history when a few individuals had seized all the property and appropriated it to themselves. In order to give license to their deed, they invented religion. They then established the institution of marriage to give them the same privilege with women that they enjoyed with property. This enabled them to be selective in their choice of women, for through their wealth they attracted the most beautiful women and then made them their slaves. Owen claimed that the whole order of present society had been built on the exploitation of the poor and that the revered institutions of society guaranteed that the poor would always persist in their poverty as long as the present system remained. He affirmed "that man up to this hour has been in all parts of the earth a slave to a trinity of the most monstrous evils that could be combined to inflict mental and physical evil upon the whole race. I refer to private or individual property, absurd and irrational systems of religion, and marriage founded upon individual property, combined with some of these irrational systems of religion." [15]

Owen did not advocate that New Harmony become a "free love" colony. His attacks were not against marriage *per se*, but against marriages in which woman is regarded as property to be administered as the chattel of the husband; marriages which enslave two individuals for life though they come to loathe and detest one another; and marriages "of the Priesthood by which they place and keep mankind within their slavish superstitions, and render them subservient to all their purposes." [16] Owen was also opposed to polygamy, although he regarded the practice as less evil than some of the Christian customs. He believed that polygamy tended "to make men and women weak, jealous, irrational beings," and made woman a slave to man's sexual desire.[17] He was equally opposed to celibacy, which he regarded a crime that ultimately led to both physical and mental illness.[18]

It is doubtful that Robert Owen's own marriage experiences shaped his attitudes toward that institution, although his marriage to Caroline Dale in 1799 did not bear the earmarks of a truly romantic union. She was not his intellectual equal and made no attempt to interfere with his work of social reform. Hugh Stowell, meeting Owen one day in a stagecoach after Caroline's death, asked him if his home had been a happy one and if he enjoyed the peace that his wife possessed as she lay dying. Stowell reported that Owen momentarily wept and said that he would not allow himself to be overcome by an appeal to his feelings.[19] William Maclure, in a letter to Madame Fretageot, dated August 21, 1826, charged Owen with improprieties with the women at New Harmony. He wrote:

> I did not conjecture that Mr. O. was quite so amorous as the stories make him. The wives of the greatest part of those that have left you [at New Harmony] lately have declared to their husbands that it was in consequence of the freedom that Mr. O. took with them that they could not think of remaining under such a dreadful risk of their virtue. This . . . forms a nostrum that gives currency to all the stories about indiscriminate intercourse and all things being in common.[20]

Robert Owen's "Declaration of Mental Independence" and his subsequent lectures and writings altered the views of conventional marriage at New Harmony but did not turn it into a free love colony as its critics claimed. William Maclure, who disagreed with Owen on several issues and withdrew to establish his own community, Macluria, a short distance from New Harmony, declared in his *Opinions on Various Subjects* that Owen's attitude was one of permissiveness toward sexual intercourse between unmarried people.[21] There is nothing in Owen's writings to support this charge against him. Maclure earlier, in a letter to Mrs. Joseph Sistaire, admitted that New Harmony was not a brothel and that he had never been in a place "where the married are so faithful, or the young so chaste." [22] Owen did encourage early marriages of the physically and mentally fit, as the only safeguard for morality. He laid himself open to criticism when he boarded young men and women in the same house, but he passed it off by claiming that "in six months they will become so used to it that they will not mind it." [23] The critic Maclure, although a bachelor, shared his living quarters with Madame Fretageot. The Indianapolis *Indiana Journal* reported that "it would be no breach of charity to class them all with whores and whoremongers, nor to say that the whole group will constitute one great brothel." [24] Premarital sex was permitted once a couple had given notice of their intention to marry. They were required to wait three months before their legal union.[25]

The first marriage occurred at New Harmony, before Robert Owen arrived to take charge of the community, between Alfred Salmon and Elizabeth Palmer.[26] There was nothing in the report of the marriage in the community's newspaper to indicate that it was any different from other marriages performed at the time on the frontier. The following April an unusual marriage was recorded. Philip Price and Matilda Greenbree, along with Robert Robson and Elisa Parvin, agreed to comply with a resolution regarding marriage ceremonies recently passed by the community as "a protest against the usual form of marriage." [27] Each couple stood up and held hands and repeated: "I, A. B., do agree to take this man (woman) to be my husband (wife), and declare that I submit to any other ceremony upon this occasion only in conformity with the laws of the State." [28] The women involved were not compelled to promise that they would obey their husbands, nor were any of the parties asked to vow their love until separated by death. One of the brides had been scrubbing all week preceding her wedding in her New Harmony costume of black and white-striped cotton. She had planned to wear a traditional bridal gown of white, but Robert Owen persuaded her to fly in the face of custom, and wear her dirty dress, which she did, but not without shedding a few tears.[29]

Robert Dale Owen, son of the founder of New Harmony and one of the community's distinguished residents, married Mary Jane Robinson of Virginia, April 12, 1832, in a simple ceremony without benefit of clergy. On the morning of the wedding, he penned the following agreement, which was in strict keeping with his father's ideas on the subject of marriage:

> . . . we contract a legal marriage, not because we deem the ceremony necessary to us, or useful . . . to society; but because, if we become companions without a legal ceremony, we should either be perpetually exposed to annoyances. . . . We desire a tranquil life in so far as it can be obtained without a sacrifice of principle.
>
> We have selected the simplest ceremony which the laws of this state recognize, and which . . . involves not the necessity of calling in the aid of a member of the clerical profession. . . . The ceremony, too, involves not the necessity of making promises regarding that over which we have no control, the state of human affections . . . of the unjust rights which in virtue of this ceremony, an iniquitous law tacitly gives me over the person and property of another, I cannot legally, but I can morally divest myself. And I hereby distinctly and emphatically declare that I consider myself . . . as utterly divested, now and during the rest of my life, of any such rights.[30]

Both Robert Dale Owen and Mary Jane Robinson signed their names to this document, and Mary Jane added, "I concur in these sentiments." Their marriage appeared a happy union, but not without incident. Their daughter, Rosamond, recorded her memories at New Harmony with some nostalgia, writing, "well do I remember the cheer of this our home." [31] Robert Dale Owen recalled that his life at New Harmony "for many months was happy and satisfying," in which he daily met "handsome, interesting and warm-hearted girls." [32] One young lady in particular who caught his eye later married the son of Oliver Evans, inventor of the high-pressure steam engine. Robert also found a kindred spirit in Frances Wright and the two made frequent trips together, both in Europe and in America.

Although Robert Owen did not inaugurate an experiment in eugenics at New Harmony, as John Humphrey Noyes later did at Oneida, New York, he believed that measures must be taken to prohibit the reproduction of disease and the multiplication of an inferior race of people. In his *New Moral World* Owen assured the reader that in the future society no inferior human beings would be produced and that people with diseases would "not be allowed to propagate their natural defects and miseries, in order that hereditary evils may speedily cease to retard the happiness of the human race." [33] However, Owen did not propose that married couples divorce if either person contracted a disease which might be passed on to their children.

Divorce at New Harmony could not be regarded by modern standards as easy to obtain, but it was certainly so by the standards of the early nineteenth century. Owen encouraged husbands and wives to always be truthful in their expression of feelings toward each other, even if they came to loathe one another, in order that there would "be no disguise or deception regarding affection between any parties." [34] If happiness were not realized in a marriage, he advised that a divorce be procured, but not without an extended waiting period in order to give both parties opportunity to work out their differences and to make every attempt to recapture their initial love for one another. If after three publications of the mutual desire to separate, at intervals of five months, no reconciliation was possible, the community regarded their divorce as final and each was free to marry whomever he pleased. Children of the marriage presented no problem, as they were considered as belonging to the community.[35]

Robert Owen believed that the family was incompatible with communal life, although he reluctantly permitted the separate family arrangement at New Harmony. He had been unable to destroy familism at New Lanark, mainly because of the opposition of the women of the community and the objections of his business associates. He did manage to weaken family ties by making the community assume responsibilities, through socialist measures, which were once purely the concern of the individual families. Owen hoped that he could be more successful in this respect at New Harmony. In an address delivered at Harmony Hall, April 27, 1825, he admitted that

> to change from the individual to the social system, from single families with separate interests, to communities with one interest, cannot be accomplished at once; the change would be too great for the present habits of society . . . it becomes necessary, therefore, that some intermediate measures should be adopted to enable all parties, with the least inconvenience, to change their individual, selfish habits. . . . New Harmony . . . is the best half-way house I could procure for those who are going to travel this extraordinary journey with me.[36]

Robert Owen regarded the middle-class family as the main bastion of private property and selfishness; a perfect social order could not be attained without its abolition. In his *Lectures on Marriages*, he charged that the children in the nuclear family are instructed in a most efficient manner to acquire the dubious virtue of selfishness. The daily vocabulary spoken in their presence, in such expressions as "*my* house, *my* wife, *my* estate, *my* children, or *my* husband; *our* estate, *our* children; or *my* brothers, *my* sisters, and *our* house and property," were calculated to teach children that they must by all means, short of robbery, "increase the wealth, honour, and privileges of the family and every member of it." [37] Owen regarded the individual family, and not class divisions, as the most divisive factor among men. The family enjoyed the unique advantage of protection from the laws of the state as well as religious sanctions. Behind these two barriers, the family was sovereign and thus an alien element in a society which tended to isolate rather than unite men.

Robert Owen proposed to replace the family with "scientific associations of men, women and children, in their usual proportions, from about four or five hundred to about two thousand, arranged to be as one family." [38] He planned to incorporate an entire village into a single, continuous structure with gymnasiums, living quarters, schools, library, ballrooms, theatres, museums, brewery, bakery, laundries, etc. Stedman Whitewell drew up the plans from the dimensions Owen submitted which gave the appearance of a medieval castle. Owen allowed for the newly liberated family in his community plan in which a husband and wife would occupy a "lodging room" and would be expected to have no more than two children. The children would remain with their parents until the age of three, and then be sent to the community nursery and from that time forward the parents would be relieved from the burdens of their care. The community dining hall also replaced the family dinner table.

Owen's theories found only a limited practical expression at New Harmony. Many of the families occupied the private houses which the Rappites left behind. In 1826 Owen prevailed upon these families to take in other families, while at the same time their children were to be removed to a boarding school. Sarah Pears bitterly complained of this invasion of privacy. In a letter to Mrs. Benjamin Bakewell, dated March 10, 1826, she wrote:

> I will now, if I can, give you some account of our new rules. . . . All our elder children, those whom we expected to be comfort and consolation and support in our old age, are to be taken away from us, at an age, too, when they so peculiarly require the guardian care of their parents; and are to be placed in large boarding houses. The single males and females above the age of fourteen are to live together in one house, over which there is to be one married woman to superintend. . . . In stead of our own dear children each housekeeper is to receive two more families, one of which will have a child under two years old. . . . We have already got one family with us. . . . I hope it will not be necessary to take a third. . . . However, I shall prefer going into one of their miserable log cabins to being crowded so thick. . . if this is not slavery I do not know what is.[39]

A large house was constructed at New Harmony in 1826 in order to provide living quarters for the married members of the society. Each family was to have a chamber and an alcove. There were no kitchen facilities in these family quarters, as all ate in a common dining hall.

Children at Owen's New Harmony were reared much like those in Plato's *Republic*. Infants were surrendered to the community as soon as feasible without jeopardizing their health. This was done, according to Maclure, to remove them "during the formative years from the handicap of ignorant and immoral homes." [40] This removal of children to a community nursery was done forcibly when necessary. From the age of two to five years, Madame Fretageot superintended their education. At the age of five, the children were taken over by Joseph Neef, his four daughters and a son, who trained them, according to the Pestalozzian system of education, in Community House Number Two. The children were allowed to see their parents only on rare occasions. If parents insisted on visiting their children they were told to remove them from the Community House and take them home with them. One of the students, Sarah Cox, later wrote, "I saw my father and mother twice in two years. We had a little song we used to sing:

> Number 2 pigs locked up in a pen
> When they get out, it's now and then;
> When they get out, they sneak about,
> For fear old Neef will find them out.[41]

Altogether there were 130 children under the Community's charge in 1826. Owen's money, while he was willing to invest it, paid for the children's board and education. Parents, if they chose, could contribute either labor or an annual sum for the education of their children, as well as for other social benefits, including care in sickness and in old age.

Owen employed every conceivable means to neutralize the influence of the private family at New Harmony, but in the end he had to admit his failure. In his farewell address to the community, which he delivered on April 13, 1827, just three years after the advent of the Owenites to New Harmony, Owen confessed:

> This last experiment has made it evident that families trained in the individual system, founded as it is upon superstition, have not acquired those moral qualities of forbearance and charity for each other which are necessary to promote full confidence and harmony among all the members, and without which Communities cannot exist.[42]

Familism won out at New Harmony over Owenism. Owen took leave of the community, never to return. Robert Dale Owen and many of his father's associates remained for a time, hoping to salvage something worth while from the social experiment.

New Harmony inspired the establishment of at least sixteen communities in America and seven in England. The Friendly Association for Mutual Interest formed a community at Kendall, Ohio, in June 1826, at the height of the New Harmony experiment. The avowed purpose of the community at Kendall was "to carry out Owen's ideas." [43] Within a year the community was paying wages and families were allowed to manage their own internal affairs for themselves. Before a second year passed the experiment was regarded a failure and folded.[44]

The Franklin community at Haverstraw, New York, was established the same year as the Kendall community, also on the basis of the Owenite philosophy. Unitary housing at Franklin, which provided apartment-like living for families, with the exception of a common dining hall, was a source of dissension. Robert L. Jennings admitted that the community had learned a few things in their experiment, mainly that they would never again accept married couples, but only the youth who would be reared within the milieu of the new social system.[45]

The Yellow Springs community in Green County, Ohio, was another venture in Owenism. A group of Swedenborgian intellectuals had heard Owen lecture and were converted to his plan for communal living. They purchased 720 acres, on which Antioch College is now located, and began their utopian experiment. About 100 families were involved. An unidentified newspaper clipping in the Macdonald Manuscript reports that "there was no free-loveism, or other looseness of morals allowed." [46] Morris Hillquit, a sympathetic socialist, claimed: "The ministers soon found sinners more manageable and interesting than swine, merchants found the pitchforks not half as remunerative as the yardstick, and refined ladies tired of the coarse company of pots and kettles. One by one they returned to their old homes and vocations." [47] The community disbanded the same year it began, in 1825. The Owenite communities were noted for their brevity, as none exceeded three years.

V

Family Life in a Phalanx:

The Fourierites

THE FRENCHMAN, CHARLES FOURIER, INSPIRED ABOUT FIFTY COMMUNAL experiments during the nineteenth century in America, although none of them strictly measured up to his ideal. Writing after the French Revolution, Fourier found that the evils which afflicted mankind were social in nature and could be removed only by a reorganization of society in accordance with what he regarded as the "natural law of attraction." Fourier believed that he had discovered this great law of society and compared his discovery with Newton's discovery of the natural law of moving bodies. The eccentric Fourier believed everything could be reduced to mathematics. He even had his walking stick marked off in feet and half-feet in order that he might measure everything that caught his interest.[1] Fourier calculated that the ideal social unit was one in which 1,620 men, women, and children lived in a scientifically organized community, called a phalanx.[2]

All were to reside in a phalanstery, a huge six-story structure with one long body and two wings which were to be symmetrical and rectangular. There were to be inner courtyards and a parade ground in front, with the main body of the building and two wings adjoining on three of its four sides. The phalanstery was to be situated on a tract of land three miles square and was to contain private apartments for the members, general purpose rooms, and a dining hall. The phalanstery was not designed for barrack-type living, as the citizens were not to be thrown together in a dormitory, nor were they to eat in a common dining hall. Apartments were to be let at various prices, depending on their location in the phalanstery and their accommodations, much like a large resort hotel.

Fourier's plan was not communistic. Although he bemoaned the plight of the proletariat, he did not wish to destroy capitalism, but to use capitalistic principles which could benefit all mankind rather than the bourgeoisie alone. The phalanx was to be a joint-stock company in which the members in common were to engage in industry and to share the proceeds according to their capital investment, skill, and labor.[3] Fourier believed that once the scientific laws of society were demonstrated in industry, the whole world would follow and become a universal joint-stock enterprise, sharing its benefits with every man, woman, and child on earth. Fourier calculated there would be precisely two million phalanxes in the world once his views were universally accepted.

Fourierism frankly accepted industrialism as a fact of modern life, rather than attempting to repudiate it. But individualism had no place in the industrial society for Fourier, as the system demanded cooperation and association. Fourier was concerned with the greatest amount of happiness for the greatest number of people. He charged that the present order of society had isolated man through fragmentation of the social order. Each man and his family constituted the smallest possible unit of society, separated from their fellow men. Selfishness, distrust, egoism, strife, anarchical competition, and universal duplicity of action were the results.[4] Through association, founded on scientific laws, Fourier held there could be capital unity and the harmonious action of interest and feelings. While it promised numerous social benefits for the poor, including attractive industry, Fourierism also promised to increase the wealth and the enjoyments of the rich.[5] Sophia, the wife of Nathaniel Hawthorne, after reading the works of Fourier, wrote to her mother that the main thrust of Fourier's ideas was "to make as much money and luxury and enjoyment out of man's lowest passions as possible . . . to restrain, to deny, is not suggested." [6]

Before there could be social harmony, Fourier maintained that there had to be a moral harmony of the passions. He believed the miseries of mankind were mainly due to the suppression of the passions of friendship and ambition. Society, as presently constructed, held these passions in bondage, and filled the world with antagonisms, hatred, and destruction. The passion of friendship could find freedom in uninhibited association, and the passion of ambition, or the love of order, could find its freedom only when society was scientifically structured so as to give each man, woman, and child a place in the social scale according to his worth. In Fourier's community, persons would be naturally attracted to one another in groups of seven to nine persons, which he called "series." [7]

The associationism of Fourier had no place for individualism. Feudalism had once submerged the individual and he believed that industrialism threatened to do the same. Fourier accepted the loss of individualism as a fact of life. But neither feudalism nor industrialism had brought human happiness, although both systems had assigned each man his place from which there could be little or no escape. Feudalism and modern industrialism were not instituted in accordance with the natural and immutable laws of social science and were regarded by Fourier as systems of human bondage. Associationism proposed a collective submission to these scientific laws as discovered and revealed by Fourier.

The sublimation of the individual in Fourier's doctrine caused several New England intellectuals, such as Ralph Waldo Emerson, Theodore Parker, and Henry David Thoreau to refuse to join in the attempts to found associations, although they, like the Fourierists, were critical of the same evils in society. Emerson, in his essay, "Self Reliance," regarded society as "a joint-stock company, in which the members agree, for the better securing of his bread to each shareholder, to surrender the liberty and culture of the eater. The virtue in most request is conformity. Self reliance is its aversion." [8] He believed the individual was fully capable of arriving at truth without becoming involved in an association. Fourier's own mode of living, which was the antithesis of his social theory, was more in keeping with the ideals of many of the transcendentalists, since no one was more individualistic than he. He never married, and lived and died "almost as great a stranger to his own family as to the rest of society." [9]

The popularity of Fourier's ideas in America was due mainly to the support given them by Albert Brisbane and Horace Greeley. Brisbane went to Europe in 1828 and sat at the feet of Hegel in Berlin, Goethe in Weimar, and Fourier in Paris. He was disturbed over the coming industrial society and the competitive chaos which followed in its wake, and hoped he could find something in the teachings of these philosophers which would bring order to a troubled world. Fourier appeared to have found the solution in his doctrine of association. Upon return to America, Brisbane, in 1840, wrote *The Social Destiny of Man*, in which he outlined Fourier's principles for American readers. The depression of the late 1830s provided a reform climate in which Fourierism, as well as other social panaceas, gained a hearing. It is doubtful, however, that Fourierism would have received widespread publicity had it not been for the encouragement it received in the nation's press. Brisbane approached Horace Greeley, who had just begun to publish *The New York Tribune* in 1840, and encouraged him to read his book, *The Social Destiny of Man.* Greeley consented and, upon finishing the volume, became an enthusiastic believer in Fourier's plan for industrial association.[10] Greeley opened up the columns of the *Tribune* to Brisbane that he might set forth Fourier's ideas to the American public. On March 1, 1842, the latter began a series of articles entitled, "Association; or, Principles of a True Organization of Society." He announced that through the medium of the *Tribune*, he intended "to lay before the Public the practical means which that great Mind Charles Fourier has proposed for alleviating the vast amount of misery which exists in Society, and for the elevating of the social Condition of Man, and securing ultimately his happiness." [11] The response exceeded Brisbane's wildest imagination and was well worth the $500 he was supposed to have paid Greeley for space in the newspaper.[12] The doctrine of association was picked up by other newspapers across the nation. The circulation of the *Tribune* increased tremendously, to the alarm of the editors of *The New York Morning Courier* and *The New York Enquirer.* Fourieristic societies were formed and conventions were held in the winter of 1843–1844. Hundreds of delegates convened in Rochester, New York, in August 1843, and a drive was made to organize phalanxes in that area. The following April a national convention of Associationists was held in New York City and George Ripley, a transcendentalist who had founded Brook Farm in 1841, was elected president. Horace Greeley, Albert Brisbane, Parke Godwin, and Charles Dana were elected vice presidents.

Without due consideration to Fourier's mathematical scheme,

phalanxes were hastily formed in New York, Pennsylvania, Ohio, Massachusetts, New Jersey, Illinois, Michigan, Wisconsin, Indiana, and Iowa. Popular enthusiasm for security, peace, and happiness, which many thought possible only in association, ran far ahead of the architect's proposal. They did not wait for 1,600 or more individuals to vow their purpose to form a community, nor did they linger until a sufficient capital base had been accumulated.

America's experiment in Fourierism was abortive and many of the communities could survive no more than three years. Only the North American Phalanx at Red Bank, New Jersey, exceeded a decade; most of them died the first year. Brisbane became disillusioned. He once affirmed that the appearance of Fourier was the second coming of Jesus Christ, but later expressed his feeling that "If ever a man deserved to be hanged for intellectual rashness and violence, it is Fourier." [13]

Fourier is not to be blamed altogether for the failure of associationism in America, for his social system had never really been tried. The experiments which lay claim to his name were, for the most part, expressions of sentimental enthusiasm for new doctrines rather than calculated attempts to test his thesis regarding a new social system. Fourier's ideas would have necessitated a complete revolution in public sentiment, and the American associationists were too impatient for such a revolution to be effected. Greeley was too naive in his acceptance of Fourierism to realize this. He wrote: "This system requires no immediate sacrifice as a condition precedent of ultimate benefit. While it may well satisfy the most thorough Radical, it need not alarm the most timid Conservative." [14]

One of the basic tenets of Fourierism which would first require a change in traditional sentiment before an experiment could succeed was that which concerned marriage and the family. Fourier posited the theory that association could find practical application when there were families with few children and where one-third of the phalanx consisted of celibates.[15] Fourier was deliberately vague about marriage and the family in the future, for he realized that public sentiment was too deeply entrenched in their favor to demand their immediate abolition. He was content to leave this issue to the future to work out its own natural solution once association became the established social order. Fourier preferred to educate the children of the phalanx in such a way as to prevent an inculcation of traditional family sentiments. He regarded children as a neuter sex, without the passions of love and family feelings, and he wished to prolong this "neutrality" as long as possible. He was opposed to any form of sex education, including Bible stories which were frank in the discussion of sex, and the observation of copulation of animals.[16]

Families were to retain their individual identities at first, and to live in separate apartments in the phalanstery. However, through the associative life, familism would wane and gradually lose its exclusive characteristics. The Fourierist, Madame Gatti de Gammon, assured her readers that the law of social attraction,

> while it conserves the ties and affections of the family, will destroy its exclusive interests. Association will mingle it to such an extent with the great communal or phalansterian family that every narrow affection will disappear, that it will find its own interest in that of all, and will attach it sincerely and passionately to the public concern.[17]

Fourier was highly critical of the family as constituted in present society as being "the greatest obstacle to the freedom of the passions." [18] Family selfishness, which concentrated all affections within its own narrow circle and manifested a spirit of indifference toward the sufferings of those outside, was what Fourier criticized most. He complained that "the life of married households, or couples, is unsociability reduced to its simplest form." [19] Like Owen, he did not believe a husband and wife should make lifelong commitments to love one another. He reasoned:

> Civilized love, in marriage, is, at the end of a few months, or perhaps the second day, often nothing but pure brutality, chance coupling, induced by the domestic tie, devoid of any illusion of the mind or of the heart: a result very common among the masses where the husband and wife, surfeited, morose, quarrelling with each other during the day, become necessarily reconciled upon retiring, because they have not the means to purchase two beds, and contact, the brute spur of the senses, triumphs a moment over conjugal satiety.[20]

Fourier contended that the natural impulse of each member of the family is to break away from the monotonous pleasure of familial association. The father seeks to escape the home by running to a mistress or seeking the companionship of other males. The mother seeks associations outside the home. The children, upon reaching puberty, think only of escaping from the restrictions of the household. Even the very young constantly think of ways to avoid the eye of their elders that they might engage in forbidden pleasures. Fourier concluded that "individuals, considered separately, seek nothing but to escape the sweet household . . . where the moralist wants to locate happiness." [21]

The disciples of Fourier in America played down his views on marriage and the family as much as possible. These hallowed institutions were so thoroughly ingrained in American society that any threat to them was sufficient to unleash a tirade of invectives that few associationists were prepared to counter. Nathaniel Hawthorne's wife, Sophia, wrote to her mother that the American Fourierists were afraid to translate his works for all to see how his teachings undermined the foundations of the social order, particularly marriage and the family. She admitted that "this subject is often discussed in the book-room," but "it is strange . . . that among learned men, who are interested about public morals and our civil institutions, no one should take the trouble to read what Charles Fourier wrote." [22] Albert Brisbane had read all of Fourier's works and fully understood his master's views on marriage and what he anticipated for the family in his plans for a new social order. Brisbane, through his column in the *Tribune*, repeatedly hit at the separate family arrangement, with its separate houses, separate interests, separate hopes, and separate welfare to maintain. He concluded that such a social order was "opposed to capital reason, to capital judgment, and to capital truth, and should be reformed." [23]

Horace Greeley, although strongly in favor of social reform, was not interested in defending Fourier's attacks on marriage and the family. He had been responsible, by his money and through his influence, for the establishment of the Sylvania Phalanx in Pennsylvania and the North American Phalanx in New Jersey. He was also instrumental in converting Brook Farm from a transcendentalist commune to a Fourieristic phalanx. American Fourierists repeatedly embarrassed Greeley by criticizing the family and belittling marriage. Greeley felt compelled to affirm his position on these two institutions lest he be categorized as an advocate of free love and easy divorce. The revered editor debated Robert Dale Owen on the subject of divorce in 1860. His logic, however, left something to be desired in this literary duel. He contended that marriage was for life because that is the way Webster's dictionary defined it.[24]

The most telling attack against Greeley's Fourierism was made by Henry J. Raymond, editor of James Webb's *Courier* and *En-*

quirer. Raymond had worked for Greeley in the *Tribune* office and had become thoroughly acquainted with Greeley's views and his polemic inadequacies. James Webb was determined to wreck the *Tribune*, and the occasion of Raymond's joining his staff in 1844 appeared to be his opportune moment. Raymond wrote several articles against Fourierism in general and Greeley in particular for the *Courier*. Greeley challenged Raymond to a literary debate. He suggested that each paper print both sides of their argument once each week from November 20, 1846, to May 20, 1847. Raymond carried the attack against Fourierism to the point where Greeley was most sensitive: the destruction of the family and the dishonor of marriage. He contended:

> Fourierism is either communism with all its moral horrors, or it is only a new and cheap disguise for the familiar capitalistic system. If the 'passions' are free, as the scheme proposes, the result will be polygamy and other perversions destroying the family.[25]

Raymond was relentless in his attack of Fourierism on this point. He charged that the doctrine "would crumble civilization's bulwark, which was the sanctity of property. It would dissolve the family and flood the country with immorality." [26] He tried to make Greeley guilty by association by accusing him of being in agreement with Fanny Wright and Parke Godwin, who were accused of being advocates of free love.[27] Greeley countered, "I deny with disgust and indignation that there is in Socialism, as American Socialists understand and teach it, any provision or license for the gratification of criminal passions or unlawful desires." [28] Greeley, whose fervor for Fourierism waned throughout the debate, was forced to disavow the *Tribune's* responsibility for Charles Fourier, Parke Godwin, and Albert Brisbane and to declare: "What the *Tribune* advocates is, simply and solely, such organization of society as will secure to every man the opportunity of uninterrupted and profitable labor, and to every child nourishment and culture." [29] Beyond this, Greeley was content to go no further. He was in no mood to defend the individual actions of the socialists with whom he associated. When necessary he exposed their immorality through the pages of the *Tribune*. In 1855 the report of Brisbane's arrest on the charge of disorderly conduct for attending a meeting which was alleged to have involved free love was published by Greeley's paper.[30] As the subtleties of Fourier's teachings unfolded under the light of further investigation and debate, Greeley lost his initial ardor for associationism and shifted his attention to reforms which were less revolutionary in their scope.

Fourieristic phalanxes sprang up in America like spring mushrooms during the 1840s and withered just as quickly. None of them came close to approximating the ideas of Fourier, except in vocabulary. The North American Phalanx at Red Bank, New Jersey, was the most successful experiment in associationism as to duration. It was organized in 1843 and was not officially abandoned until 1856. Horace Greeley claimed that if this enterprise could not survive, there was no hope for any other.[31] The initial capital investment for the experiment exceeded $100,000, of which Greeley himself had invested $4,300 of his early *Tribune* profits.[32] Albert Brisbane, whose knowledge of Fourier's teachings was overwhelmed in the midst of popular enthusiasm, rushed the phalanx into existence with a few dozen families. Instead of a castle-like phalanstery, the members lived in squalor and erected numerous buildings for others who never came. A large house, forty by eighty feet, was constructed on the 700-acre tract with accommodations for the first families. Later a "mansion house" of three floors, 150 feet long, was built to house about 100 people.[33]

The North American Phalanx wrestled with the problem of which new institutions were to be adopted and which institutions of ordinary society were to be retained. The role of the family figured prominently in their early deliberations. In a treatise written by Charles Sears, a member of the phalanx, entitled "Social Reform, Practical Agricultural and Domestic Association—Historical Sketch of the North American Phalanx," the author admitted their struggle in the beginning in deciding which direction to take. Sears wrote:

> . . . to break up habitudes, relinquish prejudices, sunder ties, and to adopt new modes of action, accept of modified results, and readjust themselves to new relations was difficult . . . . The question at issue was vital. It was whether the infant Association should or should not have new institutions; whether it be Civilisée or Phalansterian.[34]

Sears anticipated the abolition of conventional marriage when women were fully franchised and given their property rights so that they would no longer be dependent on their husbands for support.

He admitted, however, that such prospects were not likely to be realized in the near future.

The question of the role of the family at the North American Phalanx was settled in favor of retaining the separate fireside with some slight modification. Only six to twelve families lived in the mansion house, since the structure was designed mainly to accommodate single adults. Most of the families lived in separate cabins. Fredrika Bremer, who visited the phalanx in September 1852, reported that one Marcus S. had built a small house there for his family, purely because of the fresh air and the sea-bathing opportunities nearby during the summer months.[35]

At the first, each family ate separately, but within a short time all began eating in a common dining hall. At times the food was scarce and monotonous. N. C. Meeker admitted that the menu frequently consisted only of buckwheat cakes and water.[36] Meeker also revealed that mothers were more concerned about their own offspring than they were about other children in the community, and made sure they got the choice of the small quantity of available food. Despite the privations at the North American Phalanx, some freedoms were enjoyed there that one could not find in the more affluent, but restricted, religious communities. John Gray, an ex-Shaker, said that he knew he could go away from the North American Phalanx when he pleased without any difficulty, but that he preferred the single family and isolated cottage arrangement to the unitary fare of a Shaker village.[37]

Familism at North American posed its usual problems to communal living. Meeker claimed that some of the women who were the most enthusiastic over the prospects of associationism at first were broken in both body and spirit before the experiment ran its course and collapsed. He concluded: "The idea that woman in Association was to be relieved of many cares, was not realized." [38] The usual backbiting and gossip which plagued other utopian communities were not neutralized by Fourier's natural laws of attraction in the North American Phalanx. Several members of the community went to Texas in 1853 to join Victor Considérant's experiment at La Réunion. Considérant came from France the year before to seek an ideal location for a community in America. Albert Brisbane accompanied him to Texas and the French utopian was greatly impressed with the possibilities which the southwestern part of America offered to his plans. Considérant wrote *Au Texas*, in which he described Texas in glowing terms, and pleaded with others to join him in establishing a community there.[39] He chose a site near Dallas for his enterprise. Considérant made no effort to interfere with the marriage relation and the family at La Réunion. He returned to France, however, a disillusioned figure after his experiment barely survived a year.

The Sylvania Phalanx, of which Horace Greeley was treasurer, was organized in 1842 on a 2,300 acre tract in northern Pennsylvania. The location was a poor one, as it was selected in the winter, while the snow was on the ground, by "a landscape painter, an industrious cooper, and a homeopathic doctor,"[40] who knew little about agriculture. The land was so unproductive that it barely yielded the amount of seed sown, despite the optimistic report of Albert Brisbane that "The soil of the domain is a deep loam, well calculated for tillage and grazing."[41] The experiment lasted less than two years. However, the community received a great deal of notoriety because of Horace Greeley's association with it.

Familism was retained at Sylvania, but not without discord. In "A Dialogue Concerning the Sylvania Association," an unidentified member described the living conditions as anything but desirable:

> . . . in August [1842] there were on the place 28 married men and 27 married women. 24 single young men, 6 single young women and 31 children, making a total of 136 individuals. These had to be closely packed in three very indifferent two-story frame houses. The upper-story of the grist mill, we devoted for as many as could sleep therein. These arrangements very soon brought trouble. Children with every variety of temper and habits were brought in close contact without any previous training to prepare them for it. Parents, each with his or her peculiar character and mode of educating their children, long used to very different accommodations, are brought here and literally compelled to live like a herd of animals. Some believed that their children would be taken and cared for by the society as its own family. While others claimed and practiced the rights to procure for their children all the little indulgences they had been used to; thus jealousies and ill-feelings were created, and in place of self *sacrifice* and zealous support of the constitution and officers to which they were pledged (I have no doubt by some in ignorance) there was a total disregard for all discipline and a determination in each to have the biggest share of all things going except *hard* work.[42]

If some in the community believed that their children would be taken and cared for by the society, they were simply trusting Article Nine of the Sylvania Constitution, which clearly stated that children under ten years of age would be the charge of the Association under the direction of an executive council.[43]

Among the professed Fourieristic communities, the Wisconsin Phalanx ranked second in duration to the North American, having survived for six years. The idea for the formation of an association in Wisconsin came directly out of a village lyceum in Southport, now known as Kenosha, Wisconsin. A 1,700 acre tract of government land was purchased in Fond du Lac county, near the town of Ripon, in 1844. By 1847 there were 157 resident members, consisting of thirty-two families and several unmarried adults and children. Financially, the venture was a tremendous success, as no money was lost by any of the shareholders and at the dissolution of the colony in 1850, a sizable premium was paid on all stock. Socially, however, the experiment, like so many of its sister associations, was a failure.

Warren Chase, George H. Stebbins, and Benjamin Wright were determined to apply Fourier's principles as best they could within their limited resources at the Wisconsin Phalanx. Fourier's theory of distribution, which involved unequal remuneration to laborers of different classes, was a feature of the phalanx which was found in but few other associations identified as Fourieristic. Chase, in a letter dated September 12, 1844, reported: "We adhere strictly to our constitution and by-laws, and adopt as fast as possible the system of Fourier. We have organized our groups and series in a simple manner, and thus far everything goes admirably." [44] A year later, he was still confident and proclaimed: "We are Associationists of the Fourier school, and intend to reduce his system to practice as fast as possible, consistently without our situation." [45]

At this point a problem arose at the Wisconsin Phalanx as to the type of dwellings to be constructed for the benefit of the married men with families. Several families wished to maintain their separate identity and to live in separate houses. This was contrary to the Fourieristic plan for a phalanstery. A vote was taken and those who wished to construct a large unitary house to accommodate all of the members barely succeeded in mustering sufficient numerical strength in their favor. The minority was unwilling to submit to the democratic decision and continued to live as separate families in dwellings apart from the unitary house. The phalanx was plagued by petty differences from that time forward until its dissolution. Warren Chase noted that even in the unitary house,

> Most of our families cook their board in their rooms from choice under present circumstances; some because they use no meat and do not choose to sit at a table supplied with beef, pork and mutton; others because they choose to have their children sit at the table with them . . . others because they want to ask a blessing, etc.; and others because their manner of cooking and habits of living have become so fixed as to have sufficient influence to require their continuance.[46]

Members began to complain about unequal pay for the various jobs within the phalanx. In a work entitled, "History of the Wisconsin Phalanx," an anonymous writer admitted that their system of labor and pay was complicated and unsatisfactory: "The farmers and mechanics were always jealous of each other," and some were "determined to accumulate property individually by any and every means called fair in competitive society." [47]

All of the members of the Wisconsin Phalanx were American-born and thoroughly imbued with American ideas. The community was unable to neutralize these ideas and the teachings of Fourier, although daily discussed, could never find full acceptance. The economic success of the enterprise, in part, was its own undoing. There were competitive opportunities to make money and many took advantage of them. As one expressed it, "the love of money and the want of love for association" killed the experiment.[48] The pent-up life in the unitary house, where families competitively vied for their individual benefits, brought more problems than the directors of the phalanx knew how to handle effectively.

A Fourieristic phalanx was also begun in 1844 in Clermont County, Ohio, about thirty miles east of Cincinnati. An enthusiastic convention of Socialists met in Cincinnati that year and read letters written by Horace Greeley, Albert Brisbane, William H. Channing, and others regarding the virtues of the associative life. They immediately determined to find a suitable location to put Fourier's principles into operation. A "splendid domain" was chosen on the Ohio river which was ideally situated for shipping and receiving goods.[49] The members of the Clermont Phalanx, as the community was christened, decided in favor of unitary housing for its families, without the debate which attended the decision at the Wisconsin Phalanx. The building, which resembled a steamboat, had a long, narrow corridor which ran the entire length of the structure, with little staterooms jutting off on either side. Each room, which was intended to house a man and his wife, or two single persons, had a small window, somewhat like a porthole.[50] Various types and temperaments of the members of the association, all thrown together in tight quarters, resulted in disagreements and general confusion.

The women at Clermont found it more difficult to adapt to communal living than did the men. Their roles as wives and mothers had been altered to the point where they no longer felt needed by their families. A. J. Macdonald pinpointed the source of the problem at the phalanx as directly the fault of the women.[51]

The Trumbull Phalanx at Braceville, in northeastern Ohio, began operation in 1844. At the height of their experiment, there were 250 individuals in the community. At first there was an attempt at living in unitary houses with some thirty-five families in dwellings designed to house a single family. The bill of fare was meager and discontent among the families forced a change in the housing policy. Log cabins were hastily constructed and families were removed from the intolerable unitary houses. The president of the association occupied one of the cabins apart from the community, as he could not bear the strain of so much intimacy. One by one the families departed, mainly because the food was coarse and inadequate and they had not been afforded the better life which they had anticipated. The leaders of the colony blamed the indiscriminate admission policy for the failure. As one member expressed it, the society had become "an asylum for the needy, sick and disabled, [rather] than a nucleus of efficient members, carrying out with all their powers and energies, a system on which they honestly rely for restoring their race to elevation and happiness." [52]

A Fourieristic phalanx, once established, normally ran its brief course and dissolved in a single location. This was not the case, however, with the Integral Phalanx, which had its start in Ohio and folded in Illinois. In 1845 the Integral Phalanx began operation on a 900 acre tract in Butler County, Ohio, twenty-three miles north of Cincinnati. Plans were laid for the construction of one wing of a phalanstery, which would house sixty-four families. John S. Williams, leader of the group, was one of the most ardent Fourierists in the West and was determined to make the Integral Phalanx the classic example of Fourierism at work. He realized that it would take time to secure the precise number of people necessary for an ideal phalanx and to educate the members to his projected way of life. Internal dissension wrecked the experiment in Ohio and a remnant "for the space of one year wandered like Noah's dove, finding no resting place for the sole of its feet." [53] Williams admitted the defeat of the experiment in Ohio, but he was by no means sorry for the difficulty encountered there, as it served to purge the association of the unconverted, whom he said "hankered after the flesh-pots of Egypt." [54]

The group settled in Sangamon County, Illinois, a short distance from Springfield. The secretary for the phalanx vowed that no attempt would be made to force unitary housing on the members, as it had been a source of discontent in Ohio. As true Fourierists they would wait until they had the number necessary to enable them

> to organize upon scientific principles, and in accordance with Fourier's admirable plan of industrial organization. It is better that the different families should remain separate for five years, than to bring them together under circumstances worse than civilization. Such a course will unavoidably create confusion and dissatisfaction, and we venture the assertion that it has done so in every instance where it has been attempted.[55]

Within nine months of this report, another was submitted to the *New York Tribune* which informed the public that a unitary structure was under construction, eighty feet of which had been completed and occupied by five families. The report also mentioned that separate firesides still existed within the community for those families who chose to maintain their individuality.[56] Within a year the associationists grew tired of one another's company and went their separate ways. Family life in a Fourieristic phalanx was at best tenuous.

VI

And Fools Rush In

CONCURRENT WITH THE OWENITE EXPERIMENTS IN COMMUNAL LIVING, a split occurred in the Congregational Church in New England. Lyman Beecher emerged as the leader of the orthodox faction, and William E. Channing as the leader of the social reform group of Unitarians. Channing, along with Ralph Waldo Emerson, George Ripley, Margaret Fuller, and others was mainly responsible for the development of a philosophy known as transcendentalism, although it was Emerson who gave it its fiber. The transcendentalists met frequently, discussed their ideas, and speculated on the social improvement of mankind. George Ripley was more than a dreamer; he was eager to apply the thoughts of this elite group of intellectuals in an experiment in group living. He was unable to persuade all of his transcendental cohorts to join him in forming a community, although each of them gave him a reserved endorsement. The culmination of Ripley's planning was Brook Farm, a 200 acre tract at West Roxbury, Massachusetts, about ten miles out of Boston. Brook Farm was made famous by, among other things, Nathaniel Hawthorne's *Blythedale Romance*, a fictional account of the community's daily life.

Ripley's primary objective regarding Brook Farm was to bring together people of high intellect, where all could get closer to nature by engaging in menial farm labor, but above all, where the intellectual atmosphere in their moments of leisure would be conducive to mental stimulation. He wrote to Emerson:

> Our objects, as you know, are to insure a more natural union between intellectual and manual labor than now exists; to combine the thinker and the worker, as far as possible, in the same individual . . . to prepare a society of liberal, intelligent, and cultivated persons, whose relations with each other would permit a more simple and wholesome life, than can be led amidst the pressure of our competitive institutions. To accomplish these objects, we propose to take a small tract of land, which, under skillful husbandry . . . will be adequate to the subsistence of the families; and to connect with this a school or college, in which the most complete instruction shall be given, from the first rudiments to the highest culture.[1]

"Plain living and high thinking" was a term applied in derision by the critics but welcomed by the members of Brook Farm.

Some of the brighter stars in the transcendental galaxy refused to join Ripley at Brook Farm as permanent members, although they frequently visited the community and manifested a tolerant attitude toward the experiment. The spirited Margaret Fuller found communal life too confining. She confessed:

> My hopes might lead to Association, too—An Association, if not of efforts, yet of destinies. In such an one I live with several already, feeling that each one, by acting out his own, casts light upon mutual destiny, and illustrates the thought of a master mind. It is a constellation, not a phalanx, to which I would belong.[2]

She had no reservation about leaving her sixteen-year-old brother, Lloyd, at Brook Farm. He was mentally retarded and was the charge of his sister upon the death of their mother. Margaret enjoyed visiting Brook Farm in its early stages, for there she presided over discussions and seemed to delight in others' glowing appraisals of her intellectual prowess. However, on occasion she was duly disturbed over some of the members' manners. She complained: "The people showed a good deal of the *sans-culotte* tendency in their manners,—throwing themselves on the floor, yawning, and going out when they heard enough." [3]

William Henry Channing, nephew and successor of the William Ellery Channing who inspired Ripley, also declined membership in the Brook Farm community. He had, at first, planned to join, but his wife opposed the idea.[4] He visited the community frequently and gave the experiment, in its earlier stages, his verbal support.

Ralph Waldo Emerson was too much an individualist to join Ripley's community. He claimed that "to join this body would be to traverse all my long trumpeted theory, and the instinct which spoke from it, that one man is a counter-poise to a city,—that a man is stronger than a city, that his solitude is more prevalent and beneficent than the concert of crowds." [5] Later, when the community was considering the adoption of the principles of Fourier, Emerson's response was simply: " 'And fools rush in where angels fear to tread.' So say I of Brook Farm." [6]

Brook Farm began operation as a transcendentalist colony with fifteen persons and the population never exceeded 120. Charles Lane, who lived in several utopian communities, described this one as "merely an aggregation" which lacked "that oneness of spirit" needed to make it of lasting value to man's progress.[7] Few families were involved in the experiment, as once more the maternal instinct was opposed to communal life. Arthur Sumner recalled that only three married couples lived in the community while he boarded there as a student. He remembered that there were several engagements which afterward led to marriage.[8] Amelia Russell told of a family which moved in with several small children and built a house which the members dubbed "The Nest." She said, "It was a pleasant little place, but somehow those who lived there seemed in a degree separated from us, living more by themselves, more like a separate family who visited us as neighbors, and even in that way seldom joining us in our social meetings." [9] Under the transcendental phase of Brook Farm, no attempt was made to pressure the families to live in unitary housing or to sacrifice in any way their identity. The community published its consensus that family integrity was to be held sacred and that "Any married couple with their children may live together, eat together, and have a paramount right to each other; or they may go to the commons." [10]

Accommodations were anything but commodious at Brook Farm. The main building, called "The Hive," was no more than a farm house which was on the grounds when community life began at West Roxbury. There were two rooms on either side of a wide hall on the first floor, and the rooms upstairs were used as sleeping quarters. Several smaller houses accommodated the families and single male members who preferred more privacy than "The Hive" afforded.

Marriages during the transcendental phase at Brook Farm were not always perfect matches, as the divorce rate appears to have been relatively high. There is record of but few weddings, yet Sophia

Eastman revealed that "It is nothing uncommon for people to get married and then part from there [*sic*] husbands. There are three who board here and there [*sic*] husbands have left them." [11]

Although Brook Farm residents did not interfere with the marriage relation, either to divide compatible couples or to insist that incompatible couples remain united, there is evidence to suggest that there was discussion within the community over the advisability of trying to maintain the family relation within the communal context. Charles Lane wrote in *The Dial*, early in 1844, and dwelled at length on the subject. He affirmed that a community

> cannot bring to issue the great question, whether the existence of the marital family is compatible with that of the universal family, which the term 'Community' signifies. This is now the grand problem. By mothers it has ever been felt to be so. The maternal instinct, as hitherto educated, has declared itself so strongly in favor of the separate fire-side, that association, which appears so beautiful to the young and unattached soul, has yet accomplished little progress in the affections of that important section of the human race—the mothers. With fathers, the feeling in favor of the separate family is certainly less strong; but there is an undefinable tie, a sort of magnetic *rapport*, an invisible, inseverable, umbilical chord [*sic*] between the mother and child, which in most cases circumscribes her desires and ambitions to her own immediate family. . . . This is the chief cornerstone of present society.[12]

Although Horace Greeley regarded the transcendental phase of Brook Farm as "too angelic" for its own good, and feared that "the entrance of one serpent would be as fatal as in Eden of old," [13] there were reports that indeed the tempter had already arrived and the community was not as puritanical as had been figured. The close association of the sexes, married and single, at Brook Farm gave rise to rumors of impropriety. Ora Sedgwick, who was sixteen years old when she boarded there, claimed that she had never observed any hanky panky. She affirmed "that not only was no harm done, either to young men or maidens, by the healthful and simple intercourse that was invariable between them, but that very much good came, especially to the young men." [14] Amelia Russell also admitted that "The hills around us afforded every facility for exercise, and the moonlight evenings were pleasantly employed in this merry recreation." [15]

Visitors to Brook Farm were eager to find some scandal to report to the outside. However, the reports were usually limited to those "moonlight wanderings in the pine grove," which were enough to kindle the wrath of the typical Bostonian nearby. Robert Carter defended this social diversion of the youth at Brook Farm and claimed that "it is creditable to the sound moral training of New England that little or no harm came from these wanderings—at least, not to the maidens." [16] Marianne Dwight admitted, in a letter to Anna Parsons, that she, Fred Cabot, Dora Wilder, and William Coleman stayed out in the pine woods, "lying on their backs," until 9:00 P.M. one evening, when "the dampness" warned them to go home.[17]

Love affairs and romances which went awry were common at Brook Farm. Jokingly, Charles Dana suggested that a society, known by the letters R. L. S. G. (or Rejected Lover's Sympathizing Group) be formed to console those individuals who had been jilted by their lovers in the community.[18]

George Bradford, former clergyman and a member of the Brook Farm community, spoke to Emerson about conditions at West Roxbury and assured him that passions there were not unrestrained. Bradford "expressed the conviction, shared by himself and his friends there," Emerson wrote in his *Journals*, "that plain dealing was the best defence of manners and morals between the sexes." [19] Emerson gathered from Bradford's account that bodily familiarity there was counterbalanced by a spiritual intimacy, and as their minds came nearer and met, there was no danger of physical passions getting out of control. Emerson concluded, "the remedy of impurity is to come nearer." [20] Bradford, a bachelor, later confessed that in the meeting of minds with several of the young ladies, his passions nearly got the better of him. One morning he startled the residents of "The Hive" by telling them he was leaving. Before he took his departure, he admitted to two of the ladies his love for them. He further confessed that he hated Charles Dana, and there were times when he would not have lifted a finger to save Dana's life because he had lured into his German class women whom he himself had wished to be near.[21]

The angelic Brook Farm, regardless of the pious intentions of its founders and leaders, was not spared a female temptress who could charm the piety out of the heart of the most stolid transcendentalist. She came, with her three young sons, in the person of Almira C. Barlow. Almira was a striking beauty, with long dark hair and a lofty brow. She convinced the Ripleys that her husband had forsaken her and had become an alcoholic. She played every bit the part of a queen at Brook Farm, as her physical appearance destined her to be. She sat in the parlor while the other women did the chores. At tea she often found notes under her plate from male admirers. She always responded to these gestures of admiration by sending perfumed notes of acknowledgment, and at times, suggested walks with her admirer in the moonlight. Nathaniel Hawthorne, who was engaged to marry Sophia Peabody, could not keep his eyes off Almira. He admitted that she was "a most comfortable woman to behold." [22] Almira flirted with John S. Dwight, one of the leaders at Brook Farm, and after running him a merry chase, tactfully called it off. Isaac Hecker, who later became a Catholic priest and founder of the Paulist Fathers, fell in love with Almira. Hecker was not handsome, but she was attracted to him nonetheless. Ora Sedgwick described his face as "pockmarked and not handsome, but it was earnest, highminded, and truthful." [23] In his diary, Hecker confided a conversation with Almira. He later scratched out her name and all nouns and pronouns, but enough remains to identify Almira as one to whom he expressed his love, and she to him. Hecker left Brook Farm and spent a short time at Bronson Alcott's utopian community, Fruitlands, in order to escape going contrary to his better judgment in his intimacy with Almira. She was ready to follow him to Fruitlands, but Alcott replied to her request for admission to his community and made it clear that if she became a member, she would have to submit to the ascetic discipline which Charles Lane had imposed. This was more than she was willing to promise, so she remained in her parlor at Brook Farm.

In April 1843 the Directors of Brook Farm decided to remove Almira Barlow as the queen bee from the parlor of "The Hive" in order that it might be put to public use. Almira was altogether banished from the community the following month. She managed to gain a reprieve and was allowed to return. She found the limited male companionship at Brook Farm too restrictive and therefore made frequent trips to New York and Boston, leaving her children behind under the supervision of Georgianna Bruce.[24]

The married women at Brook Farm were beset with intimate problems, the nature of which will probably never be fully known. Margaret Fuller was one frequent visitor in whom they confided. In her *Memoirs*, she told of numerous occasions when women at the community had private audiences with her, which usually ended with a walk in the pine woods to get away from eavesdropping. She claimed, "If I were to write down all . . . married women have confided to me, these three days past, it would make a canto, on one subject, in five parts [alluding to the five married women then at Brook Farm]." [25]

In 1844 Brook Farm became a Fourieristic phalanx, mainly as the result of the efforts of Albert Brisbane and Horace Greeley. Greeley visited the community and talked to Charles Dana about the merits of Fourierism. Dana was reluctant to commit himself to a new system, as Brook Farm was apparently a successful venture up to that point. Greeley criticized the transcendentalists' "cant of exclusiveness" and urged Dana to take a broader view of social reform.[26] Brisbane's articles on Fourierism were published weekly in the *Tribune* under the caption, "Social Science," and were avidly read by the residents of Brook Farm. William Henry Channing caught the Fourier fever and one by one transcendentalists fell into line behind the association movement. Elizabeth Peabody, in the last issue of *The Dial*, stated her views upon hearing that Brook Farm had become a Fourieristic phalanx: "We rejoice in this, because such persons as form that Association will give it a fair experiment. We wish it Godspeed." [27]

During the last week of December 1843, and the first week of January following, a convention of Fourierists met in Boston. Brook Farm was well represented, as both George Ripley and Charles Dana were present. Ripley was elected vice president of the convention, and Dana was elected secretary. After the convention, the residents of Brook Farm wasted little time in drawing up a new constitution, which was dated January 18, 1844. The introductory statement noted: "With a view to an ultimate expansion into a perfect Phalanx, we desire without any delay to organize the three primary departments of labor, namely, Agriculture, Domestic Industry, and the Mechanic Arts." [28] The "quiet and lazy" days at Brook Farm, of which Greeley had been critical, were over, as the pace quickened to make the community a tightly knit Fourieristic cell. Self-centeredness was replaced by a universal philanthropy and Ripley sent out appeals for aid on the behalf

> of those who perceive how little security existing institutions offer against the growth of Commercial Feudalism on the one hand, and Pauperism on the other,—of those whose sympathies are with the unfortunate and uneducated masses, of those who long for the estab-

lishment of more true and genial conditions of life, as well as of those who are made restless and fiery-souled by the universal necessities of Reform.[29]

Charles Dana was even more hopeful of Brook Farm's success as a phalanx, and of Fourier's teachings in general, than was Ripley. In a speech before the New England Fourier Society in Boston, March 7, 1844, Dana shouted: "Our ulterior aim is nothing less than Heaven on Earth,—the conversion of this globe, now exhaling pestilential vapors and possessed by unnatural climates, into the abode of beauty and health, and the restitution to Humanity of the Divine Image, now so long lost and forgotten." [30]

Brook Farm's new constitution, although it proposed to put Fourier's ideas into practice, was careful to assert in the introductory statement that no revolutionary changes regarding marriage and the family were to be made in the community. The newly converted Fourierists promised that they "would remove nothing that is truly beautiful or venerable," and that they reverenced "the religious sentiment in all its forms, the family, and whatever else has its foundations in human nature or the Divine Providence." [31] True to its constitution, the Brook Farm phalanx permitted separate family life for those who desired. Families which had been scattered because of cramped living conditions were permitted to reunite in older buildings which had been used for other purposes during the transcendental period. Unitary housing was made available for those who chose, and a common table was spread for the members who preferred a "larger fellowship." [32] Ora Sedgwick recalled that two men, Ichabod and Edward Morton, built a large house and christened it "The Phalanstery." [33] The Morton house was certainly not constructed on Fourier's plan, nor was Brook Farm for that matter. In the summer of 1844, construction was begun on a phalanstery which was more in keeping with Fourier's ideas. The building was never completed. Nearly two years afterward, on March 3, 1846, a fire leveled the incomplete phalanstery and carried with it the investments of money and labor of the phalanx. Brook Farm never recovered from the loss and folded the following year.

As an independent, transcendentalist community, Brook Farm was solely responsible for the moral life of its members. Upon becoming a Fourieristic phalanx, the colony had to share with other phalanxes the criticisms of Fourier's ideas regarding immorality, although Brook Farm was probably freer of sex scandals than any of the other associations. When the American Union of Associationists met in May 1846, in Boston, Ripley and Dana drew up a statement which was endorsed by the convention, and which was designed to relieve the reform utopians from the irksome task of trying to defend Fourier's theories regarding traditional morals. The statement, in part, read: "*Fourierists* we are not and cannot consent to be called, because Fourier is only *one* of the great teachers of mankind." [34] The members of Brook Farm were not inclined to follow Fourier's ideas on marriage and the family. Calverton asserted that "They clung to their simple, middle class code of morality and were far purer than the Puritans in practicing it." [35] Fourierism was taught in classes at Brook Farm, as a letter written by Marianne Dwight confirms. She had learned something in the classes about Fourier's views toward marriage. She wrote to Anna Parsons about the marriage of Fred Cabot, with whom she had lain on her back in the Pine Woods, to Maria Lincoln: "I cannot think of Fred as married,—and *belonging* to any *one*. . . . Why do people foolishly want to marry? I am getting to think that Fourier is right, and in full harmony there will be no marriage—at least marriage will be a very different thing from what it now is." [36] Marianne, herself, later married John Orvis, an amateur phrenologist.[37] On the occasion of their wedding, William H. Channing had the guests observe "the symbol of universal unity." All stood, joined hands in a circle, and vowed "truth to the cause of God and humanity." [38]

The marriage which caused the greatest amount of talk at Brook Farm was that between Charles Dana and Eunice Macdaniel. Marianne Dwight again wrote to Anna Parsons that there was quite a bit of gossip floating around about Charles and Eunice and that the symptoms were strong that they were in love.[39] The following March, Dana confirmed the suspicion and announced that he had married Eunice in New York in a private ceremony. Dana gave the reason for not returning to Brook Farm for the wedding as "Eunice's private movements, which then seemed to require her to stay for some time in New York." [40] Ripley was visibly upset over the marriage and the mystery surrounding it. He wrote to John S. Dwight: "The whole matter calls forth some amazement and the people are not altogether well pleased at the mystery in which it has been kept. It was an injudicious step on the part of Charles, I am sure, and I fear the influence of it will not be pleasant on his relation to the Association." [41] Dana never explained what Eunice's "private movements" were in New York which kept her from immediately returning to Brook Farm for the wedding. Gossip took over from there.

Lindsay Swift, whose mother, Sarah Edes Allen, was a frequent visitor at Brook Farm, counted fourteen marriages directly traceable to friendships created at the village.[42] The bringing together of "harmonious minds," according to Swift, accounted for the fact that the number of unhappy marriages and divorces among the members of the community was relatively small.[43]

A second utopian experiment conducted by transcendentalists was the short-lived and poverty-stricken Fruitlands. Bronson Alcott, a schoolmaster who had long experimented in educational techniques, was the proprietor of Fruitlands. In 1843, while Brook Farm was evidencing some signs of success, Charles Lane wrote to Junius Alcott, Bronson's brother, and offered to use the money he had earned in London "to redeem a small spot on the planet," where they could set an example before the world of what society should be.[44] Abigail May, Bronson Alcott's wife, unaware of the trouble which lay ahead, was elated over the prospect of founding another community. Her husband had never been a good provider and she trusted that a new beginning would give the family security. "If we can collect about us true men and women," Abigail wrote in the Alcott *Journals*, "I know not why we may not live the true life, putting away the evil customs of society and leading quiet exemplary lives." [45]

Lane's "spot on the planet" was an old rundown farmhouse and small acreage in Massachusetts. Here a small band of reformers gathered, each with his own particular idea of what a perfect society should be. In addition to Bronson Alcott, his wife and four small daughters, including Louisa May, who later wrote *Little Women*, the original members of the commune were Charles Lane and his son William, H. C. Wright, Samuel Bower, Isaac Hecker (who had barely escaped the clutches of Almira Barlow at Brook Farm), Christopher Green, Samuel Larned, Abraham Everett, Anna Page, Joseph Palmer, and Abram Wood. There were others who came and went, and who brought their own peculiar ideas and mixed them with the peculiarities already present at Fruitlands. Lane and Alcott composed a description of the activity in the colony in August 1843, in which they confessed that they did not rely as much on scientific reasoning or physiological skill as they did on the dictates of the spirit.[46] The "spirit" was apparently overworked at Fruitlands, as it "dictated" that they should eat only those foods which are grown above ground, no meat of any kind; they should bathe in cold water only; and they should till the soil manually, and not use any animals for work purposes whatsoever.[47] One member came to believe that clothes were an impediment to spiritual growth, also that daylight was equally harmful. He remained in his room stark naked during the day and roamed around at night out-of-doors wearing a white cotton gown which extended from his neck to his knees.[48]

Marriage and the family became key issues during the brief experiment at Fruitlands. Lane, who was a frequent visitor at a Shaker village at nearby Harvard, became convinced that in order for Fruitlands to succeed, the members should follow their neighbor's example of submerging the individual family into the larger communal family.[49] Lane composed a letter for the communistic periodical, *The Herald of Freedom*, on the subject of the "Consociate Family." The letter also bore Bronson Alcott's signature, but as later developments proved, it was Lane's idea from the first. The "Consociate Family," the letter explained, included "every divine, every human relation consistent with universal good . . . the home of pure social affections, the school of expanding intelligence, the sphere of unbought art, the scene of joyous employment. . . . A union in and with that spirit which alone can bless any enterprise whatsoever." [50] The letter concluded by asking for a deeper consideration in the behalf of the Shakers than they had heretofore received. The separate family, with its selfish interests, was in direct opposition to the "Consociate Family," and Lane believed that the Shakers were living examples of what could be accomplished in communal life once the nuclear family was abolished.[51]

Lane set about to break up the Alcott family, as it stood as a bulwark against all that he envisioned for Fruitlands as a "Consociate Family." The Alcotts were financially obligated to Lane, since he had not only purchased the grounds and they were in a sense his guests, but he had paid some of Alcott's outstanding debts in Concord, Massachusetts, when communal life began at Fruitlands. Lane held this over the Alcotts' head and used it to try to bend them to his will. Abigail complained that her husband had not given enough attention to the matter of supporting his family. She admitted, "I love his faith and quiet reliance on Divine Providence, but a little more activity and industry would place us beyond most of these disagreeable dependencies on friends.—For though they aid, they censure." [52]

Bronson Alcott was a religious fanatic, and it was mainly through religious arguments that Lane almost daily urged him to cease living as a husband to his wife. Lane had learned well the Shaker doctrine of celibacy and insisted at Fruitlands, which Alcott had often referred to as a "New Eden," that Adam's expulsion from paradise had been caused by the loss of his virginity. Alcott was nearly convinced that celibacy was a life of self-denial which was more in keeping with God's intended purpose for man. He admired Ann Lee and regarded her as one of the great religious leaders of her day. Fruitlands was evidencing failure with the passing of each day, while the Shakers at nearby Harvard were prospering. The argument in favor of celibacy appeared irrefutable.

Bronson Alcott experienced deep agony as he wrestled with the question of whether to heed Lane's advice and thereby please God and save Fruitlands, or to maintain his relationship with his wife and children, all of whom he dearly loved. One senses the struggle taking place in his mind when reading Louisa May Alcott's *Transcendental Wild Oats*, which she wrote after Fruitlands' failure. Her essay truly represented her father's feelings in the matter, for after he read the original draft, he suggested no changes in it. The character Abel, in the essay, represented Louisa's father. In one passage, Abel mourned:

> My faithful wife, my little girls,—they have not forsaken me, they are mine by ties that none can break. What right have I to leave them alone? What right to escape from the burden and the sorrow I have helped to bring? This duty remains to me, and I must do it manfully. For their sakes, the world will forgive me in time; for their sakes, God will sustain me now.[53]

While Bronson Alcott was undergoing the traumatic experience of trying to decide whether to turn celibate or to remain as husband and father to his family, his wife and daughters also suffered many anxious moments. Abigail was regarded by Lane as responsible for Fruitlands' failure. He charged that one reason why others had not joined the experiment was because of her selfishness over her family. Furthermore, Lane accused Alcott of paying too much attention to

Abigail, and that "constancy to his wife and inconstancy to the Spirit had blurred over his life forever." [54] Abigail had endangered her health by handling the endless chores at Fruitlands without any help, except that given her by her four very young daughters. Lane, in a letter to Henry David Thoreau, admitted that there was need of more women at Fruitlands, since "far too much labor devolved on Mrs. Alcott." [55] Louisa May confided to her diary that her mother wanted to leave Fruitlands, claiming "she is so tired." [56]

Abigail and her daughters came to despise Lane because of his repeated attempts to break up their family. In December 1843, she wrote that the situation was unbearable and that Lane was "moody and enigmatical." [57] She expressed hope of leaving Fruitlands at the first opportunity. Louisa May claimed she liked Fruitlands, except "the school part and Mr. Lane." [58] On December 10, Lane went to Boston and left the Alcott family to discuss their future. They had a long talk, shed a few tears, and prayed that God would keep them together.[59]

The Alcott family resolved to stay together and Bronson thereafter extolled the virtues of separate family life as nothing less than Eden itself. In one of his poems, he wrote:

> I drank delights from every cup;
> Art, institutions I drank up,
> Athirst, I quaffed life's brimming bowls,
> And sipped the flavors of all souls.
> One sparkling cup remained for me—
> The brimming cup of family.[60]

Later, Alcott wrote to "The Young Inmates of the Cottage," a community which he planned upon leaving Fruitlands, "I will show you what is beautiful, beautiful indeed: It is a pure and happy life of a family, a home where peace and gentle quiet abide." [61] Abigail was happier, too, and recorded in the *Journals:* "Fourteenth Anniversary of our wedding day. Whom confidence and love have wedded, let not doubt or distrust put asunder." [62]

During the winter of 1843–1844, the Alcotts visited several utopian communities and looked for a new home where their family might maintain its separate identity. Abigail, upon returning from their visits, wrote that she was convinced that there was nothing in any of them for the family without risking an "unwarrantable alienation" from their children.[63]

Withal, Bronson Alcott could never rid his mind of the concept of a "Consociate Family." In October 1844, he wrote to his brother, Junius, about his plans for Hillside, which Emerson had offered to buy for him. Alcott explained that he planned for several families to move onto the place, since he could not consent to live solely for one family. He preferred to "stand in neighborly relation to several, and institute a union and communion of families instead of drawing aside within the precincts of one's own acres and kindred by blood." [64] The community at Hillside, however, never materialized and the Alcotts returned to Concord, Massachusetts.

Lane sold Fruitlands to Joseph Palmer, a member of the community, and with his young son, William, joined the Shakers at Harvard in January 1844. The Shakers admitted Lane on a provisional basis, as they did all new converts. While living in the village, he wrote an article for *The Dial*, in which he bitterly attacked the institutions of marriage and the nuclear family, and declared them both to be in diametric opposition to the concept of communal life because they fostered exclusiveness.[65] Lane proved to be a "Winter Shaker." Louisa May Alcott wrote that the end of Lane's Shaker adventure came when he found that the order of things was reversed: "it was all work and no play." [66] He left the Shakers in the spring of 1844, and two years later went to England, leaving his young son with the Shakers at Harvard. While in England, Lane met Hannah Bond, who had lived at Robert Owen's community at Harmony Hall. Despite his earlier antagonism toward marriage, and his belief that one day private family life would be abolished, he and Hannah were married and became the parents of four sons and a daughter.

Joseph Palmer carried on the tradition of the transcendentalists, after a fashion, at Fruitlands for another twenty years. Reformers came and went, but no attempt was made again to tamper with the family relation. Ralph Waldo Emerson was among the visitors in the Palmer home, as well as a host of wayfarers. The people in the vicinity regarded the bearded Palmer the eccentric that he was, and referred to Fruitlands as a "Home for Tramps."

VII

Godly Communes and Saintly Families

SEVERAL RELIGIOUS UTOPIAN COMMUNITIES ESTABLISHED IN THE NINETEENTH century permitted familism with varying degrees of success. One such community was organized by Adin Ballou in 1841 at Hopedale, Massachusetts, as "A universal religious, moral, philanthropic, and social reform Association." [1] Membership was open to all who were regarded as "proper moral agents," and who were willing to be governed "by divine principles." [2] However, Ballou later admitted that the membership was mainly composed of the more substantial middle class, "the rank and file of the American people." [3]

Ballou was a social architect who was determined to revolutionize society. He hopefully called his organization, which began the experiment at Hopedale, The Universal Reform Association. He believed that

> What is morally wrong in the *individual* must be morally wrong in *society*—in every combination of men. Present human society is not based on these divine principles [of wisdom and love]. Therefore, a *new order* of society ought to be instituted on earth. . . . It cannot be instituted by force. It must be done by *moral power*, and

voluntary agreement. If so, it must of necessity have a *small* beginning.[4]

Like Fourier, Owen, Cabet, and others, Ballou drew the plans for communities on paper to be established as men felt the importance of it, until the whole world is transformed into a "Practical Christian Republic." [5]

Unlike the neighboring Brook Farm, Hopedale was able to shake off the Fourierist fever and to remain an independent, religious community. This was due mainly to the fact that Ballou had his own definite ideas regarding the nature of a communal enterprise, which were unlike those of Fourier. Furthermore, Hopedale was thoroughly religious and gave primacy to man's relationship to God. Religion, although tolerated by Fourier, was not a feature of his social theory. Abigail May Alcott found life at Hopedale "inoffensive" and "in sackcloth and ashes," which presented a sharp contrast to what she observed in the Fourieristic phalanxes.[6]

The constitution of the Hopedale community upheld marriage as one of the most important and sacred of human relations, which deserved to be guarded against caprice and abuse. The members of the community were to pledge "never to violate the dictates of chastity by adultery, polygamy, concubinage, fornication, self-pollution, lasciviousness, amative abuse, impure language, or cherished lust." [7] Ballou arranged for counselors, known as the Perceptive and the Parentive Circles, to handle all affairs related to marriage and the family. If a husband and wife were unable to settle their domestic disagreements, they were to take them before the Perceptive Circle. This action was purely voluntary on the part of the couple, as the Circles were not permitted to interfere in any way with private family life unless consulted. Divorce at Hopedale was permissible only on the ground of adultery, which must be conclusively proved against the accused party. Separations for other sufficient reasons were sanctioned, but with the distinct understanding that neither party would be free to marry again during the lifetime of the other.

Hopedale accommodated its members both in unitary housing and in private homes. The constitution called for the unitary houses, known as Habitations, to be constructed as needed, to provide room for 100 persons each. The Habitations were to have appendages consisting of barns, granaries, workshops, manufactories, and other buildings. They were all to be communally owned and controlled.

Families were permitted to live in separate apartments within the unitary houses. They did not have to eat at the common table, but could be served privately in their rooms if they chose. They were obligated to furnish their own apartments with bedding, chairs, tables, crockery, and other conveniences. If a family wished to maintain a house apart from the Habitations, they were allowed to do so. The community furnished such families with house rent, fuel, bakery products, staples, and "comforts of subsistence" at a nominal cost. Several families at Hopedale preferred to live in their own homes, but there were not very many houses available, and such as did exist were barely inhabitable.

Although community members at Hopedale shared common housing and a common table, the experiment was not communistic. In order to become a member, each paid fifty dollars for a share in the enterprise. Each individual man, woman, and child was given suitable employment and was paid wages. The adults were required to work eight hours per day, forty-eight hours per week.

Problems arose early in the Hopedale experiment which were directly the result of cramped living conditions. The official organ of the community, *The Practical Christian*, reported in the summer of 1842 that they had found themselves "in close contact" with one another and "had ample opportunities to find out each others' weaknesses, failings, and besetting sins." [8] Because of this, Ballou admitted:

> As the tinsel wore off and the hard actualities of our uncomfortable domestic situation began to overtax our nerves, we lost a portion of our spiritual enthusiasm, firmness, and patience. Our religious natures no less than our physical suffered for the want of needed solitude and repose, as they did for lack of wholesome nurture and stimulus to holy aspiration and endeavor.[9]

Some families found Hopedale intolerable, and they left it altogether. Others sought refuge in their separate domiciles, however rustic and inconvenient. Ballou confessed that almost anything was better than the crowded apartments which taxed the patience and fortitude of the members.[10] He affirmed that the women in the community never once grumbled or spoke an unkind word during those early days of privation. Ballou did not record anything about the response of the men and children, and it is highly doubtful that the fairer sex did not utter a disparaging word, if conditions were as terrible as he admitted. He did confess that the disorder, confusion, and friction which resulted from the crowded condition, did the community irreparable damage.[11]

The intimate association of the various types and temperaments of people at Hopedale brought its moments of threat to the purity of the marriage relation in the community. Despite every precaution to maintain vigilance on the part of the Perceptive Circle, and the solemn declarations regarding chastity, infidelity was detected which caused, according to Ballou, "great unpleasantness, perplexity, and scandal." [12] One case involved a married man and a young lady in the community. The offended wife revealed their indiscretion and the Council summoned the guilty pair to appear before them for "examination and discipline." They confessed their sin and promised to cease their intimacy. Soon afterward, they were again caught and made to appear before the Council a second time. The two claimed that they saw nothing wrong with their behavior, since "it was consonant with the principles of the new philosophy touching personal liberty, sexual relations, and the conjugal bond, which they had embraced." [13] They were compelled to leave Hopedale. They departed to Josiah Warren's Modern Times community, where free love was openly avowed. Ballou also admitted that there were other cases of indiscretion, but by no means of the magnitude of this one. Erring couples were always called to account, and made to confess their wrong and repent.

There was sufficient report of scandals at Hopedale outside of the community to cause Ballou, in 1853, to issue an official statement regarding the community's position on free love. The statement affirmed:

> That, with our views of Christian Chastity, we contemplate as utterly abhorrent the various 'Free Love' theories and practices propagated among susceptible minds and under the pretext of higher religious perfection, moral exaltation, social refinement, individual sovereignty, physiological research and philosophical progress; and we feel bound to bear our uncompromising testimony against all persons, communities, books and publications which inculcate such specious and subtle licentiousness.[14]

Thus, with one broad sweep, Ballou repudiated any association with John Humphrey Noyes, Josiah Warren, Frances Wright and Robert Dale Owen, since the terms in the resolution were the very ones used by these reformers in their utopian experiments and publications. Hopedale was to stand alone, if necessary, in its efforts to bring about a universal revolution of society without destroying the present society's moral framework.

But Hopedale, like her erring sister communities, quietly laid aside her case in 1858. Ballou continued to maintain his principles were right, but his people were not. An anonymous member of the community told John Humphrey Noyes, "The timber he got together was not suitable for building a community. The men and women who joined him were very enthusiastic, and commenced with great zeal; their devotion to the cause seemed to be sincere; but they did not know themselves." [15]

One of the largest and most successful of the religious utopian communities which permitted familism was that of Amana. The Society of True Inspirationists who settled Amana, like the Rappites and Zoarites, had their origin in Germany. Through the alleged inspiration of Christian Metz, a carpenter and spiritual leader, they were directed to come to America in 1842. They settled near Buffalo, New York, on an 8,000 acre tract, which they called Ebenezer. While there, Metz received another "revelation," informing him that they should share all things in common and retire to communities. The society arrived in western New York at the height of the communal movement in that state, which probably had a bearing on their decision to restructure their social order along utopian lines.

Immigrants from Germany poured into Ebenezer almost daily, and Metz began to fear that there would not be room for all who wished to come. In order to maintain the newly adopted social policy of communism in one community, he scouted the frontier regions of America for a suitable location to establish another community, and settled on a 26,000 acre tract in Iowa. The colony moved to their new home in 1845. As the population grew, seven villages were established on the domain, each near enough to the others to permit a single political organization to govern them and to preserve a common identity.

The Society of True Inspirationists did not encourage marriage, but only tolerated it. Celibacy was the Amana idéal, but relatively few were willing to deny themselves the privilege of marriage. The spiritual leaders of the community were expected to remain single. In 1868 a schoolteacher was dismissed because he chanced to marry.[16] Not until the last decade of the nineteenth century were

Amana schoolmasters allowed to marry. The "inspired instruments" (*Werkzeuge*), or those with whom God supposedly communicated directly, were expected to have no carnal relations with members of the opposite sex, either in or out of wedlock.

Everything short of outright prohibition was done to discourage marriages at Amana. The *Werkzeuge* were given complete control over the lives of the people in the community and only that inspired elite, upon a revelation from God, could give permission to a couple to marry. No male could take a wife until he attained the age of twenty-four, even if he had his parents' permission before he reached that age. Females were not permitted to wed before the age of twenty. The age limits were justified on the ground that if they married too early, the population would exceed the means to support it.[17] Permission was never granted for anyone to marry outside of the society. If one were to do so, he was promptly dismissed from the community for one year. If he wished to re-enter, an application had to be made and proof given that the alien party in the marriage had been converted to the doctrines of the society. Divorces were not recognized at Amana, but legal separation was permitted when the marriage relation became unbearable. One of the parties was required to leave the society altogether, usually the man. Remarriage under such circumstances was not regarded with favor.

Once a young man secured the consent of a young lady to marry him, the ordeal through which the couple was expected to go was designed not only to test their sincerity of love for each other, but to discourage them from taking the step. Application for marriage was first made to the village trustee, who in turn laid the matter before the *Werkzeuge* in the Great Council. The *Werkzeuge* prayed about it and asked God for inspired direction. They also examined the couple to be sure there were no spiritual, mental, or physical obstacles which might interfere with the marriage relation. Once God, through the *Werkzeuge*, consented, if the couple was still in the mood, a lecture was given them on the gravity of the step they had asked permission to take. They were reminded that upon their marriage they would lose their position (*versammlung*) in the church. If they had reached one of the two upper spiritual classes, they would be set back to the lowest, or children's order. Only through increased piety could they again work their way back to their former caste. Marriage jeopardized their spiritual well-being and imperiled their souls. If the couple persisted in their resolve to marry, the young man was spirited off to another village for a full year and he was not permitted, under any circumstances, to see his future bride. In the earlier days in Iowa, the young man was sent to Ebenezer in New York. As the community was phased out in New York, the custom was to send the young man to one of the seven neighboring villages in Iowa. After the year's probation, the young man was permitted to see his beloved, if his ardor had not cooled in the meantime, on every other Sunday. He had to rise very early in the morning to reach the community where his betrothed lived, in time for church services, as the visitation day was always on Sunday. After church he was permitted to visit her in the presence of her family for a brief time. He had to begin his homeward journey in time to get to bed at an early hour. The couple was again summoned before the *Werzeuge* to determine their spiritual status, and if it was found suitable, the wedding date was set.

Amana weddings were equally designed to discourage the couple and were more like funerals than occasions of joy. Weddings were private affairs and without ritual. The parents of the bride and groom met with two or three of the elders at the home of the bride. The wedding opened with a hymn and a prayer. Two passages from the Bible were always read: chapter five of Ephesians, wherein exhortations were given regarding the responsibilities of husband and wife; and chapter seven of I Corinthians, which opens with the startling statement: "It is good for a man not to touch a woman." With "great plainness of speech" and with "great thoroughness," the presiding elder elaborated on these two passages at length. The vows were then heard and afterward there was more singing and praying. The exhausted pair then retired to a very modest wedding dinner in the bride's home.

After the wedding, the groom was yet unable to claim his bride. He had to return to the village where he had spent the previous year on probation, and there remain another two full weeks. Upon his return, the elders assigned the newlyweds an apartment, consisting of a sitting room and a small bedroom, in one of the houses where another family resided, often in either of their parents' homes. The bedroom was furnished with small, twin beds, in order to discourage conjugal intimacy. If there were additions to their union, they could request and receive permission to move into a private dwelling. Childbirth, however, was discouraged by the *Werkzeuge*. With the birth of each child the parents, if they had regained the status which they had lost in marrying, were sent back down to the children's order as a punishment for their carnality.

Familism at Amana was uniquely incorporated into the communal system. There was no unitary housing in any of their villages, as the True Inspirationists valued spacious living. There were hotels, but these were for the guests who visited the community and not accommodations for the members. Usually the hotels were staffed by hired help from among non-members in order to shield the Amana women from outsiders. The private dwellings, which were owned and furnished by the society, were without kitchens, dining-rooms, or parlors. A series of bedrooms and sitting rooms, plainly furnished, made up the interior of an Amana home. Each person was free to decorate his room as he pleased and to collect whatever keepsakes he wished, all within the reasonable limits of economy. Two or three families often occupied the same house, but crowding was seldom a problem at Amana. Each family received a monthly allotment for incidentals, amounting to five or ten dollars, depending on the specific needs at the time.[18] Amana was never wealthy; the average per capita wealth in 1890, after fifty years of communal operation, was about ten per cent less than that of the state of Iowa. Each person had a wine ticket which allowed the men one quart per week, and the women and children a pint. The wine cellar, incidentally, was located under the church house.

Kitchens were located in the center of the house clusters where meals were prepared and served in common. Usually about thirty or forty persons ate together. In some rare instances, a few families were allowed to dine in their own houses, when one or more members were incapacitated and could not conveniently travel to the dining hall. Each house had its garden nearby, which the families worked to supply food for the common table. The women took turns preparing and serving the food in the kitchen houses. Kitchen service was for two weeks, with a rest of one week between. During meals the sexes were separated, as one spokesman explained, "to prevent silly conversation and trifling conduct." [19]

Precautions were taken at Amana to keep the sexes apart from a very early age. The catechism, "Some Pages of Rules for the Conduct of Children, at Home, in Church, at School, During Play Hours, at Meals and in All Relation of their Lives," admonished the children: "Have no pleasure in violent games or plays; do not wait on the road to look at quarrels or fights; do not keep company with bad children, for there you will only learn wickedness. Also, *do not play with children of the other sex.*" [20] On Sunday afternoons young people were allowed to take walks, but the girls were made to go in one direction and the boys in another. Although they might chance to meet during the course of the walk, this was strictly forbidden.[21] Another catechism entitled "Rules for the Examination of our Daily lives," cautioned the young men to keep away from women as much as possible, since they were regarded "as a very highly dangerous magnet and magical fire." [22]

At church services the men entered and departed from one door, the women from another, with the caution that "No vain conversation be carried on after services." [23] In all their assemblies, the women sat apart from the men. They also departed the meetings ahead of the men. Togetherness was discouraged at Amana; there were no planned social gatherings involving the whole community. Small prayer groups assembled in different parts of the village at evening, but these were solemn assemblies which were carefully supervised. As in the Shaker villages, women were not permitted to labor alongside the men. However, both sexes were taught, always by a male teacher, in the same classrooms.

Despite the lack of youthful excitement and companionship of the sexes, Amana lost relatively few of its young people. The peace and security found in the community more than compensated for the uncertain freedoms on the outside. There were a few elopements, but most of those who ran away returned to the society. The True Inspirationists never had to resort to the adoption of children to maintain the population level. The children born in the community, to the consternation of the *Werkzeuge*, were more likely to remain in the society than adopted children, as the Shakers learned through bitter experience and disappointment.

One of the surest guarantees of order and submission at Amana was that of the annual confession, or *Untersuchung*. Each member had to undergo a complete catharsis in order to purge himself of his evil thoughts. A firm resolve was demanded that each one would adjust his thoughts, life, and habits to be more in keeping with God's word and the Amana ideal. The *Untersuchung* was based on the biblical text which admonished Christians: "Confess your faults one to another, and pray one for another, that ye may be healed." [24] The love feast, or *Liebesmahl*, followed the *Untersuchung*, and none was allowed to enter into the occasion without first confessing his sins. This annual renewal was a vital part of the life of the community in the maintenance of the Amana tradition.

The Hutterites, who formed religious utopian communities in America during the nineteenth century, permitted marriage and familism without many of the restraints and discouragements which were imposed at Amana. The Hutterites originated in Moravia during the middle of the sixteenth century. Jacob Hutter, after whom the society was named, emerged as the leader of the Anabaptists who fled to Moravia from Tyrol and Bavaria to escape the violence of the Peasants' War. Here they adopted communism, mainly for economic survival, but justified it on biblical grounds. The church in the first century held its goods in common and distributed to each member according to his particular need.[25] The Hutterites wished to emulate the New Testament church, not only in its dogma, but in its practical life as well. Communism remained a principle among the Hutterites as they were forced to migrate from one European country to another, and finally to America in 1874.

The Hutterite population at one time reached 20,000, but only about 800 migrated to America. They first settled in South Dakota, where only half of them remained in the colony; the other half settled on their own private homesteads and were disassociated from the movement. Between 1874 and 1877 the remaining faithful established three colonies, or *Bruderhofs*. These three colonies spawned some 200 other colonies which exist today in the Dakotas, Montana, Minnesota, Washington, and three Canadian provinces. When a colony reached the population of about 130, they began preparations to establish another to prevent crowding. Each colony is directly traceable to one of the three original colonies, and the people, or *leut*, are known by the names of those who led in the establishment of those three colonies: the *Dariusleut*, *Lehreerleut*, and *Schmiedeleut*.[26] Before a colony was begun in a new location, the land was purchased and sometimes farmed for a few years in order to guarantee the economic success of the new venture for those who came later. Those who moved to a daughter colony were always chosen by lot.

Unlike most German utopian groups, the Hutterites taught that all adults should marry and that procreation was the will of God. Marriage to an outsider, however, was never condoned, since an unbeliever was not a part of the *Bruderhof* and had no right to reside in a Hutterite community. If the believer wished to return to the community after his marriage to an unbeliever, he had to obtain a legal separation from his spouse.

Peter Riedmann, a noted Hutterite, described their marriages as characterized by "male solicitude and female obedience," without the romantic elements normally found in marriages in Western civilization.[27] Marriage was carefully controlled by the community and a series of appointments had to be kept before a couple was united in matrimony. First, a young man asked his parents' permission. If it were secured, he then asked his preacher's permission; the preacher in turn laid the matter before the colony's council. If the council had no objection, the young man's father proceeded to ask the permission of the young lady's preacher, if she belonged to another colony. Her preacher then took the matter to his council. If the second council found no objection, the young man's father went to the home of the young lady and asked the permission of her father. If he agreed to the union, preparations were begun for the wedding ceremony. The young couple refrained from courting until an announcement was made in church concerning their engagement. The courtship was conducted on a high moral plane, and was carried out in the presence of the young lady's parents. The Hutterites did not believe in long engagements, so a marriage ceremony usually followed the engagement within a week or two.

Hutterite weddings were occasions of joy and festivity. They were always held at the church in the groom's community. The bride's entire colony and the last daughter colony of the groom's *Bruderhof* were invited. Wedding rings were not used. The groom was asked to take his bride "with gratitude as a gift of God, whether young or old, poor or rich, even as God has shown through their council." [28] The bride was simply asked to promise to obey her husband. Generally a celebration after the wedding lasted two full days, as weddings were about the only occasion of reunion of former friends. The newlyweds did not take a honeymoon, but were excused from work a few days, while they moved into an apartment in the groom's colony. The groom was then expected to grow a beard so that his newly attained marital status could be readily identified.[29]

The Hutterite marriage was for life, and only on the cause of adultery could the union be broken. They believed that marriage actually took place on three levels: (1) the union of God and the individual soul; (2) the union of soul and body; and (3) the union of bodies. If a person were unfaithful in the third union, it automatically severed the other two unions and made one subject to excommunication from the *Bruderhof.* If one had committed adultery and subsequently had been expelled from the colony, by repentance and appeal to the Council of Elders he could be restored. If his former mate was willing to again accept him, it was necessary that the wedding be repeated, but without the festivities which accompanied the first ceremony.

Hutterites were limited in their choices of marriage partners, as they were required to marry only those of their own *leut.* In order to prevent intermarriage in families, a genealogical chart was kept by the minister of each colony. They were forbidden to marry anyone nearer than a first cousin.

Familism was a feature of the Hutterite *Bruderhof,* but it was uniquely fused with communalism. Each family had as many rooms as its size demanded, but there were no kitchens or dining areas in their apartments. The entire *Bruderhof* ate in a common dining hall. Although they shared all things in common, each person was allowed to have his own personal keepsakes. At the age of fifteen the girls were given a hope chest, into which they began to collect the small articles which they would need when they were married and began families of their own.

The social intercourse of the sexes in a Hutterite community was carefully regulated, but not as strictly as at Amana or in a Shaker village. At church services, prayer meetings, and in the dining hall, members of the opposite sex sat apart. Although a Hutterite might shake hands with a member of another sex, he was not allowed to give the traditional embrace of fellowship.

The Hutterites were thoroughly grounded in the society's teachings and very few permanently left their communities. A sex crime has never been uncovered in any of their colonies, unless the ten or so illegitimate children born to unwed Hutterite women are to be regarded as the result of criminal acts. Between 1874 and 1950 only one divorce was recorded in the Hutterite communities, and only four legal separations.[30] To be born a Hutterite was regarded a privilege and the legacy of peace and security was to be handed to the next generation. The young Hutterites had this drilled into them from the time they were old enough to understand. The Hutterites never adopted children, for this seldom worked out in communal arrangements, particularly when the religion was strict and austere. As soon as adopted children reached maturity, they seldom remained in the community. The Hutterites, by condoning marriage and by encouraging propagation, never worried about their society dying out, as did the Rappites and Shakers. They did not send out missionaries to make new converts. One Hutterite preacher recently expressed what has been the attitude of their clergy for nearly a century, when he said: "If I tried to bring in converts, I'd be excommunicated from the church. My job is to keep watch over my own flock—not to gather stray sheep." [31]

The *Bruderhof* was composed of docile German peasants who would not break the traditions of their fathers. Under these circumstances, they succeeded in making the nuclear family compatible with communalism. Their experiment is not complete, as there are yet more than 200 Hutterite colonies extant.

The Bethel and Aurora communities, both established by William Kiel, permitted marriage and familism. Kiel was a religious fanatic who came to America from Germany in the 1830s. He settled first in New York, and later moved to Pittsburgh, Pennsylvania, where he began to practice medicine and to gather about him a small body of German peasants who regarded him as inspired of God. In 1844, after Bernhard Muller forsook the ex-Rappites at Phillipsburg, Kiel stepped in and persuaded several of them to follow him to Missouri to establish a utopian community.

The community at Bethel was located a short distance from Hannibal, Missouri. The ex-Rappites who joined Kiel were accustomed to communal life and were mainly responsible for the particular stamp of character which the Bethel community assumed. Since they had rejected George Rapp's prohibition on marriage when they chose to follow Muller, Kiel's repeated efforts to deprive them of their right to marry and to maintain their separate family relations met with little success. Some of the citizens of Bethel heeded the counsel of Kiel, enough of them to cause his community to gain the reputation of "Bachelor Town." [32]

Bethel prospered much as had the Rappite communities, and like George Rapp, Kiel saw the expediency of moving to a new location when accumulated wealth in the community posed a threat to his power. He chose distant Oregon as the site for his new experiment, and in 1855 an *avant garde* was dispatched to the upper Willamette

Valley to establish the Aurora community. The following year, the main body of the Bethel commune moved to Oregon, leaving only a remnant behind.

Although Kielites were encouraged to marry only those who believed in the teachings of their revered leader, exceptions were made for those who were likely prospects for conversion.[33] John Roebling, who designed the Brooklyn Bridge, became engaged to Helena Grisy, a member of the Bethel community, but she refused to marry him unless he joined the community and accepted Kiel's leadership. Roebling's architectural talents would have made him a welcome addition to Bethel, but he could not bring himself to accept Kiel's religion. John and Helena were never married, and she remained a spinster the remainder of her life.

Weddings at Bethel and Aurora were simple. The nuptial rites often took place in the schoolhouse and were conducted by a justice of the peace. A modest wedding feast followed in the home of the bride's father. Afterward the young people were permitted to dance, a pastime rarely enjoyed in religious communes in the nineteenth century. The newlyweds were allowed to move into one of the apartments furnished by the community, or, if available, they might move to a private house.

Each family was permitted to have its own garden, pigsty, chickenhouse, and cows. They did not all eat at a common table, and whatever food the family produced, they were allowed to either sell or consume. There were larger houses in the communities which accommodated the unmarried members. These had a common dining hall and resembled a typical boarding house. When Nordhoff visited Aurora, he found Kiel living in one of these houses with a dozen or more of the older unmarried people.[34] The Christian principle of sharing was to be observed. Each family was expected to join the others in communal enterprises for the benefit of all. There were larger community gardens worked in common to supply the foods that the smaller garden plots did not. In this respect, Bethel and Aurora were communistic. There were supply stores which were stocked with goods produced by the communities or purchased from the outside. No accounts were kept and members were at liberty to request whatever they wanted or needed without paying for it. The only restraints were that they act according to the principles of love and temperance, and that they not put an undue strain on the communities' expenses.

Kiel frequently preached to the members against carnality and urged them to "live as the Lord lived," and to "set their affections on things above, and not on things on the earth." [35] He adopted Rapp's practice of hearing their confessions in order to make them cognizant of their fleshly failings and to give them occasion to head off any secret desire or jealousy which might lead to a scandal. Nordhoff asked Kiel if there were any disagreements which stemmed from envy. He replied that there was some jealousy at the beginning of their experiment, but "very seldom now; the people have been too long and too thoroughly trained." [36] Kiel ruled with an iron hand and upon his death there was no one capable of succeeding him. Thus the community at Aurora, as originally conceived, ceased its operation in 1881.

The utopian communities which attempted to maintain the nuclear family within their precincts did so with varying degrees of success. The sectarian communities, such as Hopedale, Amana, Bethel, Aurora, and those founded by the Hutterites were the most successful in keeping the family intact, and in reducing the friction between families living in close association. Religious tenets, which were more in keeping with the mores of ordinary society, were cohesive forces which gave these communities greater stability than was found in the social reform communities founded on purely secular philosophies.

VIII

A Better Tomorrow

SUN-UP TO SUN-DOWN DRUDGERY IN A MILL TOWN FROM WHICH THERE appeared little hope of escaping the daily cycle of work-eat-sleep, trapped the masses in a life style that denied the slightest prospect for human happiness. Several nineteenth-century socialists were convinced that there was hope and dared to depart from the garden of the muses and put into practical application principles which had long been enunciated as contributory to a better tomorrow. One such dreamer and activist was Etienne Cabet, a French politician and utopian novelist, who founded the Icarian communal movement in America.

Cabet was the editor of *Le Populaire*, a social reform newspaper in Paris during the 1830s. In 1834 he published an article in which he attacked Louis Philippe personally, and for which he was sentenced to two years imprisonment. He managed to escape the sentence and went to London, where, for the first time, he read Sir Thomas More's *Utopia*. Cabet was inspired by it to write a similar work in which he, like More, sharply criticized the social conditions of his own times. He entitled his philosophical and social romance, first published in 1842, *Voyage en Icarie*. Icaria was a mythological country where all of Cabet's previously advocated social principles had found acceptance. Because it was a country of wisdom, peace, and happiness, Cabet called it "A Second Promised Land, an Eden, and Elysium, a new terrestrial Paradise." [1]

first settlement in Iowa.[5] Hinds questioned President Sauva about their rule on celibacy and was told: "Marriage is obligatory here; that is to say, celibacy is considered an anomalous condition, contrary to nature, to be tolerated only when the number of members is so limited as to prevent the celibates, men and women, from readily finding suitable mates." [6] The Icarian constitution, adopted May 4, 1851, specifically enjoined that all who were able and disposed to marry should do so.[7] The conjugal union and the nuclear family were regarded as the principal basis for happiness for all, particularly for the children. The Icarians accepted without question marriage and the family as "the surest guarantees of order and peace in society." [8] The perfection of the entire Icarian society was dependent, in part, on the marriage of each adult.[9]

The Icarians found marriage in ordinary society, particularly that of Europe, inhibited by three factors, which they sought to remove in their utopian communities: (1) dowries; (2) unequal education of the sexes; and (3) lack of liberty in the choice of a spouse. The preamble of the Icarian constitution of 1851 asserted: "the Old Society is based on individualism. Give us, as a basis of the new, Fraternity, Equality, and Liberty, Communism or the Community." [10] The constitution abolished "portions," or dowries, promised a free choice in the selection of a marriage partner, and the equality of husband and wife in all matters. Once fraternity, equality, liberty, and communism had been firmly established, the Icarians believed all marriages would be happy marriages. There would be no infidelity if each treated his neighbor as a brother. Furthermore, with every adult married, there would be no scandals and no prostitution. There would be no intellectual mismatches, if all were educated equally and were allowed to choose their mates for themselves. The problem of finances, which is at the basis of most domestic quarrels, would be solved when the system of communism guaranteed that each family would have the necessities of life. Women would not needle their husbands for fine clothes in a community where all were equal and no one tried to outdo another. Cabet, in outlining the plans for the Nauvoo community, stated:

> Wardrobes, because of their inequalities, have been one of the principal causes of all the discussions amonst [*sic*] women, of all the divisions and of all the difficulties for administration. As soon as the thing shall be possible, the Community will furnish the same ward-

> robes to all the men, to all the women and to all the children, taking away the old wardrobes and disposing of them on the best terms for the general interest.[11]

Although the Icarians accepted marriage for life, divorce was permitted and provided for by community law, with the condition that each of the divorced parties should remarry as quickly as possible.[12] Cabet believed that the communal life, as he envisioned it, was calculated to insure happiness in marriage, but if "this common life should be insupportable to one or the other," a divorce was the only course, since human happiness was the ultimate aim of the community.[13] Cabet was certain that the community life would be so arranged as to preclude any desire on the part of the members for a divorce from their mates.

Each family in the Icarian communities was allowed to live in its separate house and to maintain its separate identity with the father as the head of his household. The private houses were simple and uniform, in order that the principle of equality might be upheld. Cabet insisted that the houses should be commodious, since crowding gave rise to discontent. The houses and furnishings belonged to the community. Each house had a small garden for shrubs and flowers.[14] Although there were no unitary houses, each colony had a large house for cooking and dining purposes, as all ate in common. Food for snacks was allowed in each house to provide additional nutrition at the beginning of the day and before retiring. The unmarried adults, mostly old men, lived on the second floor of the dining hall.

The Icarian communities were rent by internal dissension over petty issues, which generally led to a withdrawal of a large number to form new communities. Albert Shaw, who visited New Icaria in 1883 and observed their attempt to combine individualism with communism, sensed the cause of the Icarian failures. He claimed that Frenchmen have a great deal of "individualism" and not a great deal of "patience and forbearance." [15]

The Northampton community in Massachusetts, also in search of a better tomorrow, was founded as an independent association, in 1842, on a 500 acre tract which was formerly owned by the Northampton Silk Company. Familism was both allowed and encouraged by its founders, David Mack, Samuel Hill, George Benson, and William Adams. Forty-one persons, twenty of whom were children, formed the nucleus of the community. The experiment was middle class in its composition and grew to a population of 220 before its dissolution in 1846.

The constitution of the Northampton community upheld the family relation as having "its foundation and support in the laws of Nature and the will of God, in the affections of the heart, and in the dictates of understanding." [16] The association allowed for other and wider relations of its members to be formed for the improvement of the social order, as long as such associations were not incompatible with the family, which the members regarded as the basis and the source of all human excellence and happiness.[17] Each family lived in a separate house and, although all property was shared in common, each family was able to maintain its individual identity.

The old silk factory building was used both for manufacturing purposes and for housing the unmarried members and children sent there for an education. These ate at a common table, but each family prepared and served its own food. The accommodations for the families were limited and at first, when hopes for improvement prevailed, the women were able to accept the inconveniences without much grumbling. As time passed and hopes faded, complaints arose and open dissension shattered the prospects for a better tomorrow. Abigail Alcott, after she and her family had visited Northampton in 1844, remarked that life there was "quite elementary and aimless," as their main concern appeared to be that of paying off the debt.[18]

During the final meeting, just before the community dissolved, a complaint was registered that there was "a want of harmony and brotherly feeling," and that there was an unwillingness to further endure the sacrifices which they were called on to make.[19] The Executive Council convened on November 1, 1846, and declared an end to the Northampton community. There was no dictator over the community, and no stringent rules to be subscribed to which might have suppressed individualism and given the community a longer life. The source of their problems appeared to be in the individual families, which had been accustomed "to good, spacious houses, and every facility for comfortable living." [20] As long as there was a promise of a better tomorrow, discontent had been kept to a minimum. But the spirit of individualism was allowed a free rein at Northampton and people who had been conditioned to life in competitive society found it impossible to continue living on promises.

John A. Collins, an abolitionist in the 1840s, used the platform of the Massachusetts Anti-Slavery Society in order to lay before his audiences a plan for complete social reform. This was during the great flurry of community building on the part of the Fourierists. In 1843 Collins purchased a 300 acre farm at Skaneateles, New York, and announced that he would construct a community, independent of the ideas of both Owen and Fourier. By January 1, 1844, 150 people accepted his invitation and Skaneateles began operation as a utopian community.

Collins was an atheist and forbade the practice of all organized religion at Skaneateles. But he was as orthodox as any churchman in his acceptance of the monogamous family relation. In an article which appeared in the *Skaneateles Columbian*, November 19, 1843, he advanced the community's ideas toward marriage and the family:

> That we regard as a true relation, growing out of the nature of things—repudiating licentiousness, concubinage, adultery, bigamy and polygamy; that mariage is designed for the happiness of the parties and to promote love and virtue . . . that parents are duty bound to educate their children in habits of virtue and love and industry; and that they are bound to unite with the community.[21]

Single men and women, or married couples with small families, were preferred at Skaneateles. During the initial stages of the experiment, the rule was observed that "a man with a large family of non-producing children, must possess extraordinary powers to justify his admission." [22] Each family occupied a small apartment but all were to eat at a common table. Divorce was not only permitted but encouraged at Skaneateles, "the sooner the better," when a husband and wife no longer contributed to one another's happiness.[23]

The Skaneateles Community repudiated its creed after the second year of operation and moved toward anarchism. Each person was allowed to be "free to think, believe and disbelieve, as he or she was moved by knowledge, habit or spontaneous impulse." [24] A new policy of admitting any and all made for an unusual assortment of characters at Skaneateles. John Orvis and John Allen, two Fourierist lecturers who were dispatched from Brook Farm, visited Skaneateles just before it dissolved in 1846, and reported that the members there were too ignorant "to discriminate between a true Constructive Reform and the No-God, No-Government, No-Marriage, No-Money, No-Meat, No-Salt, No-Pepper system of community." [25] The experiment was plagued with jealousies and bickering. Sarah Vanvelzer, who left her husband to join Skaneateles because they flattered her into believing that she was essential to the hope of humanity, admitted that there was nothing there but "backbiting, evil-thinking, and quarrelling." [26] She also reported that there were some "affinity affairs" among the sexes which caused considerable gossip.[27] The community found no way to reconcile differences and to settle disputes, since they denied the need for any rules or regulations. Its founder admitted that they might have succeeded "if men were angels, and angels Gods; but human nature is too low, too selfish, and too ignorant for relations so exalted." [28]

Several economic cooperatives were established in America during the last two decades of the nineteenth century, but none of them developed sophisticated social theories designed to revolutionize society completely. For the most part, they represented the hope of the average industrial worker of the period, that of a better tomorrow. However, in many respects they were as utopian in outlook as their predecessors, the religious, independent, Owenite, and Fourieristic experiments in communal living. The economic cooperatives did not depend purely on agriculture, like most of the utopian communities earlier in the century. They attempted to develop industrial production units in each community which would compete with the industries on the outside. The profits, however, were to be returned to the community for the benefit of all its members.

The forerunner of the economic cooperatives was Communia, founded in Iowa in 1850. The theoretical basis for Communia was the blueprint drawn by Andreas Dietsch in his *Das tausend-jahrige Reich*, published in 1842, while the author lived in Switzerland. A year later, Dietsch planned to go to America and establish a community where his social theories could be tested. He attempted to establish New Helvetia in Missouri, but was unable to attract sufficient capital or interested people. Dietsch died in 1846, but his social theories were published in America by Heinrich Koch, who employed them in constructing Communia.

Wilhelm Weitling, the founder of the Workingmen's League (*Arbeiterbund*) in America, who had known Dietsch personally in Europe, became interested in Koch's colony, and began to advertise it in the League's official paper, *Die Republik der Arbeiter*. Interest in the enterprise quickened and subscribers expressed their willingness to join the Workingmen's League and to invest in the colony.

Weitling called on "strong, unmarried members" of the League to pay the initiation fee of $100 and to go to Iowa and join the community.[29] Weitling, himself, was in and out of the community, but he used his influence among the German-American workers in support of the experiment.

The monogamous family relation was encouraged at Communia. Weitling believed that the marriage relation would improve when private property was abolished and when humanity in general became more important than individual families. He was careful on this point not to prejudice his readers against Communia; therefore he repudiated all theories which suggested a community of wives. Although the separate family was allowed to retain its identity, all lived, ate, and worked together. Only mothers with small children were allowed to eat apart from the common dining hall. The stores, orchards, and all industries were common property, and operated for equal benefits and profits to all the members of the community.[30]

By 1852 signs of discontent began to appear. The mothers refused to work, except in the behalf of their own families. Quarrels arose between the newly-arrived and the older members. The husbands took their wives' part in the petty domestic squabbles. The dissension ended in a division of the members. Those who chose to do so were allowed to depart and were given $800 for their investments of time, labor, and money. Some concessions were made to those who remained, particularly to the women, who had found communal living too restrictive for their maternal instinct. They were promised that they could have their individual hearths and homes.

Weitling sent out another call, both in this country and abroad, for new recruits for Communia. This time he specified for acceptance only those who were genuine communists and who would not expect heaven on earth. He further specified that he wanted no more large families with children, nor nagging women with sharp tongues and unreasonable demands. Weitling blamed Communia's distresses of 1852 on the women with children. In a letter to J. Krieg, he mourned: "If women only wouldn't get children. Children stimulate their egoism." [31]

The separate family arrangement had become entrenched at Communia and continued to be a source of dissension. The "quarrelsome society," from which members had to be recruited, refused to be educated to seek the community's welfare above that of their own individual families. Weitling conceded the experiment was a failure and took a pendulum swing in opposition to all utopian experiments. He later wrote: "I regard a communism without wages, and without the liberty to refrain from working if one wants to, and common food and equal work hours, an impossibility in our present society, and not even appealing for the future, and therefore impractical." [32] Weitling's associates at Communia charged him with exploiting the German-American workers in the name of communism and brotherly love. They affixed their signatures to a letter to Weitling in which they gave him the assurance that "If there is a hell for liars, you are ripe for it." [33]

One of the most famous of the economic cooperatives was that of Ruskin, established in 1894 near Dickson, Tennessee. The community owed its origin to the efforts of Julius A. Wayland, publisher of a socialist newspaper, *The Coming Nation*, in Greensburg, Indiana. Wayland capitalized on the discontent of the industrial workers in America, and issued a challenge in his newspaper for the establishment of a cooperative where all could live and work together and where the profits of their industry would be shared by the stockholding workers, rather than by the barons of industry and banking. Shares in the cooperative, which included the promise of room and board, sold for $500 for each family, refundable if the family decided to leave the community.[34]

Sufficient encouragement was given Wayland, and he sent an agent to Tennessee to purchase a suitable location for the community. A site was first chosen at Tennessee City, which proved unproductive and after a few months was moved four miles north. The new location was named Ruskin, in honor of the English author, John Ruskin, a sympathetic friend of the industrial workers. Ruskin was pleased that the colony was named for him, and sent autographed copies of his works to be placed in the community's library. However, the works of Ruskin had little to do with the organization and the affairs of the community. The operation began with twenty-six charter members, excluding their wives and children. The membership climbed steadily in the initial stages of the experiment and reached 300 by the turn of the twentieth century. They were mainly factory workers, but they came from India, England, Nova Scotia, and Russia, as well as from the mill towns of the United States, which were affected by the depression of 1893. The diverse membership subscribed to a constitution and obligated themselves to surrender their natural freedom "for the sake of civil or social freedom." [35]

The monogamous family relation was maintained at Ruskin. A few members advocated free love, it was claimed, "solely on philosophic ground," [36] but their ideas were never adopted as policy by the community. Rumors spread that the free lovers carried on their affairs in a cave on the property which was used to store food. One couple, a Mr. Lilygren and Hattie Bosworth, lived in a common law marriage for a short time, but afterward were legally united as husband and wife.[37]

The men outnumbered the women at Ruskin, and there were several bachelors in the community, but no spinsters. Families lived in separate houses but dined at a common table three times a day. There were twenty tables in the dining hall, which were served by the young ladies of the community. The young men did all the cooking, and each waitress was responsible for washing only the dishes for her table. The family houses were small, consisting of a single room, if there were no children, two rooms if there were. The houses were cheaply constructed and not much more than sheds. Each father was issued scrip for his family, printed by Wayland's presses and redeemable at the commonwealth store. There was some complaint about the fertility of some of the wives who gave birth annually and thus placed an economic strain on the community.[38] Ruskin maintained a nursery to care for the children, while the mothers worked in the kitchen, cannery, flour and coffee mills, or in the truck gardens.

The Ruskin community found the Tennessee soil unyielding and their industries insufficient to keep the enterprise alive. Economic distresses precipitated a quarrel which ended in a litigation and closed down the community in 1899. Wayland left for Kansas City. Later he moved to Girard, Kansas, where he married his secretary, Josephine Conger. A short time afterward, he committed suicide.

About 250 of the members decided to try again, this time choosing a site near Waycross, Georgia. Typhoid, malaria, fire, and starvation forced them to give up communal life altogether in 1901. Earl Miller, a shareholder in the community, admitted that these factors brought a hasty end to the Georgia phase of the experiment, but he added that the neighbors there were not as accommodating as those in Tennessee had been, as they did not trade at the commonwealth's store or bring grain to their mill.[39] The members of the community were able to salvage very little from their investment. The larger houses sold for as little as ten dollars each.

Georgia was the location of another economic cooperative experiment during the last decade of the nineteenth century, that of the Christian Commonwealth in Muscogee County. The Christian Commonwealth was an outgrowth of the Social Gospel Movement, which crossed denominational lines and called for less emphasis on divisive doctrines and creeds and more emphasis on the churches' responsibility in the area of social welfare. Ralph Albertson, a clergyman and founder of the Georgia community, preached that the most expedient way to transform men, in accordance with the teachings of Jesus Christ, was through "Christianizing property," or through sharing all things in common. The Christian Commonwealth was established in 1896 as an educational and religious society, whose stated purpose was "to obey the teachings of Jesus Christ in all matters of life, and labor, and in the use of property." [40]

There were no restrictions on membership in the colony, as Albertson believed that the power of brotherhood in a society where private property had been abolished was sufficient to reform any individual who wished to join them, regardless of his motives or former way of life. The society began with forty members in 1896, and before its dissolution in four years, some three to four hundred people had joined. The newcomers were a curious lot, mostly drifters on whom the small, high-principled brotherhood had little or no effect, and they were a constant source of embarrassment to the community.

The Christian Commonwealth upheld the sacredness of the monogamous relation and the private family. At first the families lived in separate houses, but as the colony grew, there were not enough houses to accommodate all of the families. A unitary structure, called "The Big House," was erected, which contained apartments for both married couples and single members. Nearly all ate in a common dining hall; but four families refused to dine with the rest of the community and were permitted to prepare their meals in their own quarters.

Because of the relaxed regulations regarding admission to the Christian Commonwealth, several joined them who had unorthodox views regarding marriage, and this caused rumors to be spread that the colony practiced free love. A motion was made in one of their assemblies by an anonymous member that they permit sexual relations between unmarried couples, a move that was promptly rejected.

The diversity of opinions which were allowed free expression in the Christian Commonwealth caused perpetual antagonism, bitterness, and jealousy. Added to this was a typhoid epidemic in 1899. The community was unable to survive both and disbanded the following year.

Several economic cooperatives established utopian communities on the American west coast during the last decade of the nineteenth century. One, which gained notoriety, was Kaweah, established in Tulare County, California, in 1884. Burnett G. Haskell, the father of the colony, affirmed that its object was "to insure its members against want or fear of want by providing happy homes, ample sustenance, educational and recreational facilities, and to promote and maintain harmonious social relations on the solid and grand basis of liberty, equality, fraternity and solidarity." [41] Haskell managed to secure about 12,000 acres of government land for the enterprise. United States Senate hearings were held in 1893 to inquire into the methods used by Haskell in acquiring the giant redwood forests. Haskell and his friends were charged with having "glued themselves" to the valuable timberland and with planning to hold them against outsiders and the federal government, "by force," if necessary.[42] A clerk in the General Land Office, G. V. N. Ogden, told the Senate that Kaweah "was conceived in illegality, born in fraud, and nurtured in falsehood and deception." [43] The community ceased its operation before the federal government moved in to reclaim the property.

While the community of Kaweah existed, familism was both permitted and encouraged. According to the bylaws, each member of the society was entitled to the use of a small tract, "not less than two hundred by two hundred feet," upon which he could build a house at his own expense, and for his private use.[44] The community promised to buy back the house if the builder chose to leave. A unitary house, no more than a crude hotel, was constructed to house those who wished to live in common at the community's expense.

Divorce was permitted at Kaweah, and in order to guarantee that marital unions did not continue after "affection, congeniality, and morality" ceased, the women were given economic independence.[45] Once a divorce was granted, the person who held the original certificate of membership, usually the husband, was allowed to remain. The other, by popular vote of the membership, could also remain. If the members were unwilling to retain the individual who did not possess an original certificate of membership, he was forced to depart from the society.

There was limited intimacy among the families at Kaweah, since there was sufficient room for each family to maintain its distinct identity. Individualism had the fullest expression in that each could design, build, and furnish his own home. Problems which arose among the families were set aside for discussion at Saturday night meetings. Kaweah appears to have been spared much of the internal wrangling that wrecked many of the utopian communities.

Utopian socialists never saw the sun dawn on their "better tomorrow" within their communities. As they packed their baggage and went their separate ways, perhaps they still entertained the hope that within ordinary society, with all of its competitive ills, tomorrow just might be better.

IX

Celestial Marriage: An Experiment in Polygyny

MORMON POLYGYNY * WAS ONE OF THE UNIQUE EXPERIMENTS AMONG the nineteenth-century American utopians to alter the marriage system of the Christian world. The practice was not altogether without precedent, as the patriarchs of biblical times and the oriental chieftains had their harems. Even in America, polygyny was an accepted practice of certain Indian tribes, particularly the Blackfoot of Utah.[1] William Hepworth Dixon, who visited the Mormons during the founding of Salt Lake City, wrote that he was convinced that they had "found their type of domestic life in the Indian's wigwam rather than in the Patriarch's tent." [2]

There had been one brief experiment in polygyny among Christians during the sixteenth century. John of Leyden, a leader of the Anabaptists in Munster, Germany, preached the doctrine of a plurality of wives as a means of producing a "holy seed." The Anabaptists, who also engaged in communal living, adopted the practice.

* The term polygyny best describes the Mormon practice, as they were opposed to a woman having more than one husband, as the broad meaning of polygamy implies. The Mormons preferred the term "celestial marriage." However, most of the sources of literature during the period used the term polygamy to describe the Mormon practice of having a plurality of wives.

John of Leyden was reported to have had seventeen wives.[3] Polygyny among the Anabaptists was short-lived, as it gave rise to persecution of an already despised sect. The Mormon experiment in polygyny lasted a little over fifty years and was met with the same stout resistance from the outside that the Anabaptists experienced.

The Mormons were utopian in their vision and established socio-religious communities to expedite their plan to construct a Zion of God on earth.[4] *The Book of Mormon*, first published in 1830, advanced the Christian philosophy of sharing one's goods with those who were in need. One passage admonished: "impart of your substance to the poor, every man according to that which he hath, such as feeding the hungry, clothing the naked, visiting the sick and administering to their relief, both spiritually and temporally, according to their wants. And see that all these things are done in wisdom and order." [5] *The Book of Mormon* did not specify the particular order to be followed. It was left to Sidney Rigdon, an erratic preacher and publisher, to conceive of the plan which was adopted and came to be known as the "United Order of Enoch."

Rigdon had been an associate of Alexander Campbell at the time of the latter's debate with Robert Owen in 1829. Owen's socialistic scheme, which received a thorough treatment during the debate, appealed to Rigdon and a breach followed between Rigdon and Campbell. Rigdon was preaching in Pittsburgh, and became acquainted with the Rappites, who had resettled in Economy, Pennsylvania, a short distance away, after they had sold their Indiana community site to Owen in 1825. Rigdon was convinced that communal living was imperative if men were ever to work out age-old social problems. He moved to Mentor, Ohio, at the time Joseph Smith and his small band of followers moved to nearby Kirtland. Rigdon, who had failed to convert his entire congregation to the virtues of communal life at Mentor, joined the Mormons and carried a large number of his flock to Kirtland with him. Alexander Campbell mourned the loss but claimed Rigdon had always been unstable. In his religious journal, *The Millennial Harbinger*, Campbell wrote that Rigdon had "a peculiar mental and corporeal malady," and that "fits of melancholy succeeded by fits of enthusiasm accompanied by some kind of nervous spasms and swoonings" characterized his former associate's behavior.[6]

Two Rappites, John and Jacob Zundel, joined Rigdon in Kirtland and were converted to Mormonism. Karl Arndt is convinced that the Harmony Society of George Rapp provided the living model for the Mormon Church.[7] The fact remains that no mention of utopian socialism was made by Joseph Smith, or by any of his followers, until Rigdon and a few Rappites joined the Mormons at Kirtland. The Mormons, while they resided in New York, were individualists as regards their property and family life. Their experiences in the midst of antagonistic non-Mormons convinced them that a satisfactory *modus vivendi* could not be reached and paved the way for the acceptance of a collectivist arrangement which would be both self-sufficient and self-defending.

After his brief association with Rigdon, who later became a high ranking official in the Mormon Church, Joseph Smith reportedly had a revelation which specified the cooperative structure of a Mormon community, or the United Order of Enoch. The Order specified that all properties were to be surrendered and consecrated to the community, and that every man was to become a steward over those properties which the community placed in his charge. From these properties, a man was entitled to support for himself and his family, and all other profits were to be donated to the community storehouse for the benefit of those who had not prospered. Smith contended for communism among the Mormons, and reasoned: "If men are not equal in earthly things, how then can they be equal in obtaining heavenly things." [8]

Joseph Smith and Sidney Rigdon set about to establish an autarky at Kirtland which would enable the Mormons to live independently. In 1837 the Mormons were charged by the state of Ohio for having violated the law in establishing a bank without having first received a charter. This, and several other factors, forced the members of the sect to flee the state and settle in Caldwell, Missouri. There they remained for three years, but met resistance from their new neighbors. Joseph Smith ordered his followers to stand firm; but in 1840, when the Missouri militia was called out to protect Missourians from the retaliatory threats of the Mormons, Smith took his faithful band to Nauvoo, Illinois.

By 1845, 15,000 Mormons had swarmed into Nauvoo, making it the largest city in Illinois, and the largest utopian community in the nineteenth century. At first the Illinois neighbors appeared more tolerant of the sect than those of previous settlements. Smith laid out the city with rectangular streets and proposed the construction of a city state that would be independent of all external governments.

He also drew up a charter which gave a Common Council the power to legislate in all matters which pertained to the community's welfare. A recorder's office was created by the Common Council to register all titles to property. Smith had learned at Kirtland that he was not authorized by the state of Ohio to perform marriage ceremonies, since he was not a regularly ordained minister. At Nauvoo, Smith, without obtaining the legal sanction of the state of Illinois, established an office to issue marriage licenses to Mormons, which gave him absolute control over the marrying propensities of his people.[9] The experience in Missouri convinced Smith that he must have an army to defend the Mormons, so he organized the Nauvoo Legion, which consisted of about 5,000 reservists who could be summoned on quick notice.

The Nauvoo plan was to establish a theocratic state which would be both self-sufficient and self-defending. Here Smith planned to gather Mormons from all over the world. The community would serve as Smith's power base, and enable him to make his influence felt in America. In 1844 he became a candidate for the presidency of the United States. The Illinois neighbors became concerned over the growth of Nauvoo, the threat of its Legion, and the intentions of Joseph Smith. But Smith also faced problems within the Nauvoo community. A group of Mormons published the first and only edition of *The Nauvoo Expositor*, June 7, 1844, in which Joseph Smith was charged with abuse of the city's charter, dictatorial rule, and embezzlement of the community's money, which he allegedly squandered on real estate gambles. He was further charged with teaching polygyny at Nauvoo. Smith countered by calling an emergency meeting of the Common Council and had the newspaper declared a nuisance and ordered it destroyed. Three days later, the presses of *The Nauvoo Expositor* were smashed and all available copies of the paper confiscated. The dissenters fled to Carthage, Illinois, and swore out a warrant for Smith's arrest on the charges of violating the freedom of the press, polygyny, and political dictatorship. Joseph Smith and his brother, Hyrum, were arrested and incarcerated in the jail at Carthage. A mob stormed the jail and both Smiths were murdered.

The Nauvoo experiment became the prototype for the Mormon communities which were founded by Smith's successor, Brigham Young. Young, outmaneuvering all contenders, replaced Smith as president of the society, and ordered the evacuation of Nauvoo in the winter of 1845–1846. His aim was to remove the settlement outside the federal limits of the United States in order to escape the contact and contamination with "Babylon," a term which the Mormons applied to their hostile environment. The remoteness of the Great Salt Lake Basin appeared to Young to be the most likely location in which to build the Zion of God. The size of the Mormon population, a factor which was partly responsible for the problems at Nauvoo, dictated that it would be expedient to disperse into smaller communities. Although Salt Lake City was the center of Mormondom, some 360 communities were established in the Far West between the years 1847 and 1877, each along the plan of the United Order of Enoch which had been announced in Kirtland, Ohio, in 1831. The Church planned and controlled all community development. Communities were laid out with rectangular streets, as at Nauvoo. Cooperative stores and industries were developed, the central office in Salt Lake City assuming part of the responsibility in providing capital, equipment, and foodstuffs for getting communities under way.

Brigham Young continued to preach the need for economic cooperation which Joseph Smith had revealed to the Latter-day Saints in Kirtland. He counseled: "If the people called Latter-day Saints do not become one in temporal things, as they are in spiritual things, they will not redeem the earth and build up the Zion of God. This cooperative movement is a stepping stone. We say to the people, take advantage of it, it is your privilege." [10] Amos Warner, writing in 1888, claimed the Mormon practice of cooperation had given them "farms, orchards, homes and population," and that the key to their successes was the adoption of the principle of "live and help live." [11] Of all the utopian experiments conducted in the nineteenth century in America, none was as successful in building a strong economic basis for communal life as were the Mormon communities.

The exact date of the origin of polygyny among the Mormons is yet a matter of debate among their historians. It was first adopted as a privilege of the hierarchy and was kept secret. Open admission of the practice was not officially made by the Church of Jesus Christ of Latter-day Saints until after they had settled in Utah in 1852. *The Book of Mormon* condemned polygyny in no uncertain terms. The harems of David and Solomon were declared "abominable" before God, and the Latter-day Saints were forbidden to follow the example of the patriarchs in having more than one wife. They were specifically ordered to have but one wife and forbidden to have concubines.[12]

The Mormons were accused of practicing free love as early as 1835, while they were living at Kirtland, Ohio. This was a common charge made against all utopian communities, particularly the Owenites, whose communal movement coincided with that of the Mormons. The accusation was of sufficient gravity to warrant the first among many denials. In *The Book of the Doctrine and Covenants*, published first in 1835, the Mormons affirmed: "Inasmuch as this Church of Christ has been reproached with the crime of fornication and polygamy, we declare that we believe that one man should have one wife, and one woman one husband, except in the case of death, when either is at liberty to marry again." [13]

A critical social problem developed at Kirtland, since several residents who had joined the Mormons there had left their unconverted spouses in order to follow Smith. The Mormons could not afford to maintain a community of unmarried men and women, as it would give rise to further charges of impropriety from the neighbors. Smith permitted them to marry, although some of them had never been legally divorced.

Joseph Smith became convinced that God sanctioned polygyny while he was working on his *Book of Abraham*, which he began at Kirtland. He studied the account of Abraham's life while he allegedly translated a book which the patriarch was supposed to have written and which had been allegedly found among some mummies brought to America from Egypt.[14] Smith was intrigued with the story of Abraham's taking his wife's handmaiden that she might bear him a son, since his wife, Sarah, was barren. When Smith later defended polygyny at Nauvoo, he cited the example of Abraham's action as a divinely approved precedent. He wrote: "God commanded Abraham, and Sarah gave Hagar to Abraham to wife. And why did he do it? Because this was the law, and from Hagar sprang many people. This, therefore, was fulfilling, among other things, the promises. Was Abraham, therefore, under condemnation? Verily, I say unto you, Nay; for I, the Lord commanded it." [15]

Although Joseph Smith accepted the doctrine of polygyny, he limited the practice to the elite in the Church, and publicly condemned all who dared to openly teach or practice it. In 1840, John Cook Bennett, a self-styled physician and Mormon convert from Ohio, joined the Nauvoo community. He rapidly ascended the ranks of the Mormon Church and became mayor of Nauvoo in 1842. Bennett learned of the secret practice of polygyny among the Mormon elders and was eager to establish it as an open feature of their domestic life. He had left a wife and three children in McConnelsville, Ohio. Smith later claimed that Bennett had committed adultery in Ohio, and had come to Nauvoo to escape punishment. Smith also reported that he had shown Bennett a letter which exposed his adultery and that he candidly admitted the charges were true.[16] While at Nauvoo, Bennett reportedly had several affairs with Mormon women "in Joseph Smith's name quite without benefit of ceremony." [17] When Smith learned of Bennett's affairs, and that he was too free with his talk of the official sanction of polygyny in the inner circle, he summoned him to appear before the Church Council. It was alleged that Bennett "acknowledged his wicked and licentious conduct toward certain females . . . and that he was worthy of the severest chastisements, and cried like a child, and begged that he might be spared." [18] He afterward tried to poison himself, but the dosage was insufficient to take his life. He was excommunicated by the Church Council.

Bennett retired from Nauvoo and circulated several letters in which he asserted that he had first-hand information that the Mormon elders both believed and practiced the doctrine of polygyny. The publicity was more than Joseph Smith could tolerate, and he countered Bennett's letters with an official Church publication entitled *Affidavits and Certificates Disproving the Statements and Affidavits in John C. Bennett's Letters*. In the fall of 1842 Bennett collected his earlier accounts, added a few new ones, and published *The History of the Saints: or an Exposé of Joe Smith and the Mormons*. The disclosures of Bennett regarding polygyny at Nauvoo were the first in a long series of anti-Mormon publications devoted to that topic.

If polygyny were an accepted practice of the Mormon hierarchy, it could not be kept secret indefinitely. There was a need for a solid theological base in its defense. Smith was aware of the value of a specific sanction from the Deity which would relate directly to the Mormons of the nineteenth century, without having to depend upon the Old Testament Scriptures in defense of a plurality of wives. *The Book of Mormon* condemned polygyny, and the Mormons had accepted that work as their rule of faith and practice. But Joseph Smith was regarded a prophet, with whom God was in daily contact. Latter-day revelations were commonplace among the Mormons and they had grown accustomed to modern visions, which always came at the precise moment when problems arose which had not been dealt with in earlier ones. In July 1843 Smith allegedly received a revelation from God which authorized Mormons to adopt polygyny, although he had already accepted it as a principle, and had secretly married several women. He now had a "thus saith the Lord," in case another of the ilk of John Cook Bennett entered into the elite circle and later decided to expose their practice. The revelation was not made public until 1852, after the death of Joseph Smith, when the Mormons settled in Utah.

Joseph Smith's alleged revelation, which gave divine sanction to polygyny, was written in typical King James English, in which all such Mormon revelations, including *The Book of Mormon*, were worded. It began with the statement that Joseph Smith had inquired of God how Abraham, Isaac, Jacob, Moses, and Solomon were justified, as they had many wives and concubines. God set his mind at ease by telling him that the patriarchs had not committed sin, and further ordered the Latter-day Saints to follow the example of these Old Testament worthies. Smith knew that his wife, Emma, would not consent to his having other wives, so the revelation specifically instructed her to submit to her husband's request or else stand condemned. If she consented, she was promised a happy and fruitful life. At this juncture in the revelation came the official sanction of polygyny to which the Utah Mormons later pointed as the divine justification for one man having a plurality of wives:

> If any man espouse a virgin, and desire to espouse another, and the first give her consent; and if he espouse the second, and they are virgins, and have vowed to no other man, then is he justified; he cannot commit adultery, for they are given unto him; for he cannot commit adultery with that which belongeth to him and to no one else. And if he have ten virgins given unto him by this law, he cannot commit adultery for they belong to him, therefore is he justified.[19]

Although the revelation specified that the first wife must give her consent, Smith was assured that he could overrule Emma's objections, for the document further stated:

> Therefore, it shall be lawful in me, if she [Emma] receive not this law, for him [Joseph] to receive all things, whatsoever I, the Lord his God, will give unto him, because she did not administer unto him

> according to my word; and she then becomes the transgressor; and he is exempt from the law of Sarah, who administered unto Abraham according to the law, when I commanded Abraham to take Hagar to wife.[20]

Joseph Smith had had ample opportunity to gauge the feelings of his wife regarding polygyny, and he realized that she, above all Mormon women, would be the most stubborn in resisting the practice. He had observed her violence when he had been accused of marital infidelity. He had had an affair, which allegedly resulted in a secret marriage, with seventeen-year-old Fannie Alger in 1835. Fannie had been taken into the Smith home as an orphan and Joseph became attracted to her. Oliver Cowdery spied on the prophet and Fannie, and reported their promiscuity to Emma. Emma became enraged and drove Fannie out of her house. Fannie moved to Indiana, saving Joseph Smith any further embarrassment. Cowdery was later excommunicated on several charges, one of which was that he had insinuated that Joseph Smith had committed adultery.

Two months before Smith allegedly received his revelation which divinely authorized polygyny, an incident is reported to have occurred in the prophet's house at Nauvoo which involved him with Eliza Snow. Eliza, like Fannie before, lived in the Smith mansion and occupied a room across the hall from the master bedroom. One morning, Emma caught her husband and Eliza in an embrace. Emma drove Eliza out of the house with a broom. The children in the house became upset and begged Emma not to be so mean to "Aunt Eliza." Smith, aware of his wife's temper and repeated assaults on the women toward whom he had shown particular affection, did not take Emma into his confidence as regards his acceptance of the practice of polygyny. He secretly married several women, of which Emma was not aware. Brigham Young confided to William Hepworth Dixon that he had secretly sealed dozens of women to Smith.[21]

Joseph Smith may have possessed a deep-rooted sexual urge which Emma did not fully satisfy, for his extramarital ventures were both many and varied. He fancied himself an irresistible and virile person. Charlotte Haven wrote to her sister, Ida, from Nauvoo, during the winter of 1845–1846, that Smith was "a great egoist and boaster, for he frequently remarked that every place he stopped to and from Springfield people crowded around him and expressed surprise that he was so handsome and good looking." [22]

Smith concealed his own polygyny and that of his limited circle of high churchmen after he had allegedly received the revelation which authorized the practice. He also continued to denounce publicly those who intimated that polygyny was an accepted practice in the Mormon Church. In February 1844, nearly a year after the revelation, he and his brother, Hyrum, acting as joint presidents of the Church, issued a statement in which they condemned one Hiram Brown for "preaching polygamy, and other false and corrupt doctrines," in Michigan.[23] Brown was notified that he had been "cut off from the Church for his iniquity," and was ordered to appear in Nauvoo on the sixth of April 1844, to answer charges. The following month, Richard Hewitt inquired of Hyrum Smith if certain members of the Mormon Apostleship were permitted to have more than one wife. Hyrum replied: "there is no such doctrine taught here at Nauvoo neither is there any such thing practiced here." [24] In spite of Joseph Smith's duplicity, Mormons at Nauvoo implicitly trusted him. Charlotte Haven, in a letter to her parents, wrote about the reports of polygyny at Nauvoo, but claimed Hyrum Smith was the originator of the practice, as she simply could not believe that Joseph Smith would ever sanction such a doctrine.[25]

Joseph Smith not only sanctioned the doctrine but convinced his wife, Emma, that she would be condemned by God if she did not concur. Reluctantly, she permitted him to take additional wives if she were allowed to make the selections for him. He agreed, and she chose nineteen-year-old Emily Patridge and her twenty-three-year-old sister, Eliza, orphans whom the Smiths had taken into their home. On May 11, 1843, Joseph Smith was married to the two young ladies in the presence of Emma. The ceremony was redundant, as they had secretly married two months before, without Emma's knowledge.

Polygyny was a privilege of the high churchmen at Nauvoo, but not all of the members of the hierarchy accepted it. William Marks, who served as Stake President, claimed that "when the doctrine of polygamy was introduced into the church I took a decided stand against it; which stand rendered me quite unpopular with many of the leading ones of the church." [26] William Law became Smith's arch opponent and leader of the anti-polygynist faction of the Mormons. Law demanded that Smith recant, or he would reveal the prophet's concupiscence and add his "facts" to those already published by John Cook Bennett.[27] Brigham Young claimed that he at first "shed many bitter tears" over the decision regarding polygyny, but after he saw the "sacred writings," and was "convinced by Joseph that the command to marry more wives was a true revelation," his former prejudices gave in to the will of God.[28]

There was no rational justification for limiting polygyny to the Mormon hierarchy, except that the men of the lower echelon could not financially afford to maintain a harem. Once the Latter-day Saints settled in Utah, where the democratic spirit had opportunity for freer expression than at Nauvoo, several Mormon males demanded an equal privilege in the selection of additional wives. In 1852, polygyny was openly declared to be an official doctrine of the Mormon Church, and the right to engage in the practice was extended to all Mormons. Brigham Young rationalized the secrecy and the limitation of polygyny as being due to the fear of a reaction from the Gentile world. Belinda Pratt, wife of the Apostle Orson Pratt, claimed that the official proclamation regarding polygyny was withheld by God until 1852 "because of the ignorance and prejudice of the nations of mystic Babylon, that peradventure he might save some of them." [29] When the Mormons had settled outside of the territorial limits of the United States and had secured their position as a separate political entity, such fear, for the time being at least, was removed.

Several reasons given for the adoption of polygyny by the Mormons do not find their bases in Mormon theology. Richard F. Burton, an English observer in 1860, claimed that their motive was economy.[30] Servants were rare and costly and it was cheaper to marry them. The increase in the number of wives and children did prove an important economic asset in some cases, as it provided the head of the household with a larger and cheaper labor supply than would be possible in a monogamous family. As the Mormons taught that the husband and father was the unquestioned head of his own house, he was assured that a docile body of domestic servants, called his wives and children, would be employed for his benefit. Brigham Young gave the domestic system periodic support in his sermons. On one occasion he exhorted: "let the wives and the children say Amen to what he [the head of the family] says, and be subject to his dictates, instead of their dictating [to] the man, instead of their trying to govern him." [31] Mormon women might complain of the system, but isolated on the far Western frontier, in a society which sanctioned the domestic system of cheap labor, there was little hope they could escape from it.

The adoption of polygyny assured the Mormons of an increase in population, which would be needed to fix themselves firmly on the frontier. They anticipated the establishment of a sovereign theocracy which would strike fear in the hearts of any would-be assailants. Missionary activity among the Gentiles brought its quota of people who were eager to join their compatriots in Utah, but the evangelizing process was slow and not always rewarding. One method of increasing the Mormon population was to require early marriages and to maintain no spinsters or widows who were capable of bearing children. Jules Remy heard Brigham Young say in one of his sermons: "Make haste and get married. Let me see no more boys above sixteen and girls above fourteen unmarried." [32] Every Mormon father fancied himself the prince or head of a tribe, as the patriarch Abraham. Belinda Pratt claimed that the Mormon husband anticipated sending forth "for the defense of his country, hundreds and thousands of his own warriors, born in his own house." [33] Brigham Young told the Saints in Salt Lake City that Lowell, Massachusetts, had 14,000 more girls than men, who "live and die in a single state and are forgotten." [34] He further stated that they had not fulfilled the purpose for which God had created them, and he urged that 2,000 Mormon males should go there and "take to themselves seven women a-piece." [35]

Mormons objected to birth control as being sinful and exhorted their women to fulfill their God-given responsibility to bear children. Brigham Young once told the wives that the key to marital happiness "is for you to bear children, in the name of the Lord . . . to receive, conceive, bear, and bring forth in the name of Israel's God." [36] He further cautioned them not to torment themselves about whether or not their husbands loved them, but to get immediately to the task of bearing children. The chief end of woman's existence was to bear all of the children God wanted her to. Barrenness was regarded as a curse, and it was a disgrace to womanhood for a Mormon to remain unmarried or to refuse to bear children.[37]

Brigham Young was a living example of all that he taught regarding the propagation of the species. In the spring of 1854 he had nine children born to his household within a single week.[38] Special lectures were held in Salt Lake City during the winter of

1856–1857 to train the young women in the virtues of polygyny and the rewards of motherhood. *The New York Times* reported that at this time the number of polygynous marriages rose more rapidly than at any time before.[39]

The population of Utah grew at an alarming rate. Missionaries brought thousands of people to Utah, but the Utah women are to be credited with the bulk of the population increase. Approximately 5,000 Mormons had settled in Utah by 1849. In 1860 there were 40,000. Within another ten years, the population more than doubled and stood at nearly 87,000.

Polygyny was defended by the Mormons on the ground that it was healthy, not only for the men and women, but for their offspring. In January 1870, while the Cullom Bill to outlaw the practice was before the United States Congress, an assembly of Mormon women composed a resolution to send to the Congress which stated their faith in "the institutions of the Church of Jesus Christ of Latter-day Saints as the only reliable safeguard of female virtue and innocence; and . . . the only sure protection against the fearful sin of prostitution and its attendant evils." [40] Polygyny made it possible for all women to be married, even when the sex ratio favored the male. This permitted women to bear children, and thus, as Belinda Pratt explained, allowed "the stream of life to flow through them that they might be the healthy creatures God intended." [41]

Burton also observed in 1860 that polygynous marriages had resulted in "sound health and morals in the constitutions of their offspring." [42] Horace Greeley, on the other hand, noted that during his visit to Salt Lake City, the year before Burton arrived: "Children born in polygamy seemed to have subnormal heads." [43] Benjamin Ferris, who spent six months in Salt Lake City in 1856 as the Secretary of the Utah Territory, claimed: "The children are subject to a frightful degree of sickness and mortality," and he blamed it on "the combined result of the gross sensuality of the parents, and want of care toward their offspring." [44]

Apparently Mormon women were not particularly sensuous, as they at no time demanded the same sexual variety that the men enjoyed. They were enjoined to refrain from sexual intercourse from the time of conception until the child was weaned from breast feeding. Continence during this period was for the mother and child's health, not a matter of theology. The Mormons defended polygyny on the grounds that it was also healthy and invigorating for the men. Heber Kimball, in one of his sermons, claimed:

> I would not be afraid to promise a man who is sixty years of age, if he will take the counsel of Brother Brigham and his brethren, that he will renew his age. I have noticed that a man who has but one wife, and is inclined to that doctrine, soon begins to wither and dry up, while a man who goes into plurality looks fresh, young, and sprightly.[45]

Had polygyny been defended only on the grounds of economy, propagation, or health reasons, the practice would not have received the endorsement of the Mormons, nor would it have remained an official doctrine of the Latter-day Saints for nearly fifty years. The practice needed a plausible theological base which would make its denial sufficient grounds for one to lose his soul. The alleged revelation regarding polygyny reported by Joseph Smith in 1843, which was openly published by Brigham Young in 1852, was hardly sufficient to convince the puritanical Mormons that one's eternal status depended on it. A theology was needed also to make the eternal reward attractive to the women who consented to share their husbands. If polygyny had been merely a civil contract, which ended in death, there is no ground to assume that the women would have endorsed it. Orson Pratt contended that polygyny could not be regarded as purely a domestic arrangement, but as a part of their religion and necessary for their "exaltation to the fulness of the Lord's glory in the eternal world." [46]

The Mormon women did not gleefully accept the idea of husband-sharing when it was first introduced. Brigham Young, in an interview with Horace Greeley, admitted that they were reluctant at first, but claimed they came to accept it "as the will of God." [47] Burton charged that the Mormon elders bribed them with promises of paradise and threatened them with annihilation, "well knowing without the hearty co-operation of mothers, and wives, sisters and daughters, no institution can live long." [48] William Hepworth Dixon observed that it was necessary to preach sermons, compose poetry, and to send female missionaries to work among the womenfolk, "to encourage every Sarah to bring forth her Hagar." [49]

The stupendous theological edifice which served to support polygyny was constructed to complement the entire structure of Mormonism. Polygyny became, not merely an appendage to the

Church, but its vital center. Dixon claimed that Sidney Rigdon, the architect of the communal plan of Mormonism, was also the theological genius who devised the theory of celestial marriage, which, in part, was borrowed from the Methodists in Vermont.[50] The theory stated that the immortal soul resides in three successive states: (1) the spiritual state before it is admitted to the earth; (2) the mortal state within the human body; and (3) the celestial state after physical death. The celestial state is divided into three "heavens," the highest of which is reserved for those who have entered into the Order of the Priesthood through celestial marriage.[51] God has created millions of souls who are yet in the spiritual state and who are waiting to obtain bodies on earth.[52] These souls will not prolong their stay in the spiritual state, waiting for good parents to produce children for them to inhabit. Brigham Young asserted: "Spirits must be born, even if they have to come to brothels for their fleshly coverings, and many of them will take the lowest and meanest spirit house that there is in the world, rather than do without." [53] The urgency of the souls to inhabit fleshly bodies is due to the divine requirement that they must be "perfected" in a human body before they can inherit the superior celestial state. The duty of every Mormon, therefore, was "to prepare tabernacles for them; to take a course that will not tend to drive these spirits into the families of the wicked, where they will be trained in wickedness, debauchery, and every species of crime." [54] Brigham Young affirmed: "the reason why the doctrine of plurality of wives was revealed was that the noble spirits which are waiting for tabernacles might be brought forth." [55] The monogamous marriage was limited in the number of bodies it could provide for these spirits, whereas polygynous marriages could supply myriads of earthly tabernacles. Joseph Smith expressed confidence that "The result of our endless union will be offspring as numerous as the stars of heaven, or the sands of the seashore." [56]

The theory also held out greater incentives than the fulfilling of God's purpose in providing earthly habitations for wandering spirits. The third celestial state into which one could enter, by being a member of the Order of the Priesthood, was one in which Latter-day Saints would rule as kings and queens, and be on an equality with God. A man's kingdom in the celestial state would be proportionate to the size of his progeny on earth. Fanny Stenhouse explained:

> We shall not marry there or be given in marriage; hence it is necessary for us to marry here, and to marry as much as we can, for then in heaven a man will take the wives whom he married on earth, or who have been sealed to him by proxy; they will be his queens, and their children will be his subjects . . . hence we shall ourselves be gods! [57]

The alternative for those who did not subscribe to the system of celestial marriages was to become lowly servants for ever and ever.[58]

Celestial marriages were for both "time and eternity," and the vow, "until death do us part," was not a part of the wedding ceremony. Only the Mormon priesthood was empowered to perform celestial marriages, since the civil government was limited to purely earthly affairs. Only those Mormons who were adjudged "worthy of participation in the special blessings of the House of the Lord" could be sealed in marriages for time and eternity in the "temples reared and dedicated for such holy service." [59] All other marriages were contracted for "time" only, and the relation ceased at death. If a man wished to enter into a celestial marriage, he first must ask the permission of the president of the Church before he made his proposal to a woman. The president was to await a revelation from God before he could give his consent.[60]

The doctrine of celestial marriage also included a provision for the establishment of a union for eternity only. This made it possible for one to be sealed to his deceased wife, if she had not been converted to Mormonism before her death. The couple was promised a reunion in eternity. A proxy was needed as a stand-in for the deceased woman, and, likely as not, the same ceremony which sealed a deceased wife to her husband for eternity also sealed the proxy to him for time here on earth. In order to assure the women that they would share in the joys of the third heaven, and there reign as queens, they were sometimes sealed to a deceased prophet, whose eternal destiny was assured in the third estate. In January 1846 thirty women were sealed to Joseph Smith for eternity in the Nauvoo temple, and to various other men for time. Old women, who were beyond the years of bearing children, found it advantageous to be sealed for eternity to a Mormon bureaucrat who could afford to care for them in their remaining years. Brigham Young admitted, in an interview with Horace Greeley, that several old ladies whom he regarded more as mothers than as wives had been sealed to him for eternity.[61]

Celestial marriage was regarded as one of their most sacred and essential principles, since without it, no Mormon husband could claim his wives in eternity, nor could a Mormon woman hope for eternal exaltation. Orson Pratt's first of nine wives, Belinda, was convinced that her own salvation, as well as that of all women, was dependent on being "adopted into the great family of Polygamists." [62] The doctrine of plural wives was made a solemn and sacred duty for those who entertained the hope of salvation. All good Mormons were expected to accept the principle, even if they refused to enter into the practice. Apostle Taylor accused Colonel Hooper, Utah's representative in the United States Congress, of being "only half a Mormon," because he had not consented to take additional wives.[63]

Mormon theology which supported polygyny drew most of its strength from the Old Testament and the examples of the patriarchs. The Jews in Utah, who were confirmed monogamists, were critical of the Mormons for appealing to Abraham in support of polygyny. One Hebrew remarked: "If the ancient Hebrews were as wicked as the Latter-day Saints, I am sorry the Philistines did not clean them out." [64] Richard Burton, who lived in Utah in 1861, and who tried to give an objective view of Mormonism, was convinced that polygyny was divinely sanctioned in the Old Testament, since

> the most righteous men who ever lived on the earth: holy Prophets and Patriarchs, who were inspired by the Holy Ghost—who were enwrapt in the visions of the Almighty—who conversed with holy angels—who saw God face to face, and talked with Him as a man talks with his friends—were 'Polygamists.' [65]

The Mormons had considerably more difficulty in reconciling their theory of celestial marriage with the New Testament, particularly the writings of the apostle Paul. Celibate communities made an issue of the unmarried status of Jesus Christ, and partly justified their ban on marriage as an attempt to follow his example of perfection. The Mormons did not concede that Jesus was a celibate. To give further credence to their practice of polygyny, they asserted that Jesus was the husband of several wives. In a sermon delivered in the Salt Lake City Tabernacle in March 1857 Orson Hyde gave the following exposé of the marital status of Christ:

> It will be borne in mind that, once on a time, there was a marriage in Cana of Galilee; and on a careful reading of that transaction it

> will be discovered that no less a person than Jesus Christ was married on that occasion. If he was never married, his intimacy with Mary and Martha, and the other Mary also, whom Jesus loved, must have been highly unbecoming and improper, to say the best of it. I will venture to say that, if Jesus Christ was now to pass through the most pious countries in Christendom, with a train of women such as used to follow him, fondling about him, combing his hair, anointing him with precious ointments, washing his feet with tears and wiping them with the hair of their heads, and unmarried, or even married, he would be mobbed, tarred and feathered, and rode [*sic*], not on an ass, but on a rail.[66]

Hyde added that "when he arose from the dead, instead of showing himself to his chosen witnesses, the Apostles, he appeared first to these women Mary, Martha, and Mary Magdalene. . . . Now, it would be very natural for a husband in the resurrection to appear to his own dear wives, and afterwards show himself to his other friends." [67]

The Mormon Church did not specify the particular procedure that a polygynist must follow when he selected a new bride. The romantic interlude which preceded a monogamous marriage was an inexpedient precedent when applied to polygyny, since it could give rise to jealousies. Nonromantic wives were better adapted to the polygynous family arrangement. Sarah Comstock, who visited the remote Mormon communities of the region of St. George, Utah, where polygyny was practiced after it had been outlawed by the federal government and officially renounced by the Mormon Church in 1890, claimed: "The practical lady will find polygamy convenient, and the lugubrious one will find it dreary, the pretty one will find it annoying, and the spiritual one will find it exalting." [68]

Occasionally romance was a strong factor in both the courtship and during the marriage which followed, but it was by no means essential. Brigham Young is said to have turned romantic when he pursued the beautiful Amelia Folsom, daughter of William Folsom, the architect who designed the Tabernacle in Salt Lake City. He reportedly "curled his hair and changed his homespun broadcloth when he courted her." [69] She led him a merry chase and finally agreed to join his bevy of wives on the condition that she have her own house apart from his other wives and a carriage. Ann Eliza, the last of Brigham's wives, bitterly complained over the special attention which he showed Amelia and asserted that under her influence he became a monogamist in all but the name.[70]

The procedure in selecting a bride usually followed the format explained by a Mormon elder in 1860:

> I have two wives living, and one wife dead. I am thinking of taking another, as I can well afford the expense, and a man is not much respected in the church who has less than three wives. Well, I fix my mind on a young lady, and consider within myself whether it is the will of God that I should seek her. If I feel, in my own heart, that it would be right to try, I speak to my bishop, who advises and approves, as he shall see fit; on which I go to the President, who will consider whether I am a good man and worthy husband, capable of ruling my little household, keeping peace among my wives, bringing up my children in the fear of God; and if I am found worthy, in his sight, of the blessing, I shall obtain permission to go on with the chase. Then I lay the whole matter of my desire, my permission and my choice, before my first wife, as head of my house, and take her counsel as to the young lady's habits, character and accomplishments. Perhaps I may speak with my second wife; perhaps not; since it is not so much her business as it is that of my first wife; besides which, my first wife is older in years, has seen more of life, and is much more of a friend to me than the second. An objection on the first wife's part would have great weight with me; I should not care much for what the second either said or thought. Supposing all to go well, I should next have a talk with the young lady's father; and if he consented to my suit, I should then address the young lady herself.[71]

If the first wife refused to give her consent, and her husband was determined to take an additional wife, it became necessary for her to appear before the president of the Church and state her reasons. If her reasons were deemed justifiable, the president ordered her husband to take no further steps toward securing an additional wife. But if they were judged invalid, the president ordered her to comply with her husband's wishes and permit him to marry another woman. If she persisted in her refusal, the Church regarded her as condemned, "because she did not give unto him, as Sarah gave Hagar to Abraham, and as Rachel and Leah gave Gilhal and Zilpah to their husband Jacob." [72]

The woman on whom a polygynist set his eye for marriage also had the right to refuse to enter into the relationship. Juanita Brooks claimed that she heard older women relate their experiences of being pursued by polygynists whose advances they rejected. One woman expressed her revulsion toward a suitor: "He had his nerve to ask me after the way he treats his first wife." [73] Another exclaimed: "He's like that—tried to play up every girl he met and couldn't stay true to any." [74]

Not all polygynous marriages among the Mormons were the results of male pursuit. Mormon women frequently sought the comfort and convenience of the home of a member of the Church hierarchy, since "they would rather be the fifteenth 'sealing' of Dives than the toilsome single wife of Lazarus." [75] Younger women were cautioned against marrying younger men, for it was better to marry a well-tested patriarch so that their chance of "exaltation" in the kingdom of heaven was certain.[76] *The New York Times* reported that two girls, aged ten and eleven, were married to men old enough to be their grandfathers.[77] Jane Woolsy proposed marriage to the polygynist, John D. Lee, who told her that she was too young for him, as he was fifty-five and she was yet in her teens, and that she would be better satisfied with someone near her own age. She replied, "A home is what I want & a Kind Friend to protect me. You are the man of my choice & can furnish me with the home I want." [78] Lee asked her to wait until the following autumn, and if she yet felt like marrying him, he would take her. However, in the meantime, she and four other youths took two Colt revolvers, some clothing, and $200 from Lee without his knowledge and he promptly sent her away.

Marriage was put in the forefront of the duties of faithful Latter-day Saints. Not only was it the responsibility of Mormons to provide tabernacles for the spirits who were waiting to be born in the flesh, but the marriage relation itself provided satisfaction of "the yearning for a higher state of existence," and allowed "the passions to feed the spiritual life." [79] Mormons were cautioned against marrying non-Mormons, as such relations would tend to destroy, rather than edify, the spiritual life. Brigham Young warned mothers not to teach their daughters to "marry out of Israel," with the threat that they would lose their own crowns if they did.[80] Fanny Stenhouse claimed that frequently a man was admonished to marry, but could not find an available woman in his home community, and was forced to make a trip to Salt Lake City in order to find a new bride.[81] Missionaries were urged to bring as many unmarried women to Utah as possible to support the polygynous system. Heber Kimball specified that attractive women should be sought in order to provide a better selection. He claimed that "the brother missionaries have been in the habit of picking out the prettiest women for themselves before they get here and bringing on the ugly ones for us." [82] He demanded that they afterward bring all women to Utah before they married any of them, therefore giving everyone "a fair shake." [83]

Brigham Young insisted that there were four women for every three men in Utah; yet Jules Remy, who visited Utah in 1860, claimed there were many bachelors there who could not marry because there were not enough available women.[84] The official United States Census of 1860 placed the number of females in Salt Lake City slightly above that of the males, but the men outnumbered the women in the territory.

The majority of Mormons did not practice polygyny, and those who did usually had no more than two or three wives. Stanley Ivins took a sample of one thousand, seven hundred eighty-four polygynists and found that sixty-six per cent had two wives, twenty-one per cent had three, and nearly seven per cent had four or more.[85] Kimball Young estimated that in some communities 20 to 25 per cent of the families were polygynous.[86] The number of wives a polygynist had was determined by his wealth and his status in the Mormon hierarchy. Dixon reported in 1860 that no Apostle had fewer than three wives.[87] There was a correlation between the wealth of a polygynist and the absence of conflict within his household. Kimball Young, who maintained a file of the records of 125 polygynist families, found that the number of household conflicts decreased as the wealth of the head of the household increased.[88] The wealthier Mormon could afford a larger house, which served to reduce the tensions between the members of their households.

Because of the insufficient number of available women for marriage in Utah, would-be polygynists on occasion resorted to ways of procuring wives that incensed non-Mormon Americans. *New York Times* reporters in the territory periodically related such incidents. One such incident involved the sale of two young sisters to one Horace Eldredge "for some groceries." [89] The *Times* also published an account of a man in Ogden, Utah, who allegedly sold his nagging wife to a neighbor for a wagonload of pumpkins. When the neighbor failed to provide delivery of the pumpkins, the man took back his wife.[90] Heber Kimball reportedly proposed an exchange of a yoke of oxen and a wagon for a sixteen-year-old girl.[91]

The charge of incest was also commonly made against the Mormon polygynists. Dixon alleged: "It is known that in some of these saintly harems, the female occupants stand to their lords in relationship of blood closer than the American law permits." [92] *The New York Times* published an account of a man named Winchester who allegedly married his own mother.[93]

Although Horace Greeley was at first disposed to defend the Mormons, he published accounts of the degradation of their women in Utah. In one of his reports Greeley asserted:

> No where else on the Continent of North America are white women to be seen working like slaves, barefooted in the fields. It is notorious to all here that large numbers of Mormon women are in a state of great want and destitution, and that their husbands do not pretend to provide them even with the necessities of life.[94]

The newspaper accounts, whether based on facts or concocted to sate the appetite of an already indignant public, brought a storm of protest from the East, and, in time, the outlawing of polygyny in the territories.

The Mormons were willing to make few admissions of irregularities, other than the system of polygyny itself. John D. Lee, who married sixteen women and was the father of sixty-five children, had few reservations about recording the intimate details of his own household. In an entry in his *Diaries*, dated January 18, 1859, Lee related an account of his sixteenth wife's dissatisfaction over her marriage to him. She asked for a divorce that she might marry Lee's eldest son by his first wife. Lee consented, performed the ceremony, and gave a dinner in their honor in his home.[95]

Polygynous wedding ceremonies followed a ritual prescribed by the Mormon Church. All marriages were performed by the president of the Church, or by one of his delegates. The first wife stood to the left of her husband, and his new bride stood on his right. The wife was asked:

> Are you willing to give this woman to your husband to be his lawful and wedded wife, for time and for all eternity? If you are, you will manifest it by placing her right hand within the right hand of your husband.[96]

At this point in the ceremony, the husband and his new bride exchanged the customary vows, without the phrase "until death do us part." The officiant pronounced them "legally and lawfully, husband and wife for time and for all eternity." [97]

X

No Cross, No Crown

It might seem that woman's natural capacity for jealousy would have been sufficient to destroy the system of Mormon polygyny from its outset. Yet with relatively few exceptions the Mormon women defended the institution and were responsible for its perpetuation. J. H. Beadle, who was a close observer of the practice, claimed that during his long residence in Salt Lake City he never met a woman who defended polygyny.[1] Either Beadle's acquaintance with Mormon women was limited, or he was so antagonistic toward polygyny that he ignored the number of feminine defenses made in its behalf. Richard Burton, a non-Mormon observer in Utah, claimed that he had heard a Mormon woman plead with her husband, "in the presence of a Gentile sister," to take an additional wife on the pretext that if she did not bear a cross, she would not be permitted to wear a crown.[2]

The first wife of a polygynist, in most cases, was regarded as the queen of the household. This privilege was granted when polygyny was first introduced, to secure the wives' approval. Occasions of jealousy and bitterness sometimes arose in polygynous households, as often the first wife could not adjust to the sight of her husband making amorous advances toward other women, although they had been given him by the Church and with the Mormon blessing. One first wife is alleged to have confessed that she tolerated the arrangement "until she could hear her husband's boots drop on the floor in the second wife's room." The daughter of Hyrum Stratton, who related the story, claimed, "You know, it's those little things that must have hurt." [3] The wives of Ephe Roberts, Maria and Luce, were unable to tolerate one another. Beadle claimed that he had first-hand information about an argument between Maria and Luce over a churn. Luce picked up a boiling kettle of water and scalded Maria's feet amid Ephe's shouts for Luce to kill her.[4]

Some Mormon women were able to adapt to polygyny without serious incident. Susan Young Gates, a daughter of Brigham Young, claimed the wives of her father "lived together without friction," and that she never once heard any of them quarrel.[5] In some cases the wives were closely related to one another before they joined a polygynous household. Lieutenant Sylvester Mowery, a cavalry officer in Utah, reported that a physician there had married a mother and her two daughters, and that the domestic arrangement was quite cozy. Mowery claimed that "the mother did the cooking for the household and her daughters slept with the saintly doctor." [6]

Eliza Snow, one of Joseph Smith's wives, became one of the outstanding defenders of polygyny. She admitted her revulsion to the idea when it was first introduced, but when she realized that she was "living in the Dispensation of the fulness of times," she not only accepted it but felt that it was her duty to convince her sisters in the Church of the necessity of accepting it as their Christian responsibility.[7] She also called on the wife of President Ulysses S. Grant and urged her to use her influence on her husband to manifest a more tolerant attitude toward polygyny. In January 1870 an assembly of Mormon women passed a resolution stating that they stood united behind their brethren in the defense "against each and every encroachment" by the federal government to outlaw polygyny. In November 1878 a resolution was signed by 2,000 Mormon women which, in part, read:

> We solemnly avow our belief in the doctrine of the patriarchal order of marriage, a doctrine which was revealed to, and practiced by, God's people in past ages, and is now re-established on earth by divine command of Him who is the same yesterday, today and forever—a doctrine which, if lived up to and carried out under the direction of the precepts pertaining to it, and of the higher principles of our own nature, would conduce to the long life, strength and glory of the people practicing it; and we therefore endorse it as one of the most important principles of our holy religion, and claim the right of its practice.[8]

The women were in the forefront in defense of polygyny when the federal government began to legislate against the practice. Had the institution not been bound by Mormon theology to the women's hope of salvation, it is likely that it would have been without the support of this vital segment of the Mormon population. In each defense which they made, it was their eternal status about which the women were most concerned.

There was little in polygynous familism that was worth defending from the point of view of the wives. The wealthy Mormon could provide a limited measure of comfort and convenience for his wives, but the day-to-day intimacy of women who shared a single husband at best proved unnerving. Unless the women were completely otherworldly in outlook, the patterns of monogamy, by which many Mormon wives attempted to live, posed a constant threat to the tranquility of the polygynous household. The poorer families were the most adversely affected, as they could not afford the privacy which would alleviate the strain of forced intimacy. Benjamin Ferris recounted a visit to a wretched hut where a Mormon, his two wives, and a grown daughter lived. He claimed that they all dwelled in one room containing two beds: "It was their parlor, kitchen, and bed-room . . . [with] filth enough to manure a garden." [9] Fanny Stenhouse related an interview with a man, his three wives, and eleven children, who lived in a small house of four rooms. One wife had been forced to give up her room that it might be used as a parlor, while she slept in a wagonbox. Another wife shared her room with six children. His youngest wife, because she was "young and inexperienced," and could not tolerate the inconvenience, had her own private room.[10]

Most wives of polygynists were given private quarters, since the greater percentage of them were men of means and could provide this luxury for their wives. Some men found it advantageous to build a separate house for each wife. If a wife was incompatible with the others, a separate house was built for her, while the others resided in the unitary dwelling. Juanita Brooks claimed that her grandfather built a separate house for his fourth wife, an Indian girl, because "she did not fit so well with the other wives." [11] In the single, or joint household, each wife had a separate apartment, but all ate at a common table. The typical home of a polygynist was a long, low-roofed house with a row of doors and windows alternating. As wives were added, other rooms were built to complement the overall architectural design. By counting the entrances one could estimate the number of wives claimed by the head of the household. This type of house was a status symbol, since the more wives a Mormon maintained, the higher his ecclesiastical position.

Most children born to polygynous unions were not as adversely affected by the arrangement as those born to the first wife before the husband took additional wives. John D. Lee complained that the children by his first wife were rebellious and that "the spirit of aleanation [*sic*] & disafection [*sic*] were entailed upon them." [12] Those children born later accepted the unique system of plural familism as a matter of course, since they had no other experiences with which to compare their lives. The children regarded their father's wives, with the exception of their own mother, as aunts.

Polygynous fathers were proud of their large family of children, but generally did not take particular interest in their individual needs. Benjamin Ferris observed that they took "as little care of their wives as of their children; and both, less than a careful farmer in the States would of his cattle." [13] William Hepworth Dixon once inquired of a merchant in Salt Lake City, who was the head of a polygynous household, how many children he had. Dixon was aghast that the father had to consult a book lying on his desk before he could reply.[14] Although the wives might have their separate quarters, if a Mormon could afford the convenience, the children were tumbled into a single room, or two rooms, divided according to their sex, without regard to which mother they belonged to.

A Mormon husband would tolerate almost any condition in his home rather than openly admit that he could not keep his house in order. Udney Hay Jacobs, in a work published by Joseph Smith at Nauvoo in 1842, urged a husband to continue living with his wife, even though she "despise him in her heart, abuse him before his children, and drive him like a menial slave," since the Bible did not condone divorce.[15] Adultery was the only legal ground on which men were permitted to divorce their wives. In 1860 Brigham Young made some exceptions to the rule and allowed a husband to obtain a divorce from a wife of whom he had grown tired. If he had been married to her for "time" only, the fee for the separation was ten dollars; if married for "time and eternity," it was twenty-five dollars.[16] Young reportedly told Horace Greeley the year before: "I hold that no man should ever put away a wife except for adultery —not always for that. Such is *my* individual view of the matter. I do not say that wives have never been put away in our Church, but that I do not approve of the practice." [17] A Mormon wife had greater liberty in obtaining a divorce than her husband. She could declare neglect, desertion, or cruelty as grounds for the dissolution of the marital bond. "Church Divorces," as they were called, were issued by the hierarchy when the above charges were proven, and were regarded as legal documents.

In order to maintain the chastity of Mormon women, and to defend them from the lustful eyes of the men, they were repeatedly warned about their dress. Men were first cautioned against "committing adultery in their hearts." In one of his alleged revelations, Joseph Smith counseled: "He that looketh on a woman to lust after her, or if any shall commit adultery in their hearts, they shall not have the Spirit, but they shall deny the faith and shall fear." [18] In the earlier days of the Mormon experience in Utah, the women offered very little in the way of sexual temptation. Dixon described them as "plainly, not to say poorly, dressed: with no bright colors, no gay flounces and furebelows. They are very quiet and subdued in a manner . . . as if all dash, all sportiveness, all life, had been preached out of them." [19] Mark Twain, who visited Salt Lake City in 1861, did not commit adultery in his heart when he looked at the Mormon women. In his own inimitable style he wrote:

> With the gushing self-sufficiency of youth I was feverish to plunge in headlong and achieve a great reform here—until I saw the Mormon women. Then I was touched. My heart was wiser than my head. It warmed toward these poor, ungainly and pathetically 'homely' creatures, as I turned to hide the generous moisture in my eyes, I said, 'No—the man that married one of them has done an act of Christian charity which entitles him to the kindly applause of mankind, not their harsh censure—and the man that marries sixty of them has done a deed of open-handed generosity so sublime that the nations should stand uncovered in his presence and worship in silence. . . .' [20]

As prosperity came to Utah and the railroad brought women dressed in the latest Eastern styles, Mormon women made a radical change in their dress and appearance which called for scathing denunciations from the pulpits. Brigham Young once thundered:

> Give us a little Gentileism for heaven's sake, you say. The women say, let us wear hoops, because the whores wear them.

> I believe if they were to come with a cob stuck in their behind you would want to do the same. . . . There is not a day I go out but I see the women's legs, and if the wind blows you see them up to their bodies.
>
> If you must wear their hoops, tie them down with weights, and don't let your petticoats be over your heads. . . . Who cares about these infernal Gentiles? If they were to wear a s—t pot on their heads, must I do so? I know I ought to be ashamed but when you show your tother [*sic*] end I have a right to talk about tother [*sic*] end. If you keep them hid, I'll be modest and not talk about them.[21]

In another sermon, Young told of a visitor who attended one of their parties where the Mormon women were dressed in the latest Eastern fashions, who was asked: "Did you ever see the like of this?" The visitor replied: "No, sir, never since I was weaned." [22]

Brigham Young, who professed to be "ashamed to see the tight clothes—to see the shape of the ladies," [23] attempted to impose a non-revealing uniform as standard dress for the ladies. The costume consisted of a sunbonnet to replace the feathered hats, and a cape, similar to the one worn by the Amana women. The dress was shortened, that it not drag the ground, but it was not short enough to reveal the tops of their stockings. A few pious women adopted the costume for a short time, but Eastern fashions prevailed and the drab uniform was discarded. In order to try to curb the ladies' extravagance in their dress, Young founded the Retrenchment Association, the forerunner of the Young Ladies Mutual Improvement Association.

The dress of the Mormon males also stirred the wrath of the pulpiteers. The youth adopted the style of tight-fitting trousers, which the preachers preferred to call "hermaphrodite pantaloons." Brigham Young asserted that the new style was created to make it easier for whores to unbutton. Heber Kimball charged that the men were "weakening their backs and their kidneys by girting themselves" in the new style of pants. He further claimed that such a garment would "destroy the strength of their loins" and "injure their posterity." [24]

The Mormon communities, unlike most religious utopian communities of the nineteenth century in America, enjoyed festive occasions which included games and dancing. While at Nauvoo, Charlotte Haven wrote to her family about a party given by Sidney Rigdon which began with dancing and ended with petting.[25] Formal balls in Salt Lake City were lengthy affairs which generally began at 4:00 P.M., with a prayer, and ended with another prayer at 5:00 A.M.[26] Captain Howard Stansbury, of the Corps of Topographical Engineers, who spent the spring of 1849 surveying the valley of the Great Salt Lake, remarked that "The balls, parties, and merry making at each others' houses, formed a prominent and agreeable feature of the society." [27]

The Mormons suffered a three-way split soon after the death of their founder and prophet, Joseph Smith. One group, which was vehemently opposed to polygyny, settled in Missouri after the main body followed the leadership of Brigham Young to Utah. A third faction rallied around James Jesse Strang in Wisconsin. Strang claimed to be the divinely ordained successor of Joseph Smith. The Missouri Mormons formed the Church of Jesus Christ of Latter-day Saints Reorganized. Joseph Smith's widow, Emma, joined the Reorganized Church, and later married Lewis Crum Bidamon. She, along with the Reorganized Church group, fought the polygynists and claimed her first husband was never involved in a system of multiple marriages. She vowed: "There was no revelation on either polygamy or spiritual wives . . . [Joseph] had no other wife but me." [28] The Reorganized Church in the first edition of their official organ, *The True Latter-day Saints Herald*, did admit that Joseph Smith had advocated polygyny. In an editorial, it was asserted that the people at Nauvoo were determined to adopt the practice and prevailed on Smith to supply the divine sanction and he gave them the revelation.[29] In the same issue of the *Herald* William Marks claimed Joseph Smith had "said it eventually would prove the overthrow of the Church, and we should soon be obliged to leave the United States unless it could be speedily put down." [30] Isaac Sheen asserted: "Joseph Smith repented of his connection with this doctrine [of polygyny] and said it was of the devil," [31] just before he left for Carthage, Illinois, where he met his death. These statements in the *Herald* proved embarrassing to the Reorganized Church, as they contradicted their later claim that Joseph Smith at no time advocated polygyny or gave the movement the revelation which authorized the practice.[32]

After the death of Joseph Smith a third faction of Mormons settled first in Wisconsin, and later on a small group of islands in Lake Michigan, under the leadership of the eccentric, James Jesse Strang. Strang visited Nauvoo in January 1844, and was converted to Mormonism.[33] He returned to his native Wisconsin to establish a community on the order of the Nauvoo plan. Soon after Smith's death he produced a letter which he claimed was written by the prophet on June 18, nine days before his murder in 1844, which named him as Smith's successor. The followers of Brigham Young denied the authenticity of the letter on the ground that it bore a black postmark, whereas all mail sent from the Nauvoo postoffice had red postmarks.[34] The letter, now in the Strang Collection at the Yale Library, was written in Smith's typically prophetic language. It read in part:

> And now behold my servant James J. Strang hath come to thee from far for truth when he knew it not, and hath not rejected it, but had faith in thee, the Shepherd and Stone of Israel, and to him shall the gathering of the people be, for he shall plant a stake of Zion in Wisconsin, and I will establish it; and there shall my people have peace and rest, and shall not be moved. . . . And I will have a house built unto me there of stone, and there will I show myself to my people by many mighty works, and the name of the city shall be called Voree, which is, being interpreted, garden of peace, for there shall my people have peace and rest, and wax fat and pleasant in the presence of their enemies.[35]

Strang further claimed that at 5:30 P.M., on June 27, 1844, at the exact moment of Smith's murder, an angel appeared to him in Wisconsin and anointed him as the new head of the Mormon Church. Orson Hyde, a Brighamite, also claimed an inspiration which he related on March 14, 1846, in which God reportedly said:

> Behold James J. Strang hath cursed my people by his own spirit and not mine. Never, at any time, have I appointed that wicked man to lead my people, neither by my own voice or by the voice of my servant JOSEPH SMITH, neither by the voice of mine angel . . . .[36]

Strang's following was small compared to the number of Mormons who went with Brigham Young to Utah; it never exceeded 500 families.

Strang's efforts were mainly directed to maintaining the chastity of his disciples. When George Adams was accused of bringing a prostitute to the settlement, Strang threatened to drive her away after first making her ride a black-horn buck backward while the boys hooted at her.[37] Public whipping was a common punishment for all offenders at Voree. Strang ordered all Mormon women to wear the costume fashioned by Amelia Bloomer, a garment which other utopian communities had adopted. Thomas Bedford and Alexander Wentworth were publicly whipped on Strang's orders "because they had upheld their wives' refusal to wear bloomers." [38] Another lawbreaker was given thirty-nine lashes with birch rods for spreading rumors and trying to incite "mischief and crime." [39]

James Strang was at first opposed to polygyny. The Strangites held a convention at Kirtland, Ohio, the site of the first Mormon community, in August 1846, and adopted a unanimous resolution which stated:

> we utterly disclaim the whole system of polygamy known as the spiritual wife system lately set up in Nauvoo, by the apostates who claim the authority there, and will neither practice such things nor hold any fellowship with those that teach or practice such things.[40]

Some Mormons at Voree advocated polygyny in 1847, but they were promptly excommunicated. One of the Apostles, James M. Adams, was denounced as an apostate for "believing the spiritual wife system," and Benjamin C. Ellsworth was excommunicated for both "teaching and practicing polygamy." [41] John Cook Bennett, who had suffered a similar fate at Nauvoo, went to Voree and was there again tried and condemned for polygyny and concubinage. Strang appeared determined to prevent the practice from spreading to Voree. He asserted:

> I now say distinctly, and I defy contradiction, that the man or woman does not exist on earth, or under the earth, who ever heard me say one word, or saw me do one act, savoring the least of *spiritual wifery*, or any of the attending abominations. My opinions on this subject are unchanged, and I regard them as unchangeable.[42]

However, Strang did change his views and later accepted polygyny as fully as the Utah Mormons, once he removed his settlement from Voree, Wisconsin, to Beaver Island in Lake Michigan.

The letter produced by Strang in Nauvoo, which purportedly named him as successor to Joseph Smith, and which called on all Mormons to move to Wisconsin, specifically stated that they were to maintain Voree permanently, once the community had been established. Strang had the illusion of setting up a kingdom with himself as king. He sensed the need to withdraw his following to an isolated area, far removed from the democratic frontier. He chose Beaver Island, one of the Manitou group, in Lake Michigan, and in the winter of 1847–1848 the settlement of Voree was transferred to their new home, to the Kingdom of St. James, named for James Strang.

Beaver Island was transformed into a carbon copy of the Palestine of biblical times. Its highest peak was labeled Mount Pisgah, its main stream was christened the Jordan River, and the Jordan flowed into the Sea of Galilee, known by others as Lake Michigan. Communism, which had been a feature at Voree, was abandoned and each subject of the king was permitted to own his own homestead.[43] Strang was crowned the king of St. James on July 8, 1850, in an elaborate ceremony. He was dressed in a red robe borrowed from George Adams, an actor who had used it in a Shakespearean play. Adams, on that day, played the role of the Apostle Paul, and wore his King Richard III costume. He crowned Strang king "with a deliberate and theatrical gesture of outstretched arms." [44] The eighth of July thereafter was marked by a burnt offering of a heifer at the community's expense, and the gift of a fowl to the king, which was expected of every family.

Once he established himself as king, Strang contradicted his earlier statements regarding the system of plural marriage and avowed his conversion to the doctrine of polygyny. As Joseph Smith had found justification for the practice through a heavenly vision, Strang received his divine sanction in 1849. He, like Smith, claimed he had discovered some golden plates of Laban from which he translated *The Book of the Law*, which authorized polygyny.[45] Strang chose as his first polygynous wife Elvira Field, a nineteen-year-old Mormon schoolteacher. His first wife, Mary, remained at St. James until May 1851, serving for a short while on her husband's Royal Council. In her official capacity as a Council member, she repeatedly opposed the king's policies until he was forced to send her away. She was exiled to western New York, where she lived with some of Strang's relatives. Strang also married Betsy McNutt, and two sisters, Phoebe and Sarah Wright, all of whom lived with him in the "castle." [46] Nine children were born to these polygynous unions. Sarah gave birth to a son after Strang's death, and she refused to tell her child his father's identity for fear that he might later attempt to follow in his father's footsteps and restore his kingdom.[47]

Polygyny was not a widespread practice in the Kingdom of St. James. Of the 2,500 subjects there, not more than twenty families were polygynous. Strang, with a total of five, had the largest number of wives. L. D. Hickey reportedly had three. Two factors account for the relatively low number of polygynous unions at Beaver Island: the scarcity of unattached women, and the prohibitive cost of maintaining more than one wife.

Polygyny at St. James did not have sufficient opportunity to become as rigidly formalized as it did in Utah for the kingdom came to an end after six years upon the death of Strang. His strict discipline was the major cause of the fall of his kingdom. He was determined to control the private lives of his subjects. Discontent mounted until Thomas Bedford and Alexander Wentworth, the two whom Strang had earlier ordered beaten because they would not compel their wives to wear bloomers, shot him in the back and proceeded to beat him over the head with their weapons.[48] Strang never recovered from the attack. Bedford and Wentworth were never brought to trial for the crime. Upon the demise of their king, the subjects of the Kingdom of St. James quickly dispersed, as there was no one to take his place.

Not until ten years after the open avowal of polygyny in Utah did the federal government move to attempt to put an end to the practice. In 1856 Benjamin Ferris, Secretary of the territory, offered three suggestions for neutralizing the Mormon influence in political affairs to enable the federal government to eradicate polgyny: (1) cease extending patronage to the territory; (2) establish a strong military post in the vicinity of Salt Lake City to provide protection and encouragement to those who opposed the Mormons; and (3) divide the territory into parcels and annex them to New Mexico, Nebraska, and Oregon.[49] The federal government did not act on Ferris's suggestions. The Mormons stoutly resisted any attempt to interfere with their religion or their political control of the area. Polygyny was regarded as a vital part of their religious belief, and therefore guaranteed immunity by the First Amendment to the American Constitution. Orson Pratt, in a sermon delivered in 1852, asserted:

> the constitution gives the privilege to all of the inhabitants of this country, of the free exercise of their religious notions, and the freedom of their faith and the practice of it. Then, if it can be proved to be a demonstration that the Latter-day Saints have actually embraced, as a part and portion of their religion, the doctrine of a plurality of wives, it is constitutional. And should there ever be laws enacted by this government to restrict them from the free exercise of their religion, such laws must be unconstitutional.[50]

Brigham Young utilized his prophetic powers to serve warning on any American president who attempted to interfere with the Mormons in the free practice of their religion. In a speech delivered July 24, 1851, he said: "Zachary Taylor is dead and gone to hell, and I am glad of it . . . . I prophesy, in the name of Jesus Christ, by the power of the priesthood that is upon me, that any other President of the United States, who shall lift his finger against this people, will die an untimely death and go to hell." [51] American presidents showed little fear of Young's prophetic utterances. Presidents Lincoln, Grant, Hayes, Garfield, Arthur, and Cleveland each took a strong stand against polygyny in the Utah Territory. On July 2, 1862, Lincoln signed the Morill Bill, which authorized the federal government to punish and prevent the practice in the territories of the United States. However, the federal government was virtually powerless in the enforcement of the law, because of the political entrenchment of the Mormons in Utah. In his Third Annual Message to the United States Congress, Grant was forced to admit that "In Utah there still remains a remnant of barbarism repugnant to civilization, to decency, and to the laws of the United States." [52] He vowed the Mormons would not be permitted to violate the laws of the land under the guise of religion.

In 1879 President Hayes took up the fight and called for more stringent methods in dealing with and punishing the "crime" of polygyny.[53] The following year, Hayes asked that polygynists not be permitted to vote, hold office, or sit on juries in the Utah Territory.[54] President Garfield left no doubt as to where he stood on the issue. In his Inaugural Address he stated: "The Mormon Church not only offends the moral sense of mankind by sanctioning polygamy, but prevents the administration of justice through the ordinary instrumentality of the law." [55]

Senator Edmunds introduced a bill to Congress in 1882 to amend the anti-polygamy law of 1862, in order to give the federal government greater powers to enforce the law. The Edmunds Bill passed, but the federal government found enforcement as difficult as ever. President Arthur, in his Fourth Annual Message to Congress, was forced to admit that, "if that abominable practice can be suppressed by law it can only be by the most radical legislation consistent with the restraints of the Constitution." [56] In 1885, President Cleveland made an impassioned plea for stronger legislation against the Mormon practice. In his First Annual Message he asserted: "The strength, the perpetuity, and the destiny of the nation rests upon our homes, established by the law of God, guarded by parental care, regulated by parental authority, and sanctioned by parental love. These are not the homes of polygamy."[57] He further charged that the Mormons were undermining the nation with their open defiance of its laws.

The Edmunds Act was strengthened in 1887 by the passage of the Edmunds-Tucker Bill, which disenfranchised convicted polygamists and allowed one wife to testify against another. The act also permitted the federal government to confiscate certain church properties where flagrant violation of the law was determined. One year after the passage of the Edmunds-Tucker Act, President Cleveland reported to the United States Congress that nearly 600 convictions had been obtained against those who had violated the act in Utah.[58] Thomas O'Dea has recently set the figure of convictions at 573. O'Dea also claimed that the federal government confiscated approximately $1,000,000 in property from the Mormons, including about $400,000 in cash.[59]

The United States Supreme Court upheld the constitutionality of the anti-polygamy laws, despite the appeal of the Mormons to the First Amendment. In the case of *Reynolds vs U.S.*, in 1878, the Court reasoned:

> Laws are made for the government of actions, and while they cannot interfere with mere religious beliefs and opinions, they may with practices. Suppose one believed that human sacrifices were a necessary part of religious worship, would it be seriously contended that the civil government under which he lived could not interfere to prevent a sacrifice? Or, if a wife religiously believed it was her duty to burn herself on the funeral pile of her dead husband, would it be beyond the power of the civil government to prevent her carrying her belief into practice?[60]

The executive, legislative, and judicial branches of the federal government acted in unison to eradicate polygyny on the ground that it posed a threat to the basic institutions of American society. Perhaps a deeper underlying cause of the anti-polygynous crusade was the fear of the growth of the political power of the Mormons in the Utah Territory. Statehood was withheld from Utah for thirty years after the territory was otherwise qualified for admission into the Union while the politicians in the East used the issue of polygyny as a lever to unseat the Mormon hierarchy from political offices and send them to penitentiaries as common criminals.

The Mormons were forced to bow to political pressure or face extinction. Wilford Woodruff, acting in his official capacity as the President of the Church of Jesus Christ of Latter-day Saints, issued the following proclamation on October 6, 1890:

> Inasmuch as laws have been enacted by Congress forbidding plural marriages, which have been pronounced unconstitutional by the court of last resort, I hereby declare my intention to submit to those laws, and to use my influence with the members of the Church over which I preside to have them do likewise.[61]

Immediately following the proclamation, Woodruff delivered a sermon in which he claimed that the federal government alone was responsible for the destruction of the principle of plural marriages.

Woodruff's proclamation, although it paved the way for statehood for Utah, did not bring an end to the practice of polygyny among the Mormons. Many regarded the proclamation as a sacrifice of religious principle for the sake of political expedience. These left Salt Lake City and went into hiding in remote settlements of Arizona and New Mexico. Some left America altogether and settled with their polygynous families in Mexico and Canada. The federal government pursued offenders within the borders of the United States and Mormon folklore accounts of many tales of "cohab hunts" and "running from the feds." [62]

It was no easy matter for the Mormons to comply with federal laws against polygyny. Those who firmly believed in Mormon theology, which made one's eternal status dependent on the system of celestial marriages, would rather sacrifice their bodies than run the risk of losing their souls. From a more practical vantage point, there were closely knit families which could not be easily severed by official proclamations. Either a husband would have to send his wives and children away homeless, an act contrary to Christian charity, or carry out his duties as a husband and father in defiance of the law. Many chose the latter course. Austin and Alta Fife, who lived among the Mormons who resisted the federal ban on polygyny, asserted that the institution of polygyny was actually strengthened in the remote areas of Utah, New Mexico, and Arizona as a result of the attempts of the federal government to destroy it. The Fifes maintained that polygynists not only retained their wives in these areas, but added new ones, if they felt they could evade detection and imprisonment.[63]

Polygyny among the Mormons began and ended in secrecy. Licentiousness may well have given rise to the practice, but its theological justification, which was accepted by its practitioners in Utah, removed it from the pale of purely sensual lust. The objective observers who visited Utah were generally impressed with the sacredness with which the Mormons endowed the institution. William Chandless, a perceptive British observer, reported, "they are not a specially sensual people." [64] Richard Burton was impressed that there were rules and regulations "which disprove the popular statement that such marriages are made to gratify licentiousness, and which render polygamy a positive necessity." He further observed that "All sensuality in the married state is strictly forbidden beyond the requisite for ensuring progeny." [65]

Mormon men had approved access to more than one woman, but the women were not given equal privileges, since there was no theological justification which could be offered for polyandry. Mormons were essentially puritans, and sex for its own sake was not tolerated. Intercourse had conception for its prime objective. One potent male could impregnate one woman, but during the long period of pregnancy, her husband could perform the same function with numerous women. The ultimate goal was a "kingdom" for the male, and if his sexual relations were limited to a single wife, his future "subjects" would be limited in number. The moral question was one of ends, rather than of means. If a kingdom, which would number "as the stars of the heavens or the sands of the seashore," was the ultimate purpose of life for the Mormon male, a plurality of wives was of no moral consequence. The woman who expected to share in her husband's heavenly kingdom would gladly bear her cross and trust that she would be crowned a queen in eternity. After the passage of the Edmunds Bill in 1882, one old lady reportedly told John Coyner, "I would not abandon it [polygyny] to exchange with Queen Victoria and all her dependencies." [66] Yet Mormon women like Fanny Stenhouse, who left the Mormons and wrote a vociferous attack on polygyny, were never converted to the principle of spiritual wifery and viewed the institution as nothing more than male license for adultery.

Mormon polygyny was too short-lived to permit the development of standard procedures for dealing with conflicts within families. The monogamous patterns were not adaptable, but often a source of problems. Romantic love, a salient feature of monogamy, when applied to polygyny became a cause of jealousy among the wives within a household. Although the first wife had status in the family, the amorous attachment of the husband to a younger wife would sometimes cause resentment. Each husband was on his own to chart a course for his family. If he were forced to admit to failure in the management of his household affairs, it was tantamount to an admission that he was unqualified to rule a celestial kingdom in the world to come. The pulpit aided him in the control of his wives with periodic counsel and threats to the womenfolk who got out of line. But the husband alone was accountable to both God and the community for the conduct of his family. No set patterns existed for living arrangements within polygynous households. The material wealth of the husband determined whether each wife had her separate quarters or whether they had to share rooms, and even beds, with other wives and their children. Children lived as members of a commune, separated only by sex, but without regard to maternal distinctions. The polygynous arrangement was the only one that the children, except those of the first wife, had experienced, and they adapted to it in most cases reasonably well. Their attachment to their mothers was generally weak.

It appears that polygyny among the Mormons did last long enough to show that such a system was workable in America. But two factors emerged as essential: (1) in order to eradicate the influence of former habits and training which would tend to destroy the multiple wife arrangement, the patterns of monogamy in courtship and family life had to be dropped; and (2) a theology which held greater rewards in eternity than that which the institution offered on earth had to be developed and imposed in order to compensate for the sacrifice of values which Mormon women were required to make when joining a saintly harem.

XI

Complex Marriage at Oneida

COMPLEX MARRIAGE, A TERM COINED BY JOHN HUMPHREY NOYES, WAS the most revolutionary of all social experiments associated with the communitarian movements of the nineteenth century in America. The pantagamous arrangement, where each male was theoretically married to each female, and where each regarded the other as either a brother or a sister, was first practiced at Putney, Vermont, and later at Oneida, New York, and Wallingford, Connecticut. Free love was practiced in other utopian communities, but without the systemization and rigorous supervision which prevailed in the communities directed by John Humphrey Noyes. The Oneidans were accused of trying to "out-Mormon the Mormons" in their arrangement of complex marriage.[1] Unlike the Mormons, they never attempted to conceal their sexual unorthodoxy, nor did they seek refuge in remote frontier regions that they might engage in their practice unmolested. Sexual variety was not a privilege of the males alone, as in the case of Mormon polygyny. The women of Oneida were permitted to engage in sexual intercourse with as many men and as often as they wished without the loss of their honor.

Born in Brattleboro, Vermont, in 1811, John Humphrey Noyes was the son of a small-town banker and reared in the finest tradition of puritan ethics. He graduated from Dartmouth College and studied theology at Andover and at Yale. While at Yale he confessed that he "landed in a new experience and new views on the way of salvation, which took the name of Perfectionism." [2] The Perfectionists did not regard man as naturally depraved, as did the Calvinists in New England, from whom they revolted. Human perfection was thought to be attained when one ceased sinning. Noyes compared Perfectionism with two other popular reform doctrines of his time: temperance and abolition of slavery. He explained: "as the doctrine of temperance is total abstinence from alcoholic drinks, and the doctrine of anti-slavery is immediate abolition of human bondage, so the doctrine of Perfectionism is immediate and total cessation from sin." [3]

In 1835 Noyes organized an adult Bible School at Putney, Vermont, and gathered around him students of Perfectionism who were of the most reputable families in Vermont and who had been educated in the best schools of New England. Noyes also began publication of *The Perfectionist* at Putney, in order to disseminate his ideas and to serve as a forum for the ideas of others. This history of the establishment of the utopian community at Putney was one of gradual progression, as "the school advanced from a community of faith, to a community of property, to a community of households, to a community of affections." [4]

Noyes taught that any successful attempt to reorder the structure of society must have its basis in religion. He argued "that religion, not as a mere doctrine, but as an afflatus having in itself a tendency to make many into one, is the first essential of successful communism; and secondly, that the afflatus must be strong enough to decompose the old family unit and make communism the home center." [5] He was convinced that Perfectionism could be best realized when people entered into communal life, where all private property was abolished. He admitted that he became interested in the idea of communal living through reading Fourieristic literature and by the example of Brook Farm.

The Fourierists did not base their concepts of communalism on religion, a fault which Noyes repeatedly emphasized in his discussions of Fourierism. He preferred the term "Bible Communism" when he wrote of his own social theory. The church of the first century practiced communism, according to his interpretation of the New Testament. Noyes did not believe that all men were equal in every respect, but "that every man, woman and child should be surrounded by circumstances favoring the best development of heart, mind, and body."[6] A communistic community, according to Noyes, was the best of all possible environments.

By March 1843, some thirty-five people had been converted to Noyes' social theory. They renounced their claims to private property and were supported from a common purse. Noyes was proud of his accomplishment at Putney, and wrote: "What if there is not another bright spot in the wide world, and what if this is a very small one? Turn your eye toward it when you are tired of looking into chaos, and you will catch a glimpse of a better world."[7]

In the Bible School at Putney, Noyes taught that celibacy was the ideal practice for the Perfectionists who wished to prepare themselves for the imminent establishment of the kingdom of God on earth, a kingdom in which there would be no monogamous marriages. Noyes had earlier been disappointed in a love affair with one of his converts, Abigail Merwin, who deserted the Perfectionists at Putney and married. He rationalized his disappointment by developing the doctrine of "spiritual affinity," in which he advanced the idea that a spiritual relationship between members of the opposite sex could and did exist outside of a physical union. Although Abigail was physically the wife of another man, spiritually she belonged to Noyes. The principle of "spiritual affinity" was a cohesive force which united the Perfectionists at Putney, and which included bachelors, spinsters and a few married couples.

The theology developed by Noyes in the Putney Bible School strongly resembled that of the Shakers. He taught that God was a dual being, both male and female, and capable of reproducing himself, as he did in the case of Jesus Christ. Noyes found but one fault with the Shaker theology: that regarding the nature of the kingdom of heaven. He claimed that if it had not been for this one barrier, he would have become a Shaker.[8]

Some of the Putney disciples saw little distinction between themselves and the Shakers, and suggested that they retire to one of the latter's villages. Noyes realized his control over the Putney society was ebbing, and in a surprise move he proposed marriage to one of his most ardent followers, Harriet Holton, and requested the other members to also marry. He explained that the principle of "spiritual affinity" would in no way be jeopardized by entering into the physical union of wedlock. In his formal proposal of marriage to Harriet, he asked that they enter into no arrangement which would limit the range of their affections with others. He gave his bride the liberty to "love all who love God, whether man or woman . . . as freely as if she stood in no particular connection" with him.[9] Putney marriages served to dispel further notions about joining the Shakers, as the move was never again mentioned by the disciples of Noyes.

Noyes disavowed all connections with the doctrine of "spiritual wifery," or free love, which some Perfectionists, who were not directly associated with the Putney experiment, advocated. He was too much of a puritan to endorse licentious behavior under the pretext of religion. Noyes once dealt firmly with one couple who had committed adultery. Abram Smith and the wife of George Cragin, Mary, had a clandestine romance which came to the attention of the community when Abram forced his wife out of his house and Mary became his mistress.[10] Noyes assessed their impropriety as having been "characterized by two vices—licentiousness and deception. . . . Mrs. Cragin took the lead and was the principal agent in the licentiousness, and then Mr. Smith took the lead and was the principal agent in the deception. She kindled the fire and he excused and justified and concealed it."[11] Both Abram and Mary acknowledged their sin and promised it would never happen again. George Cragin was persuaded to forgive his wife and to take her back. Later, Mary and Abram resumed their affair. John B. Lyvere was also expelled from the Putney community because of his advances toward Almira Edson. Noyes attempted to keep his community as free of the cause for gossip as possible.

In 1843, the thirty-seven members of the Putney Bible School adopted communism and began community life in earnest. They lived in three houses, maintained a store, and worshiped together in a small chapel. The monogamous family presented a problem for Noyes from the outset, since it fostered an exclusiveness which ran counter to the principle of pure communism. The Shakers, by abolishing marriage, had created a community spirit devoid of exclusive attachments. This was the ideal. But Noyes feared celibacy would bring stagnation and eventual death to the community. He sensed the need for the development of a principle which would make the community the center of each member's aspirations, and, at the same time, would not sterilize the society. The mere dissolution of the monogamous family and the adoption of free love were impractical, from Noyes' point of view, since such a course "tended toward anarchy."[12] The physical passions, according to Noyes, must be channeled in such a direction so as to serve communism, rather than to pose a constant threat to the community's survival.

The principle of "spiritual affinity" at Putney allowed social intercourse between the sexes, without the attendant jealousy found in ordinary society. But there was a limit to how far two members of the opposite sex could go before physical passion was aroused and the marital bonds threatened. One evening in May 1846 Noyes and Mary Cragin went for a walk and he later confessed that he had taken some personal liberties with her and that "the temptation to go further was tremendous."[13] He managed to restrain his passion and he and Mary returned to the community, called their respective spouses, and laid bare their feelings for each other. Noyes admitted that "Mr. Cragin was tempted to think that I was following the course of Abram C. Smith."[14] However, Cragin was convinced that no wrong had been committed. John Humphrey Noyes' wife, Harriet, showed no signs of jealousy over his intimacy with Mary Cragin, and the four agreed to give each other "full liberty" with one another's spouses.

The Noyeses and Cragins had earlier gone through the formalities of expressing their love for each other but Noyes had placed a ban on kissing and petting, which smacked of licentiousness.[15] His experiences in the woods convinced him that the time had come when the restriction against fondling should be removed. Mary had given Noyes to understand that she was ready to go all the way in love-making.[16] John and Harriet, along with George and Mary, entered into marriage in quartette form and a full consummation followed. The following year, George Cragin's wife, Mary, gave birth to twins, a boy and a girl. She named her son, appropriately enough, Victor Cragin Noyes. The quartette form of marriage was expanded toward the end of 1846 to include Noyes' sisters, Charlotte and Harriet, and their husbands, John R. Miller and John L. Skinner. Noyes, who was accustomed to coining phrases where none existed which adequately described his innovations, used the term complex marriage for the first time to designate the practice.

Noyes was faced with two dangers when he introduced complex marriage at Putney: (1) the arrangement could very easily degenerate into out-and-out lasciviousness, as it had in the free love collectives; and (2) exclusive attachments between couples could undermine the communal spirit which he deemed essential to the community's welfare. In order to cope with these potential perils, Noyes kept a firm grip on the arrangement and supervised the pairing of couples. He insisted on the right to designate which couples could cohabit and when. He cautioned: "Whoever meddles with the affairs of the inner sanctuary . . . will plunge himself into consuming fire." [17] One couple reportedly ignored Noyes' advice, fell in love, and were expelled from the Putney community. Mary Cragin expressed the true spirit of the system of complex marriage when she claimed: "Our love is of God; it is destitute of exclusiveness, each one rejoicing in the happiness of others." [18]

The practice of complex marriage at Putney created a storm of protest in New England. Noyes wrote to David Harrison, in September 1836, and explained his views of the relation between the sexes at Putney. Theophilus Gates published the letter in his paper, *The Battle Axe and Weapons of War,* and it became known as "The Battle Axe Letter." Noyes had written to Harrison:

> When the will of God is done on earth, as it is in heaven, there will be no marriage. The marriage supper of the Lamb is a feast at which every dish is free to every guest. Exclusiveness, jealousy, quarreling, have no place there, for the same reason as that which forbids the guests at a thanksgiving-dinner to claim each his separate dish, and quarrel with the rest for his rights. In a holy community, there is no more reason why sexual intercourse should be restrained by law, than why eating and drinking should be—and there is as little occasion for shame in the one case as in the other. God has placed a wall of partition between the male and female during the apostacy, for good reasons, which will be broken down in the resurrection, for equally good reasons. . . . The guests of the marriage supper may have each his favorite dish, each a dish of his own procuring, and that without the jealousy of exclusiveness. I call a certain woman my wife—she is yours, she is Christ's, and in him she is the bride of all saints. She is dear in the hand of a stranger, and according to my promise to her I rejoice. My claim upon her cuts directly across the marriage covenant of this world, and God knows the end.[19]

At the time Noyes composed "The Battle Axe Letter" he did not believe the Kingdom of God had been established on earth, and he was describing the nature of the relations between the sexes as they would be in "the resurrection," without the restraints of monogamy which characterized the "apostacy," or the period between the New Testament era and the coming of the kingdom. In 1838 Noyes said that he did not believe that they had arrived at that state.[20] However, the Putney experience convinced Noyes that the Kingdom of God indeed had been established on earth. He calculated that "The second advent of Christ took place at the period of the destruction of Jerusalem," in 70 A. D., and "that at that time, there was a primary resurrection and judgment in the Spiritual World."[21] Once Noyes was convinced that the Kingdom of God was among men, the relation of the sexes, without regard to earthly marital ties, underwent a transition which resulted in complex marriage. Those who had taken part in the resurrection, that is, the Perfectionists, were alone capable of entering into the practice of complex marriage. Noyes cautioned against the adoption of the practice before a conversion to Perfectionism. In one of his "Home Talks" he asserted:

> Woe to him who abolishes the law of the apostacy before he stands in the holiness of the resurrection. The law of the apostacy is the law of marriage; and it is true that whoever undertakes to enter into the liberty of the resurrection, will get woe and not happiness. It is . . . important . . . they should know that holiness of heart is what they must have before they get liberty in love. They must put first things first; they must be *Perfectionists* before they are *Communists.*[22]

A convention of Perfectionists was held in September 1847 at Lairdsville, New York, at which Noyes announced the plan of complex marriage as practiced at Putney. Thirty-six delegates at the convention voted their approval of the practice. No doubt Noyes would have persisted in support of complex marriage even if Perfectionists elsewhere had not sanctioned it, but the vote of confidence at Lairdsville gave him the determination to follow through with it in the face of certain opposition from his Vermont neighbors. The Lairdsville convention moved to Genoa, New York, and plans were here laid to form a Perfectionist community at Oneida. This action on the part of the convention was significant for Noyes, since he and his disciples at Putney chose to go to Oneida, New York, when the Putney community was forced to disband.

When Noyes returned to Putney after attending the convention he found the neighbors in an uproar over the reports of sexual improprieties in the community. Daniel Hall lodged a formal complaint against him for introducing the doctrine of complex marriage to his wife. Further investigation revealed that Noyes had committed adultery with Fanny Leonard and Achsah Campbell as well. He was arrested on October 26, 1847, charged with adultery and released on a $2,000 bond. He insisted that "the head and front and whole of our offense is communism of love. . . . If this is the unpardonable sin in the world, we are sure it is the beauty and glory of heaven." [23] Warrants were also issued for the arrest of George and Mary Cragin.

Enraged New Englanders would give no quarter and Noyes chose to jump bail rather than become a martyr. He gave as his reason for a hasty retreat that he feared mob violence if he remained at Putney. He fled first to New York City, and there continued his defense of the ideals of Perfectionism. He affirmed:

> Our warfare is an assertion of human rights; first, the right of man to be governed by God and to live in the social state of heaven; second, the right of woman to dispose of her sexual nature by attraction instead of by law and routine and to bear children only when she chooses; third, the right of all to diminish the labors and increase the advantages of life by association.[24]

Noyes found the people of New York more tolerant than those of Vermont, and he decided to move to the new community which was being formed at an abandoned sawmill site on Oneida Creek. Forty-five of his Putney associates joined him there; and by the end of 1848, their number had swelled to eighty-seven.

Complex marriage was adopted at the outset of the Oneida experiment. The principle of sharing all things in common was not restricted by the legal ties of a marriage license and a civil ceremony. The "we" and "our" spirit replaced the "me" and "my" spirit which characterized an apostate society. Leon Rymarkiewiez, a Polish gentleman who visited Oneida in 1852, reported: "The whole family is one marriage circle. The hearts are conscious of one love; consequently all things are common among them—women, goods, ideas, and inventive skill." [25]

Noyes was extremely careful regarding admission to membership at Oneida. Nordhoff observed that most of the applicants were men who were no doubt attracted by the prospects of sexual variation and who were for this cause rejected. He claimed that "The Perfectionists are sincerely and almost fanatically attached to the peculiar faith, and accept new members only with great care and many precautions."[26] Noyes insisted that no community could succeed unless there was a "very careful selection of material."[27] The lack of restrictions on admission was considered a major factor in the failure of the communities which Noyes surveyed in his book, *The History of American Socialisms*. A stock answer given to those who inquired of the membership qualifications at Oneida was: "We receive no new members (except by deception and mistake) who do not give heart and hand to the family interest for life and forever."[28]

The principle that men should become Perfectionists before they became communists was one to which Noyes adhered throughout the Oneida experiment. He was opposed to the mere amalgamation of the sexes, as some of the utopian communities had encouraged. The Noyesian doctrine was one of progression toward eternal redemption in which the observance of each step was paramount. He cautioned that "Holiness, free love, association in labor, and immortality, constitute the chain of redemption, and must come together in their true order. . . . Holiness must go before free love."[29] Stow Persons asserted that Oneida was "the first noncelibate community in which sexual irresponsibility ceased to exist."[30]

Noyes justified complex marriage on theological as well as practical grounds. "Religion," he declared, "is the first interest, and sexual morality the second in the great enterprise of establishing the kingdom of God on earth."[31] Noyes contended that the monogamous relation fostered exclusiveness and selfishness, which worked to counter communism. Celibacy had proved impractical at Putney, and was therefore abandoned. Noyes was delighted to be free from the reproach and evil surmisings occasioned by their celibacy.[32] He later counseled, "You must not make monks of yourself; if you do you will be damned."[33]

Unlike the Shakers, the Perfectionists claimed that sex relations were not sinful but were practiced in heaven as well as on earth, and in both places with God's approval. Noyes taught that "shame gives rise to the theory that sexual offices have no place in heaven. Anyone who has true modesty would sooner banish singing from heaven than sexual music."[34] In heaven, he asserted, the monogamous relation does not exist, since this would isolate certain saints and keep them from the enjoyment of a broader association within the kingdom. If the Kingdom of God were now among men, as Noyes believed that it was, sexual relations must not be limited to a single mate within the kingdom. Monogamy made it impossible for one to obey two of the cardinal tenets of Christianity: to love God; and to love one's neighbor.

No shame was attached to the sexual act in the Noyesian theology. Adam and Eve, the first Perfectionists, were totally without shame before they sinned. Noyes affirmed that sin and shame go hand in hand; therefore, when one ceases sinning, he ceases being ashamed.[35] He wrote: "To be ashamed of the sex organs, is to be ashamed of God's workmanship . . . of the most perfect instruments of love and unity . . . of the agencies which gave us existence . . . of the image and the glory of God." [36] True love finds its fulfillment in the sexual act, as it is love in its most natural and beautiful form. To deny this privilege to the saints of God on earth is equal to denying them their normal and healthful desires. Noyes asserted: "We need love as much as we need food and clothing, and God knows it; and if we trust him for those things, why not for love?" [37] To ignore man's biological drives is irrational and those who attempt to do so are engaged in a hopeless war with nature, since "Nature is constantly thrusting . . . sexual subjects upon the mind." [38] Sex, as an end in itself, was not supported by the theories of Noyes. He was mainly interested in clearing away the debasing associations that generally crowd around it. It was not sex which was sinful, but the motives which prompted the sexual union which determined its righteousness or sinfulness. If one engaged in the sexual act purely for selfish purposes, that is, his own physical satisfaction without regard to the feelings of his partner, the act was sinful. The true Perfectionist could never think only of himself, as this was contrary to the principles of Christ, who taught self-denial. The sexual act, when properly performed, permitted one to escape from selfishness into the delight of communion with others.[39]

Communism, according to Noyes, was not merely limited to the mutual sharing of material things. He affirmed: "There is no intrinsic difference between property in persons and property in things . . . as the same spirit which abolished exclusiveness in regard to money, would abolish . . . exclusiveness in regard to women and children." [40] Noyes based his argument on the Apostle Paul's statement to the Corinthians in which he made no distinction between wives and material property. Paul wrote: "The time is short; it remaineth that they that have wives be as though they had none; and they that buy as though they possessed not . . . for the fashion of this world passeth away." [41] The Kingdom of God on earth, therefore, was to be one in which all possessions were to be shared. Christ prayed that all his disciples might be one, even as he and the Father were one.[42] In that oneness, the ego is submerged and all possessiveness is abolished. Noyes concluded:

> the possessive pronoun *mine*, is derived from the pronoun *I*; and so the possessive feeling, whether amative or acquisitive, flows from the personal feeling, that is, it is a branch of egotism. Now egotism is abolished by the gospel relation to Christ . . . the extinguishment of the pronoun *I* at the spiritual center. . . . The grand distinction between the Christian and the unbeliever . . . is that in one reigns the We-spirit, and in the other the I-spirit. From *I* comes *mine*, and from the I-spirit comes exclusive appropriation of money, women, etc. From *we* comes *ours*, and from the we-spirit comes universal community of interests.[43]

Noyes contended that the traditional one-man one-woman relationship limited one in his relationship to his fellow men to the point where he could not truly obey the injunction of Christ to "love one another." The command did not specify believers to love in pairs, but *en masse*. Noyes added that the command is to love one another fervently, which was certainly more than forming a passing acquaintance. He claimed that if one were to insist that this love not be expressed in a physical way, he would "strain at a gnat and swallow a camel" in his attempt to justify the prohibition.[44] Noyes admitted that at times it may not be expedient to express one's love to another in a physical way. The Apostle Paul, because of hostile surroundings, claimed that there were things lawful for him which were not expedient. Noyes concluded that the apostle had written this when defending his right to engage in sexual intercourse.[45]

Monogamous marriage was an expedient arrangement in the ancient Jewish world before God's kingdom was established on earth. Noyes stood this domestic institution alongside the other Jewish practices, such as ceremonial observances which the Apostle Paul said had been abolished when Jesus died on the cross.[46] Noyes regarded monogamous marriages as being contrary to human nature. Second marriages often turned out to be the happiest, as "Men and women find universally (however the fact may be concealed) that their susceptibility to love is not burnt out by one honeymoon, or satisfied by one lover."[47]

Noyes found the monogamous marriage relation a violation to both reason and revelation on five counts: (1) it caused one to commit secret adultery, either in a clandestine affair or in the heart; (2) it often united couples with unmatched natures; (3) it deprived one of the mutual and elevating experience with another whose nature matched his own; (4) it gave the sexual appetite only a scanty and monotonous allowance; and (5) it made no provision for the sexual appetite at that time when it was strongest, in those adolescent years before marriage. Complex marriage, Noyes argued, removed each of these impediments to human happiness. There was no need for clandestine affairs, since it was perfectly permissible at Oneida to show openly one's affection toward any member of the opposite sex. There was no permanent pairing off of unmatched natures, nor was one deprived of association with a member of the opposite sex who appeared more compatible to him than his own wife. Variation in love-making, it was claimed, gave a fuller and deeper satisfaction to the sexual urge. The system of complex marriage permitted teenagers to engage in the sexual act without censure during the very flush of life. Noyes claimed the discrepancy between the monogamous marriage system and human nature was one of the principal causes of female diseases, prostitution, masturbation, and licentiousness in general.[48]

Eternal salvation was the ultimate goal of the Perfectionist, and the abolition of marital ties at Oneida was but one step in a progression toward that goal. Noyes taught that there are four links in a chain which bind man to evil and that each of these must be broken in their proper sequence if he is to be free to dwell with God: (1) a breach with God; (2) a disruption of the sexes and a curse on woman; (3) the curse of labor; (4) death and disease. "These are all inextricably complicated with each other," Noyes wrote, and "the true scheme of redemption begins with reconciliation with God, proceeds first to a restoration of a true relation between the sexes, then to a reform of the industrial system, and ends with a victory over death . . . the sin-system, the marriage-system, the work-system, and the death-system, are all one, and must be abolished together." [49] Once the Perfectionist ceased sinning and abolished marriage, work would become attractive. Women would not be confined to the house and men to the field in their labors. "Loving companionship in labor, and especially the mingling of the sexes,"

Noyes confidently remarked, "makes labor more attractive." [50] At Oneida, men learned to sew with the women and women learned to hoe with the men. Noyes was also confident that death would be abolished for the Perfectionist, just like sin, marriage, and oppressive labor. The fact that Perfectionists died at Oneida in no way daunted Noyes, as he stoutly maintained that the abolition of death would be the last triumph of God's kingdom on earth.

The principal fault Noyes found with the Fourierists was that they attempted to abolish oppressive labor without first abolishing sin and marriage. The Fourierists were non-religionists and attempted to maintain the nuclear family in their associations, both of which doomed them to failure according to Noyes. "Fourierism," he declared, "has no eye to the final victory over death . . . and confines itself to the rectifying of the industrial system. . . . Fourierism neither begins at the beginning nor looks to the end of the chain, but fastens its whole interest on the third link, neglecting the two that precede it, and ignoring that which follows it." [51] The Oneida Perfectionists disavowed any responsibility for those who meddled with the sexual relationships before they had laid a foundation of true faith in God.

Noyes admitted that even the Perfectionists had to be constantly alerted to the dangers of placing the institution of complex marriage ahead of true holiness. In *The Oneida Circular*, February 2, 1874, he wrote:

> We have got into the position of Communism, where without genuine salvation from sin our passions will overwhelm us, and nothing but confusion and misery can be expected. On the other hand . . . if we have the grace of God triumphant in our hearts and flowing through all our nature, there is an opportunity for harmony and happiness beyond all that imagination has conceived. So it is hell behind us, and heaven before us.[52]

The love of God was to exceed the love between the sexes. Charles Nordhoff visited Oneida and noted a song which they sang at one of their religious services. A man, while looking at one of the women, sang:

> I Love you, O my sister,
> But the Love of God is better;
> Yes the Love of God is better—
> O the Love of God is best.

The woman replied in song:

I Love you, O my brother,
But the Love of God is better;
Yes the Love of God is better—
O the Love of God is best.

The congregation then joined in the chorus:

Yes, the Love of God is better,
O the Love of God is better;
Hallelujah, Hallelujah—
Yes, the Love of God is best.[53]

Noyes contended that the relation of the sexes at Oneida was that of a marriage. Each person was married to every other member of the opposite sex in the community, regardless of age differentiation. This, Noyes affirmed, kept the arrangement from being mere licentiousness. Complex marriage consisted of permanent unions rather than temporary associations. Each person was held responsible for the consequences of his acts of love toward another. The maintenance and education of the children were not neglected, as might be the case if the society practiced unregulated free love. Noyes assured the public that they were not free lovers in the sense that made love less binding or responsible than it was in an ordinary marriage. He insisted that "Our communities are *families*, as distinctly bounded and separated from promiscuous society as ordinary households. The tie that binds us together is as permanent and sacred . . . as that of marriage, for it is our religion." [54] The Perfectionists adhered to the maxim, "The normal man loves the normal woman." [55] In the Oneida co-sexual fraternity this love was not to be inhibited but allowed to express itself as freely as love was permitted to be expressed between a husband and wife in the monogamous family.

The institution of complex marriage was without precedent and Noyes formulated the rules mainly through the process of trial and error. In the early stages of the experiment, a man could approach any woman who appealed to him and ask if she were willing to have intercourse with him. She was at liberty to accept or to refuse, as no one was allowed to force himself on another. Under such a system, there was no accurate way to account for the number of propositions which a virile male might make in a given period.

There were no courtship periods which preceded cohabitation; these were thought unnecessary since membership in the community was generally regarded as sufficient basis for compatibility. Courtships might also occasion exclusive attachments, which the community attempted to avoid. Flirting was not permitted, but it was permissible for the woman, since advances in the kingdom of nature were generally made by the female, to smile or flash her eyes if she wished to attract a male's attention.

In order to check the amativeness of some overly eager males, the system of requiring a third party to act as an intermediary between the seeker and the sought was adopted. The intermediary was required to post the account of the request in a ledger.[56] In order to assure complete control of all sexual relations in the community, a committee of elders, headed by Noyes, was formed in the 1860s to receive all requests for cohabitation. In this manner, an overly active member was restrained by having his request denied. The committee made its decision under the pretext of "spiritual considerations." Even if the committee of elders approved, the mate who was besought still had the right to refuse to have sexual relations with her suitor. The freedom to accept or to reject the advances of lovers kept the community members alert as to their personal appearance and manners. None dared to be offensive to the members of the opposite sex for fear of being refused or neglected. Pierrepont Noyes observed that "the opportunity for romantic friendships also played a part in rendering life more colorful than elsewhere. Even elderly people, whose physical passions had burned low, preserved the fine essence of earlier associations." [57] William Mills, after repeated attempts to get a female's approval to have intercourse with him had failed, requested that a better system would be to draw lots from a hat. Noyes promptly refused the suggestion and proceeded to lecture Mills on the community rights of the women and his obligation to respect those rights or go elsewhere. Mills was later expelled from the community for allegedly giving some home-made wine to some of the children.

Couples who were married before they entered the Oneida community were expected to forgo their exclusive attachment and become married to all in the society. Noyes claimed: "No matter what his other qualifications may be, if a man cannot love a woman and be happy seeing her loved by others, he is a selfish man, and his place is with the potsherds of the earth." [58] Allan Estlake observed that some men found it difficult to relinquish all authority over their wives, but on the whole they surrendered them to the married circle.[59] Married women were under no obligation to accept the proposals to cohabit from their husbands, any more than from any other man in the community. The selfish possession of another was regarded as making one unfit to practice the Perfectionist's ideal of "loving his neighbor without discrimination." [60]

Noyes exerted strenuous effort to abolish exclusive attachments to both persons and things, which he regarded as the very antithesis of communism. Members were counseled to "keep in circulation," in order that they might not grow too fond of specific individuals and thereby limit their association with others. At social functions the members were to take care that they not dance in successive sets with a particular partner.[61] Mothers were not permitted to show special affection to their own children. Pierrepont Noyes admitted that the community rules regarding exclusive love were harder on the mothers than on the children. He recalled:

> Whenever I was permitted to visit my mother in her mansard room —once a week or twice (I have forgotten which)—she always seemed trying to make up for lost opportunity, lavishing affection on me until as much as I loved her, I have grudged the time taken from play with those toys which she had—I think somewhat surreptitiously—collected for my visits.[62]

If a mother showed too much attachment to her child, the number of visits between them would be reduced or altogether denied. Pierrepont Noyes recalled that when he was once denied a visit with his mother he threw a tantrum, lay down on the sinkroom floor, and exhausted infantile vocabulary in "vehement protestations and accusations." [63] If a child called to its mother from a window in the children's house, the mother was forbidden to acknowledge its plea. Charles Nordhoff observed while he visited Oneida that the children, although healthy, appeared "a little subdued and desolate, as though they missed the exclusive love and care of a father and mother." He admitted that he may have misjudged their feelings, but said that he would "grieve to see in the eyes of my own little ones an expression which I thought I saw in the Oneida children." [64]

Noyes forbade exclusive attachments to personal property as well as to persons. Members were given a small allotment to buy incidentals and on one occasion, when Noyes noticed that they generally spent it for jewelry and other articles of personal adornment, he requested that they give him all their trinkets lest they seek to outdo one another.[65] Oneida children were taught at an early age to share their toys and if a child grew too fond of a particular toy, it was taken from him. Once, around 1850, when it was observed that the little girls were getting too possessive with particular dolls, which they regarded as their own "babies," they were persuaded to form a circle around the stove and each girl was asked to commit her doll to the fire. From that time forward, dolls were never allowed at Oneida.

The Oneida marriage circle practiced "perpetual courtship," but rigorously dealt with those couples who limited their amorous associations to each other. Noyes once told a man who evidenced affection to one particular woman, "you do not love her, you love happiness." [66] Noyes not only regarded such attachments as inexpedient in the practice of communism, but as selfish and sinful. There was to be no "pairing off" at social functions or at work. Pierrepont Noyes admitted that there were occasions when couples who worked together in a particular community enterprise would form an attachment to one another.[67] In such event, Noyes arranged to have one or the other taken from the job and placed elsewhere. If an offender deserved to be punished for his exclusive devotion to someone, he might be given an unpleasant job in the community in order to bring about his reform. If a couple persisted in their limited devotions, one or the other would be sent to the branch community at Wallingford, Connecticut. George Cragin was compelled to go to Wallingford because he saw too much of the eighteen-year-old Edith Walters. Sarah Bradley and a Mr. Delatre were accused of forming an exclusive attachment in 1863 and were ordered to separate. Delatre refused to abide by Noyes' decision and Sarah chose to relieve him of further embarrassment and departed to Wallingford. A manuscript record of the daily events at Oneida reveals that Delatre refused to give her up and wrote to her frequently. He followed her to Wallingford and continued his relationship with her.[68] All else having failed, Noyes refused to allow the couple to have sexual relations from that time forward.

In order to properly introduce virgins into the system of complex marriage, Noyes developed the principle of "ascending fellowship." The principle also worked to prevent the young members from falling in love with one another and limiting the range of their affections. Noyes did not believe all Perfectionists were equal. Some members, because of their experience and holiness of life, maintained a closer association with God than did others. These were regarded as the Central Members. They were less likely to yield to the temptation of exclusive love and were charged with the responsibility of caring for the spiritual welfare of their inferiors. The Central Members, or those of the ascending fellowship, had first choice in the selection of sexual partners and the women of the lower ranks felt compelled to accept their requests for intercourse. By the same token, the men of the lower order were obliged to honor the requests of the older women of the ascending fellowship. In order to maintain a rigid control over the community, and to prevent internal division of loyalties, Noyes forbade the young to mate exclusively with the young. Each sex was introduced into the system of complex marriage by the older members of the ascending fellowship of the opposite sex. The virgins were to be spared the abuse which impatient and inexperienced lads might inflict upon them during the initial sexual intercourse. The young men were to be taught proper pleasure-giving and pleasure-receiving techniques by the older and experienced women. Women who were past the menopause were generally regarded as the ideal ones to introduce the young males into the mysteries of sex, since it would spare the community unwanted pregnancies until the youths learned the art of restraining ejaculation. The system of having the older members initiate the younger into complex marriage also served to prolong the active sex life of the older members and to supply them with partners which otherwise might not be available to them. Noyes regarded himself as spiritually superior to the other Perfectionists at Oneida and assumed the role of "first husband" to the young women. As he grew older, he delegated this role to other men of the ascending fellowship. The arrangement established an emotional bond between the youth and the older members which prevented a generation gap at Oneida, a divisive factor in every other utopian community which survived two or more generations. There were, however, some complaints late in the Oneida experiment that the young women were called on as often as seven or eight times a week while the older women were altogether neglected.[69]

The Mansion House served as the main living quarters of the members at Oneida and was specifically designed to accommodate the system of complex marriage. The structure was sixty feet long, thirty-five feet wide, three stories high, and topped with a habitable garret. There were three large basement rooms. The unitary dining room and kitchen were located on the first floor. There was an all-purpose room on the second floor and the remainder of the Mansion House was divided into small bedrooms and sitting rooms, the latter "to make association easy and attractive." [70] The children were kept in a separate wing of the house. Since overt courting in public was forbidden, all petting and fondling were to be limited to the privacy of the lady's bedroom. Rarely did the Oneida male spend the entire night with a lady, as this might lead to an exclusive attachment, the worst of all Oneida sins.

Anita Newcomb McGee, who interviewed several women in 1891, after the breakup of Oneida, reported that they had intercourse every two to four days.[71] Some women were more popular than others, as might be expected, and they were propositioned oftener. When a woman conceived, it was difficult to determine the identity of the father. The children were given their father's surname; but when the father was unknown, the child was given the mother's surname. Visitors to Oneida, upon observing the children there, frequently asked if they knew who their fathers were. The stock answer was: "They have no more proof than other children—only the testimony of their mothers." [72]

The members of the Oneida community apparently suffered no ill effects from their frequent and varied sexual relations. William Hepworth Dixon, during his visit there in the 1860s, was told to observe their apparent happiness: "We work, we rest, we study, we enjoy; peace reigns in our household; our young men are healthy, our young women bright; we live well, and we do not multiply beyond our wishes." [73] Leon Rymarkiewiez noted, during his visit in 1852, "That the Perfectionists are not sensual, is proved by their healthy appearance, their physical energy, and their blooming children. That they are not often carried away with the animal drift, is proved by the fact that in three years only one child was born among them." [74] In 1877 Ely Van de Warker, a physician, was invited to come to Oneida to examine the women, since even the Oneidans themselves feared that the system of complex marriage might have had a harmful effect on their physical condition. Van de Warker examined forty-two women between the ages of fifteen and eighty years, or less than one-third of the adult female population at

Oneida. He found no more significant difference in the physical condition of the Oneida women than one would find with a random sample of women anywhere else in America.[75] George Noyes Miller told Havelock Ellis that the incidence of nervous disorders at Oneida was considerably less than the average among non-Perfectionists. He did admit that possibly two women had had a nervous condition which might in some way be attributed to male abuse.[76]

XII

On To Perfection

THE SYSTEM OF COMPLEX MARRIAGE, WITHOUT STRINGENT CONTROLS, would have multiplied the population at Oneida several times over. Noyes was opposed to their women giving birth to children, except under controlled conditions. His objection to excessive childbirths was mainly based on the experiences of his own wife, Harriet, who had been pregnant five times in six years and who had given birth to four stillborn children. Only a son, Theodore, had survived. Noyes was a Perfectionist, and concluded that there must be a way to overcome this affliction of pain and agony. He promised his wife that he would never again expose her to such "fruitless suffering." [1] He refrained from having sexual intercourse with his wife for two years. In the summer of 1848 he worked out a theory which would permit the enjoyment of the sexual act without running the risk of an unwanted pregnancy and without the use of a contraceptive device. He had paved the way for the art of sexual intercourse to move toward perfection.

Robert Dale Owen, whose interest in the equality of women had led him to write *Moral Physiology, or a Brief and Plain Treatise on the Population Question* in 1830, suggested the practice of *coitus interruptus* as a means of preventing conception while at the same time permitting satisfaction in the sexual act. Charles Knowlton, in 1832, had written *The Fruits of Philosophy, or the Private Companion of Young Married People*, in which he advocated the use of contraceptives mainly for medical and economic purposes. Noyes read both of these volumes and concluded that neither fulfilled the Perfectionist ideal of maximum satisfaction. The practice of *coitus interruptus* was specifically condemned in the Bible. Onan was ordered to marry his deceased brother's wife and to father children in his brother's behalf. Onan had intercourse with her but refused to ejaculate his "seed" within her. Instead, he "spilled it on the ground, lest that he should give seed to his brother." [2] Noyes was opposed to Onanism on theological grounds. He not only regarded it as sinful, but as a substitute of self-indulgence for self-control. With equal vehemence Noyes rejected contraceptives as "those tricks of the French voluptuaries." [3] He preferred a practice which was more in keeping with the ideal of puritan discipline and therefore developed his own theory, which he labeled male continence.

Male continence was rooted in Noyes' philosophy regarding spiritual and physical love. Spiritual love, he believed, is expressed by the actions of filling and enveloping. God fills the soul of the Perfectionist and the Perfectionist is enveloped by the Godhead. Jesus prayed that his disciples might be one, "as thou father, art in me, and I in thee, that they also may be one in us." [4] Physical love is likewise expressed by filling and enveloping: the male desires to fill and to be enveloped, and the female desires to be filled and to envelop. "Love in the highest form," Noyes wrote, "is the reciprocal and satisfied attraction of these two forms of desire." [5] The sex organs serve two distinct functions in the act of love: that of social magnetism, or the amative function; and that of conducting the semen, or the propagative function.[6] Noyes regarded the amative function as superior to the propagative. It was the latter which had brought his wife so much anguish and disappointment in childbirth. He believed that God had originally made Eve for social purposes rather than for propagation. Her maternal office did not emerge until after the original couple had sinned. For her share in the transgression God said, "I will greatly multiply thy sorrow and thy conception; in sorrow thou shalt bring forth children." [7] The Perfectionists sought to restore the pure state of innocence which Adam and Eve enjoyed in the Garden of Eden. The original pair enjoyed intercourse, but propagation was not the objective of the act. The first commandment of the eternal law of love was to love God; the second was to love thy neighbor. Since Eve was Adam's only neighbor, he was to love her, and she him. According to Noyes' theory, love involved the desire to fill and to be enveloped, and for the female to be filled and to envelop; sexual intercourse was the only possible physical manifestation of that love. Propagation, therefore, could not possibly be the purpose in the fulfillment of the law of God to love one's neighbor. Propagation, Noyes asserted, not only brought misery to the female, but drained life from the male. When the male's semen was habitually expelled, it brought disease to his body. Noyes claimed, "It is as foolish and cruel to expend one's seed on a wife merely for the sake of getting rid of it, as it would be to fire a gun at one's best friend merely for the sake of unloading it." [8] He further asserted that God did not intend men to "sow seed by the wayside, where they do not expect it to grow, or in the same field where seed has already been sown and is growing." [9]

Noyes was determined to elevate the amative office of the sex organs, since he was convinced that celibacy was contrary to God's purpose for them. Expending one's semen in *coitus interruptus*, as Robert Dale Owen suggested, or in a contraceptive, drained life from the male. In the summer of 1844 Noyes wrote:

> I conceive the idea that the sexual organs have a social function which is distinct from the propagative function, and that these functions may be separated practically. I experimented . . . and found that the self-control which it required was not difficult; also that my enjoyment was increased; also that my wife's experience was very satisfactory, as it had never been before.[10]

He had "discovered" the art of male continence, which he was convinced would "elevate the race to new vigor and nobility," when it was adopted by all.[11] Sexual intercourse involving male restraint became a form of worship at Oneida. The female orgasm was the ultimate objective in every sexual encounter. Women were expected to enjoy sex, as well as the men, and when they did not, the men were to blame for not having mastered the Noyesian technique.

Noyes analyzed the sexual act as consisting of three phases: (1) the presence, or when the penis is introduced into the vagina; (2) the motion, to induce friction and bring about the female orgasm; and (3) the crisis, or male ejaculation. He insisted that the entire process, up to the point of ejaculation, is within the voluntary control of one's moral faculty.[12] Noyes contended that Perfectionists must exercise self-control in all things, and the sexual act was no exception. "Only brutes, animals or human," he claimed, "tolerate none

. . . it is the glory of man to control himself." [13] He illustrated how one might control his passions during intercourse by comparing it with a man who rows a boat in a stream above a waterfall. He wrote: "If he is willing to learn, experience will teach him the wisdom of confining his excursions to the region of easy rowing, unless he had an object in view that is worth the cost of going over the falls." [14] Noyes claimed that the male could constrict the ejaculatory ducts and that the process was easy, once the technique was mastered. Alfred Kinsey, in his recent study of human sexual behavior, confirmed the Noyesian thesis that the human male can have an orgasm without ejaculation.[15] Havelock Ellis, writing in 1911, claimed that the male could engage in intercourse for an hour or more without emission and without a pressure which demanded a release of the semen after withdrawal.[16]

Noyes first communicated his discovery to George Cragin, who later reported that he found the technique both simple and satisfying. One elated Perfectionist exclaimed that the discovery of male continence by Noyes "surpassed that of the steam engine and the electric telegraph." [17] Noyes himself regarded the practice as one of the fine arts which some day would excel music, painting, and sculpture. Aldous Huxley, in his utopian novel, *Island*, called the practice of male continence "maithuna," and captured the essence of the technique in the following dialogue:

> in a word . . . it's just birth control without contraceptives. . . . Remember the point that Freud was always harping on . . . the point about the sexuality of children? What we're born with, what we experience all through infancy and childhood, is a sexuality that isn't concentrated on the genitals; it's a sexuality diffused throughout the whole organism. That's the paradise we inherit. But the paradise gets lost as the child grows up. *Maithuna* is the organized attempt to regain that paradise.[18]

Male continence, as practiced at Oneida, was not altogether easy nor foolproof, as approximately thirty children were accidentally conceived during the first twenty years of the experiment. This in no way accounts for the number of "upsets," as they called the ejaculations of those who had not mastered the secrets of male continence. Careless and unskilled men were open to rebuke and the women avoided encounters with them for fear of pregnancy, which served as a controlling force on the side of the practice.

Male continence was discovered before complex marriage was adopted and, indeed, made the unique marital arrangement at Oneida possible. Noyes needed a guarantee that the sexual liberty which he envisioned for his utopia would not result in overpopulation in the community, which would serve as an economic drain on its resources. Other utopian communities had suffered grave economic distress because of an excessive number of unproductive citizens. Noyes was too practical to allow his experiment to be overburdened by unwanted children. "It is still self-evident," he asserted, "that the birth of children, viewed either as a vital or a mechanical operation, is in its nature expensive." [19] Male continence assured him that Oneida could engage in free love without the consequences of unwanted pregnancies and a proliferation of unproductive children.

The system of mutual criticism served to curb the passions of the members of the Oneida community and to check the abuses of the practice of complex marriage. Other religious utopian communities had practiced a form of catharsis which allowed their members to relieve the psychological tensions through a confession of their deviations from the expected community norms. Shakers acknowledged their faults to their elders, and the Amanaites had their annual *Untersuching*, which served as cohesive forces within their respective communities. Noyes adopted the practice of mutual criticism at Putney and Oneida, mainly out of his experiences as a theology student at Andover. In order to correct their personal lives that they might be more godly, Andover students, in the spirit of brotherly love, agreed to single out each other's disagreeable traits in meetings called for the purpose. Noyes had benefited from these sessions and realized the value of such an institution as a social force to maintain conformity to the community's ideals. Mutual criticism, therefore, became "the regulator of industry and amusement—the incentive to all improvement—the corrector of all excesses." [20] Any manifestation of individualism which threatened the communal spirit was certain to be exposed and condemned in a criticism session. Noyes claimed: "the moral health of the Association depends on the freest circulation of this plainness of speech; and all are ambitious to balance accounts in this way as often as possible." [21] Ill will and complaints were thereby forced out into the open and were not permitted to fester and threaten the community from within.

There was no set routine as to the time or to the method of mutual criticism. Noyes told A. J. Macdonald:

> We tell each other plainly and kindly our thoughts about each other in various ways. Sometimes the whole Association criticises a member in a meeting. Sometimes it is done more privately, by committees, and sometimes by individuals. In come cases, criticism is directed to general characteristics, and in others to special faults and offences.[22]

Generally the criticisms were accepted with good grace and the members promised to correct their faults. One member acknowledged: "I felt as though I had been washed; I felt clean through the advice and criticism given. I would call the truth the soap; the critics the scrubbers; Christ's spirit the water." [23] Noyes asserted that the members themselves invited criticism and regarded it as a privilege and a blessing. Some members, however, were incensed at first when their faults were openly criticized, but afterward they came to regard the experience as beneficial. One person claimed that every trait of his character in which he had taken pride or comfort was cruelly discounted. He admitted: "I felt like pouring out my soul in tears, but there was too much pride left in me yet to make an exhibition of myself." Later he confessed that he had changed his mind about the criticism and that he would gladly give his life if he could have "*just one more criticism* from John H. Noyes." [24]

The criticisms usually began with pointing out the virtues of the individual before moving toward his faults. One young lady was said to be "a fine specimen of the vital temperament," but her elders accused her of being disrespectful and inattentive: "She will fly through a room, on some impulsive errand of generosity, perhaps, leave both doors open, and half knock down anybody in her way." The critics concluded: "We must cure her of her coarseness, and teach her to be gay without being rude, and respectful without being demure." [25]

Much of mutual criticism was devoted to curbing exclusive attachments and other abuses of the system of complex marriage. Charles Nordhoff related an account of the criticism which he was permitted to observe in which a young man was charged with "having fallen under the too common temptation of selfish love, and a desire to wait upon and cultivate an exclusive intimacy" with a certain woman in the community. The young man admitted his guilt and chose to isolate himself entirely from the woman. To help him get his mind off the woman, he agreed to go sleep with the children and care for them during the nights.[26] The dead as well as the living were subject to scathing criticisms when warranted. On one occasion the notebook and letters of a deceased member, in which he had recorded his innermost private thoughts, were passed about in the community. It was found that he had been guilty of exclusive love and thus merited a "rousing criticism." [27]

One of the unique experiments at Oneida was conducted in the field of eugenics. John Humphrey Noyes was a Perfectionist and he carried his faith in human perfectibility to its logical extreme. If horses, cattle, and pigs could be bred in such a way as to produce better stocks of animals, it seemed the natural thing for a better breed of human beings to be produced by using the same scientific principles. Society condoned a system which produced mentally deranged and physically deformed human beings. Noyes was certain that there was a better way, once propagation was no longer regarded the exclusive prerogative of the monogamous relation. Monogamy could not be depended upon to always produce perfectly fit human beings, since "it discriminates against the best and in favor of the worst; for while the good man will be limited by his conscience to what the law allows, the bad man, free from moral check, will distribute his seed beyond the legal limits, as widely as he dares," Noyes contended.[28] Monogamy gave the same rights of propagation to the unfit as it did to the fit, and it appeared to the Perfectionist that the unfit were more prolific. Noyes did admit that immoral people could disseminate good seed, as the notorious escapades of Pierrepont Edwards, son of the saintly Jonathan Edwards, proved. Noyes asserted: "who can say how much the present race of men in Connecticut owe to the numberless fornications and adulteries of Pierrepont Edwards. Corrupt as he was, he must have distributed a good deal of the good blood of his noble father . . . . Such are the compensations of nature and providence." [29] Although Noyes did not respect the promiscuity of Jonathan Edwards' son, he did his talents, and named one of his own sons in his honor.

Noyes was confident that the time would come when common sense would dictate and enforce the rule that women would bear children only when they chose, since it was the women, not the men, who had the principal burdens of childbirth.[30] He was equally confident that science would some day take charge of human propagation and only perfect specimens would be born. Noyes believed that his experiments in complex marriage and male continence had paved the way for a scientific system of select breeding. The monogamous marriage relation had been abolished at Oneida, and the system of complex marriage had its built-in controls which put the sexual relations of the community under the supervision of committees and ultimately into the hands of Noyes himself. The practice of male continence gave a measure of assurance that conception need not be the inevitable consequence of satisfying sexual relations over a long period of time. Both complex marriage and male continence were heavily bolstered by religious sanctions so that there was no immorality of illegitimacy associated with the pantagamous system on the conscience of those who implicitly trusted in Noyes. The Oneida community was ideally constituted for a bold experiment in select human breeding before the term "eugenics" was coined.

Noyes conceived the idea of breeding future Perfectionists while studying the works of Charles Darwin and Charles Galton. The concept of the "survival of the fittest" appealed to Noyes, who regarded perfectibility as within the range of the human potential. However, he accused Galton of having written too vaguely about the application of scientific principles in order to produce a more fit human being. Since Galton also defended the monogamous family, Noyes claimed that he was too conservative. Noyes was no conservative. "Duty is plain," he asserted, "we say we ought to do it—we want to do it; but we cannot. The boldest course is the safest. . . . It is only in the timidity of ignorance that the duty seems impracticable." [31] As in the defense of complex marriage and male continence, Noyes assured the members of the Oneida community that select human breeding was the will of God. To refuse to accept it was to defy God.

Although Plato had written about a system of select breeding in his *Republic*, he did not use the Greek term "eugenics" to describe it. Noyes coined the word "stirpiculture," from the Latin *stirps*, meaning stem or root, and applied it to the practice at Oneida. There was to be no compulsory acceptance on the part of either the males or the females in the pilot program of stirpiculture, for that would have been contrary to the principle of individualism which Noyes advocated. The decision to enter into the experiment was voluntary on the part of those who were devoted to both God and science. The experiment in select breeding of humans began at Oneida during the year 1869.

Not everyone who volunteered for the experiment could be accepted, for this would have run counter to the purpose of the venture. It was to be "select" breeding. To provide subjects for the experiment, young men and young women signed documents in which they volunteered to be used in any capacity Noyes saw fit. The men, with solemn religious conviction, declared:

> we most heartily sympathize with your purposes in regard to scientific propagation and offer ourselves to be used in forming any combinations that might seem to you desirable. We claim no rights. We ask no privileges. We desire to be the servants of the truth. With a prayer that the grace of God will help us in this resolution, we are your true soldiers.[32]

The women who were willing to bear the discomforts of pregnancy and the agony of childbirth without the reward of subsequent pleasures of motherhood declared:

> 1. . . . we do not belong to *ourselves* in any respect, but that we *do* belong first to *God*, and second to Mr. Noyes as God's true representative.
>
> 2. . . . we have no rights or personal feelings in regard to childbearing which shall in the least degree oppose or embarrass him in his choice of scientific combinations.
>
> 3. . . . we will put aside all envy, childishness and self seeking, and rejoice with those who are chosen candidates; that we will, if necessary, become martyrs to science, and cheerfully resign all desire to become mothers, if for any reason Mr. Noyes deem us unfit material for propagation. Above all, we offer ourselves "living sacrifices" to God and true Communism.[33]

Ninety-one members signed the agreement to enter into the experiment in eugenics. Fifty-three women signed the declaration as compared to thirty men. No rationale was ever given as to why the female volunteers outnumbered the males, since the male to female ratio was nearly even at Oneida. The maternal instinct, which had been curtailed during the practice of male continence, quite possibly manifested itself in the women's declaration. The men were seemingly more content to continue the practice of sexual variation without the necessity of an emission. The community had proved economically successful for twenty years with only a minimum of accidental conceptions and the men may have feared the innovation would encumber the growth of the community with nonproductive children. Possibly the fear that the maternal instinct would tend toward exclusive love and make the women less receptive to their advances troubled some of the males. The most likely factor, however, which may account for the imbalance in the ratio of females to males who volunteered, is that the Oneida women, most of whom had been initiated into the system of complex marriage by John Humphrey Noyes, were emotionally attached to him, implicitly trusted him, and secretly entertained the hope that they might become the mother of his child. There was little doubt that he was regarded as the "fittest of the fit," and would sire most of the children of the new race of Perfectionists in the experiment.

The volunteers cushioned themselves for possible rejection in their signed statements by agreeing to accept, with good grace, Noyes' criteria for intellectual, physical, and spiritual fitness. Those of the ascending fellowship were obviously the first on the list to be selected, as Noyes explained: "Persons must themselves improve, before they can transmit improvement to their offspring." [34] Noyes chose a committee to examine the applicants and to determine who should be asked to participate in the experiment. As in the case of all activities of any serious magnitude at Oneida, Noyes was not only the chief architect, but the chief engineer. Bernard Shaw is credited with observing: "The existence of Noyes simplified the breeding problem for the Communists, the question of what sort of men they should strive to breed being settled at once by the obvious desirability of breeding another Noyes." [35]

The selection of those for breeding purposes was to follow two principles: breed from the best; and breed in-and-in with an occasional introduction of new blood. The same principles were observed in producing thoroughbred horses. Noyes also believed the ancient Hebrews practiced the same principles in select breeding and that this accounted for the superior lineage of Jesus Christ.

Twenty-four men and twenty-four women were originally chosen from the ninety-one applicants. Noyes justified the selection on the ground that they had been the most ardent practitioners of the Oneida social theory.[36] As time passed, another fifty subjects were added to the select breeding circle. The average age of the women selected was thirty years, and that of the men, forty-one. The oldest woman in the experiment was forty-two and the oldest man was sixty-eight. The youngest woman was twenty and the youngest man was twenty-five.

A committee of six men and six women, headed by Noyes, was selected to decide when the couples would propagate and with whom. Hilda and George Noyes claimed that the couples were given some liberty in deciding with whom they would cohabit for eugenic purposes, and that actually the Stirpiculture Committee dictated only about one-fourth of the pairings.[37] Pierrepont Noyes claimed that his father "used his head in administering the details of selection for breeding and forestalled trouble." [38] Noyes would rather risk having a few imperfect children born in the community than to have to face a group of disgruntled members who had been plainly told that they were unfit by being ignored in the experiment. Pierrepont Noyes noted that almost every man fathered one child, but only one.[39] Between 1869 and 1879 fifty-eight "stirps" were born at Oneida, nine of whom were children by John Humphrey Noyes, who was at that time in his sixties. One child fathered by Noyes was stillborn. His wife, Harriet, had given birth to four stillborn infants before communal life was begun at Putney.

Noyes was certain that the experiment in eugenics would provide Oneida with future Perfectionists so that the community would not have to resort to the practice of adopting children from the outside, which was never a reliable method of ensuring the perpetuation of communal ideals. He arranged for the children to be put into a laboratory-nursery to be sure that they were reared from their earliest remembrances in keeping with his ideas of Perfectionism. The nursery was operated under homelike conditions as much as possible, in order to give the children the love and attention which they would have received in any middle-class American home. Three men and fifteen women were in charge of the Children's House. The children were allowed to sleep as long as they wished in the mornings. The mothers were permitted to visit their children for two hours each week, but were cautioned against forming an exclusive attachment to their particular son or daughter. The children, who knew no other mode of life, accepted their laboratory-nursery with but few exceptions. There were moments when they craved the coddling which only a natural mother could give them. But most children, who later in their adult lives reflected on their childhood at Oneida, regarded those times as happy ones. One woman recalled: "Everybody was good to us. You knew you were loved because it was like a big family. Also, there were so many activities for the youngsters, so many things to do, well—believe me—we were happy children. Everybody around here will give you the same answer on that." [40]

No thoroughly scientific study was ever made of the breed of human beings produced in the eugenic experiment at Oneida. It is a tragedy that no more was accomplished in the way of an accurate assessment of the modern world's first systematic attempt at human eugenics. Ten years after the experiment ceased, Anita Newcomb McGee interviewed several of the children and recorded the following about the older ones:

> The boys are tall—several over six feet—broad-shouldered and finely proportioned; the girls are robust and well-built. The present occupations of the older youths are interesting in connection with the fact that with the exception of the Noyes family and half a dozen lawyers, doctors, and clergymen, the Oneida community was composed of farmers and merchants, and that mothers generally belonged to the classes employed in manual labor. Of the oldest sixteen boys, ten are in business, chiefly employed as clerks, foremen, etc., in manufactories of the joint-stock company [Oneida Limited]. The eleventh is a musician of repute, another, a medical student, one has passed through college and is studying law, one is a college senior and one is entering college after winning state and local scholarships. . . . Finally, the sixteenth boy is a mechanic, the only one engaged in manual labor. Of the six girls between eighteen and twenty-two years, three are especially intellectual . . . . The children are markedly superior to the maternal stock.
>
> As an index of the calibre of the offspring of stirpiculture, it may be mentioned that a favorite amusement is found in a debating society of three girls and four boys, which meets during the summer when all are at home.[41]

No systematic follow-up was ever attempted to fully determine how the stirpiculture children fared during their adult life. In 1921 Hilda and George Noyes claimed that only six of the fifty-eight "stirps" were deceased at that time, and those who survived were between the ages of forty-two and fifty-two. There were no mentally or physically handicapped children in the experiment and they were all in apparently good health. The environment in which they were reared, the special attention shown them, and the concerted efforts of the community to educate them probably accounted for their apparent intellectual and physical superiority as much as, or more than, their breeding. The experiment was not of long enough duration nor of sufficient scope to warrant a positive statement regarding its scientific value. Stirpiculture was a feature of Oneida near the end of their experiment in communalism, and when complex marriage ceased, the experiment in eugenics also ceased.

The Oneida community, like its predecessor, Putney, lived under the constant threat of attack from the outside. In 1850 Oneida and Madison county residents brought independent suits accusing the community of immorality and being a public nuisance. Several neighbors came to the defense of Oneida, and signed a petition declaring that the members minded their own business and whatever went on in the colony brought no harm to anyone on the outside. The petition further declared the Oneidans to be of good moral character.[42] The case against Oneida was dropped and the community continued the practice of complex marriage for another thirty years.

In the mid-seventies internal strife threatened to disintegrate the utopian experiment at Oneida. A faction led by a new convert, James W. Towner, challenged the autocratic leadership of John Humphrey Noyes. A loyal body of members stood by Noyes and continued to acknowledge him as the "permanent medium of the spirit of Christ."[43] Noyes, in recent years, had delegated his assumed right to introduce virgins into the system of complex marriage to other members of the elite circle of the ascending fellowship. Those who were excluded from this privilege were urged by Towner to follow his direction in opposition to Noyes. The Townerites charged Noyes with statutory rape, since the girls who were first introduced into complex marriage were under age. Ely Van de Warker discovered, during his gynecological study of Oneida women, that on the average, the girls were about thirteen when Noyes or one of his delegates first had intercourse with them.[44] The fact that the Townerites were equally guilty of statutory rape, since they had relations with the same girls soon afterward, had little bearing on their charges. Noyes and his delegates had been the "first husbands," and this was regarded as the more serious offence. The squabble was carried outside the community. John W. Mears, a professor at nearby Hamilton College, led the attack and was joined by the Methodist Association of Central New York, the Congregational Association of New York, the Baptist State Convention, and the New York Presbyterian Synod. Mears summoned a conference of forty-seven clergymen and prepared to carry a case against Oneida into court. Pierrepont Noyes claimed that his father "had, it seems, definite information that certain men inside the community were about to ally themselves with the outside crusaders." [45] John Humphrey Noyes elected once more to escape, rather than face mutiny and possible martyrdom. On June 23, 1879, he fled first to Strathroy, Ontario, and nine months later he took up residence on the Canadian side of Niagara Falls. A small group of loyal disciples followed him to Canada, where they continued communal life, but without complex marriage. Noyes maintained communication with Oneida, but with the master spirit departed, there was little question that the enterprise, as originally conceived and operated for more than thirty years, would cease.

In August 1879 Noyes proposed that the Oneida community "give up the practice of complex marriage, not as renouncing belief in the principles and prospective finality of that institution, but in deference to the public sentiment which is arising against it." [46] He further proposed that a thorough study be made of the seventh chapter of I Corinthians in regard to proper sexual relations, but he strongly urged them to adopt celibacy. He expressed his belief that Oneida could continue to operate as a communistic society, live together in a common household, and all eat at a common table. He did not, however, venture to predict how long they could continue as a community under this arrangement. Earlier, he had contended that complex marriage was essential both to communism and to the fulfillment of God's purpose on earth. His former theories and present advice for the future were poles apart. On the evening of August 28, 1879, a meeting was called at Oneida to consider Noyes' proposals. Only one member, William Alfred Hinds, voted against the abandonment of complex marriage. Hinds was hopelessly outvoted and the unique marital institution officially ended.

The proposal of Noyes that the Oneidans become celibates was heeded by only a few. Some were already married, since they joined the community as husband and wife. Despite his aversion to monogamy, Noyes had united several couples in the marriage bond in order to prepare them for the possible abandonment of the community. Thirty-seven couples married soon after the abolition of complex marriage, and where possible, the men married the mothers of their children. Some of the mothers were unable to marry the father of their children, particularly those who had borne children by John Humphrey Noyes. Pierrepont Noyes inquired of his mother whom she planned to marry. She replied, "Perhaps no one, as your father is already married; so is Ormond's [Pierrepont's half brother] father." [47] The children, who had been protected from taunts from the outside, were now labeled by their neighboring peers as "bastards."

When Oneida adopted monogamy, its communism was seriously threatened. The individual families became concerned about their selfish economic interests and the rights of private property were established for the first time at Oneida. Pierrepont Noyes recalled that the members hoped that they might continue the experiment, but, he added, "They did not know that this change made the dissolution of their community inevitable." [48]

The charismatic leadership of Noyes had departed, faith in Perfectionism had lost its fervor, and complex marriage, which had been regarded as a sacred part of their religion, had been abandoned. Oneida lost its purpose for being. Under the inept leadership of Myron Kinsley, the community struggled under the monogamous family arrangement for a year. In September 1880 the members signed an agreement to divide and reorganize, and the following January communal ownership of property ended. The Oneida enterprises were converted into a joint-stock company and each person received stocks equal in value to one-half of the property which he had brought into the community. Children born at Oneida received $200 in stock.[49] The corporation was obliged to furnish living quarters for the members and their children at cost, and each was given $60 in cash to provide a new start in a competitive society when he began to work for a salary in the community industries.

Complex marriage was a unique system devised by Noyes to provide an outlet for man's sexual drive without admitting the monogamous relation into the practice of communism, which would serve to augment selfishness and undermine the community spirit. The puritanical Noyes established a plausible theology to support the system and to give it divine sanction. To prevent the practice from degenerating into sheer lasciviousness, he developed a social structure which gave him full control over every encounter between the sexes. The institution of mutual criticism served to break up exclusive attachments and to guarantee conformity to the mores of the society. Each member served as a confidant and there was no need for a police force, judges, juries, or jails. The technique of male continence gave some assurance that the community would not propagate beyond its means to support itself, and this without the denial of the pleasures of sexual intercourse. A unique balance between individualism and communism was effected at Oneida. Each person was given the right to accept or to refuse the advances of a member of the opposite sex. Intermediaries served to shield each individual from the embarrassment of a negative response and to check the overly amorous Perfectionists. The members were free to associate with one another without the morbid fear of gossip and scandal. There were no divorces, wife-beatings, prostitution, merciless stepmothers, or other such social evils which characterized the outside world. For more than thirty years Oneida existed as one family in excess of 300 members, all of whom possessed the "we" spirit. Unlike the Mormons, the Oneidans did not attempt to conceal their unorthodox sexual behavior. Oneida Limited, the modern corporation formed to conduct the communal enterprises, later ordered that the private records of the members of the utopian community be destroyed on the pretext that divulging their contents would have served no useful purpose.[50] Noyes, however, encouraged the keeping of records, for he did not try to hide the community's activities behind a façade of Victorian prudery. Shame was evidence of sin, and if any were ashamed of their relationships at Oneida, they had no fellowship with the Perfectionists.

Oneida failed, as did most utopian communities in America during the nineteenth century, because it lost its vital center when Noyes departed and when the basic tenets which gave justification for its existence were no longer honored. The abolition of complex marriage completed the task of dismantling the society. The hollow shell which remained for a year after its denial lay gasping and cried for euthanasia. When the private families shut themselves up in their separate domiciles and out from the community at large, communism took a backward step at Oneida and never regained its footing. When husbands refused to share their wives, they ceased sharing all things.

Noyes had been proud of his accomplishments at Oneida and he often pointed to the results of the social system he had engineered. He once told A. J. Macdonald: "we live in peace, have good health, and are not troubled with involuntary propagation—which facts could not exist in a licentious state of society." [51] But the Oneidans paid dearly for their style of life. They were not permitted to follow their natural urge in the culmination of the sexual act. They were under the perpetual scrutiny of every other member of the community and their slightest deviation from the norm made them liable to public ridicule and scorn. They were not free while they chose to live in the Oneida community. They were only free to leave it, and several did. Mothers were denied the free expression of love toward the children whom they brought into the world, and this gave rise to duplicity. Mothers disclaimed their children openly, but behind closed doors they nestled their little ones to their bosoms during those rare intervals when they had occasion to be alone with them. There was no democracy at Oneida. No one dared question Noyes, for to do so was to question the justification for Oneida's existence. The first crack in the system appeared when the Towner faction challenged Noyes. From that moment forward the breach widened and Oneida community prepared to join her sister utopians in a march toward oblivion.

XIII

Unusual Sexual Practices, Fact and Rumor

UTOPIAN COMMUNITIES IN NINETEENTH-CENTURY AMERICA, ONCE THEY modified or abolished the monogamous family, took occasion to experiment in the whole range of human relations between the sexes. Novel experiments were generally admitted with caution, and as they fossilized into institutions, they were supported on theological or theoretical grounds, depending on the orientation of the masterminds of the community. Unorthodox sexual practices were varied, but not always as rumored. Utopian communities were accused of every conceivable sexual deviation and were the objects of both curiosity and righteous censure. Visitors, both foreign and domestic, exhibited a mania for prying into the cloistered affairs of the utopias, and often carried away frightful tales of degenerate activities, which make it difficult to distinguish between actual practices and the figments of the observers' imagination. Not all of the communities kept written records of their activities, and our only source of information, whether fact or rumor, must come from the accounts of those who claimed to have first-hand information.

The Nashoba community, established by Frances Wright in 1825 near Memphis, Tennessee, was known for its unorthodox views toward marriage and the family. The community was founded with the hope of providing a pattern for the emancipation of Negro slaves by integrating them into white society through education and association. However, rumors of free love and miscegenation at Nashoba overshadowed the philanthropic aims of Frances Wright.

Frances Wright and her sister, Camilla, were orphaned at an early age and were reared by Jeremy Bentham, a former business associate of Robert Owen of New Lanark, Scotland. Frances was thoroughly schooled in the Benthamite utilitarian tradition and became a critic of the institutions of society which she thought perpetuated human misery. She held that monogamous marriage, as defined and upheld in society by the law, was one of man's worst institutions. In 1827, she wrote:

> There can, indeed, be nothing more anomalous or productive of greater misery than the laws which now regulate the relation between the sexes; a fictitious sanctity has been ascribed to the exercise of an unnatural restraint. In wedded life the woman sacrifices her independence, and becomes part of the property of her husband; affections are outraged by a union that cannot be dissolved when the heart is chilled; a connection, unhallowed by sacerdotal benediction, inflicts a crushing penalty on the woman, and brands with infamy the offspring of love.[1]

Frances Wright regarded marriage as an invention of religionists to assist them in maintaining a hold on every relationship in society.[2] She had not always viewed matrimony in such a dim light, and it was not until she met Robert Owen that her views changed regarding that institution. She admitted, upon coming to America and observing the position of women in the new world, that "Love at an early age gives place to domestic affection, and pleasure to domestic comfort; the sober happiness of married life is here found in perfection. Let the idler smile at this; it is assuredly the best of heaven's gifts to man." [3] A visit with Owen changed her attitude and her carpings thereafter about the degraded position of married women took on the sound of Owen's ridicule of marriage, even to the exact terminology. She came to regard women as slaves in the marital relationship, who by saying "I do" had placed themselves "in their tender, ignorant and unsuspecting youth, as completely at the disposal and mercy of an individual, as the negro slave who is bought for gold in the slave market of Kingston or New Orleans." [4]

Frances Wright was extremely distressed upon witnessing Negro slavery in America during her tour of the country with Lafayette in 1818. There was too much of the reformer in her to leave the institution untouched. During the tour she was also introduced to the idea of communal living. She visited the Rappite community at Harmony, Indiana, and several of the Shaker villages. George Rapp, in one of his sermons, complained that she visited Harmony for the purpose of spying on the society.[5] It was not Harmony which appealed to Frances, but Robert Owen's New Harmony, which later settled on the site of the Rappite village in Indiana. She saw in this experiment a method for effecting reform, including Negro emancipation and rehabilitation.

Frances Wright laid her plans before Lafayette for a utopian community in which Negroes, who were either purchased or donated, might be educated for responsible citizenship and relocated in a colony outside America as free people. Lafayette corresponded with Andrew Jackson and asked him to advise her about this "delicate but very interesting subject."[6] Frances Wright and George Fowler, the latter also an ardent emancipationist, visited Jackson at Nashville, Tennessee, and Old Hickory advised them to seek some land in the Chickasaw Purchase in West Tennessee which he had earlier sold. In October 1825 Frances Wright and Fowler went to Memphis, a newly incorporated town of 500, made friends with the new mayor, Marcus B. Winchester, and purchased nearly 2,000 acres of land traversed by a small creek. The stream was called Wolf Creek by the white settlers in the vicinity, but the Chickasaw word for wolf was "Nashoba," and Frances Wright chose the more romantic Indian name as the one for her bold experiment.

Nashoba was in time to incorporate all of Frances Wright's ideas regarding reform and what society should be. Women, as well as Negro slaves, were to be emancipated. There was to be no religion, no private property and no class distinctions. There was to be complete freedom and none was to be expelled for any reason whatsoever.[7] Frances Wright was, above all, an advocate of personal independence, and she inserted a provision for membership in Nashoba's bylaws to the effect that the admission of a husband or a wife did not automatically admit his or her spouse. Each was to be voted on individually. Unless a husband and wife were able to get along in harmony, there was no need for them to apply jointly for membership, as Nashoba was not to be a community for reconciling domestic incompatibility. Frances Wright insisted that "If there be introduced into such a society thoughts of evil and unkindness, feelings of intoleration and words of dissention [*sic*] it cannot prosper. That which produces in the world only commonplace jealousies and every day squabbles is sufficient to destroy a community." [8]

Frances Wright planned to bring together people from all nations who were sympathetic to her views. Slaves who were admitted were to purchase their freedom through labor for the community.[9] Once they had aided the community with their cooperative labor and had helped create a sufficient profit to pay for their transportation to Africa, they would be resettled on that continent. The idea was not altogether a new one, as the National Society for Colonization of Negroes had advocated a similar plan.

Frances Trollope visited Nashoba in 1827 and found only a small clearing in the forests with six or seven log cabins and thirty or forty slaves and their children, and an overseer who was reportedly suffering from malaria.[10] Richeson Whitby, an ex-Shaker, was the manager of the slaves, who took advantage of his gentle ways and did pretty much as they pleased. No whipping was allowed. The slaves exploited the opportunity to exercise their newly-found freedoms at Nashoba, the accounts of which were recorded by James Richardson and freely passed on to Benjamin Lundy, who published them in his paper, *Genius of Universal Emancipation*. Lundy, a sympathetic supporter of the Nashoba experiment, printed Richardson's accounts without editing them, which did little to help the cause of Frances Wright. One account concerning the sexual improprieties of the Negroes created a storm of protest against the experiment. It ran:

> Friday, June 1, 1827.
>
> Met the slaves at dinner time—Isabel had laid a complaint against Redrick, for coming during the night of Wednesday to her bedroom, uninvited and endeavoring without her consent, to take liberties with her person. Our views on the sexual relation had been repeatedly given to the slaves . . . that we consider the proper basis of sexual intercourse to be the unconstrained and unrestrained choice of *both parties*. Nelly having requested a lock for the door of the room in which she and Isabel sleep, with the view of preventing future uninvited entrance of any man, the lock was refused, as being, in its proposed use, inconsistent with the doctrine just explained; a doctrine we are determined to enforce and which will give to every woman a much greater security, than any lock can possibly do.[11]

An unidentified critic, who wrote Lundy under the pseudonym "Mentor," complained: "What is all this but the creation of one great brothal [*sic*] disgraceful to its institutions, and most reprehensible, as a public example in the vicinity." [12] Richardson's release of the news of the improprieties at Nashoba to the sympathetic Lundy was transparently honest, but unwise, for it did nothing for the community's public relations but to create further gossip about its operations.

Frances Wright was in Europe, seeking support for her Nashoba project, when these reports were being published. Her own published views of the marriage relation, coupled with the reports of free love at Nashoba, gave credence to the charge that she was an advocate of open fornication. In December 1827, on her return voyage to America, she did little to quiet the fears of those who observed the inner workings of her Tennessee enterprise. She published her "Explanatory Notes Respecting the Nature and Objects of the Institution of Nashoba," in which she further confirmed the rumor about the Nashoba orgies. She claimed:

> The marriage law existing without the pale of the institution [Nashoba] is of no force within that pale . . . . Let us not teach, that virtue consists in crucifying of the affections & appetites, but in their judicious government: Let us not attach ideas of purity to monastic chastity, impossible to man or to woman . . . . Let us enquire—not if a mother be a wife, or a father be a husband, but if parents can supply to the creatures they have brought into being all things requisite to make existence a blessing.[13]

Frances Wright let the world know that in her plan to educate Negroes for the responsibilities of freedom at Nashoba, she would teach them the virtues of sex out of wedlock.

Mademoiselle Lolotte, a free Negro from New Orleans, with her daughter, Josephine, joined Nashoba in May 1827, and was given the responsibility of caring for the children in the community. James Richardson was attracted to Josephine and the two shared the same bedroom. Richardson, not one to hide anything, reported to Benjamin Lundy the account of the miscegenation, and Lundy, as he had with Richardson's earlier reports, published it. The account ran: "Met the slaves—James Richardson informed them that last night, Mamsell [*sic*] Josephine and he began to live together; and he took this occasion of repeating to them our views on color, and on the sexual relation." [14] Negro women had been commonly accepted in the South as concubines, but Richardson's flagrant announcement of his decision to live openly with Josephine, and his subsequent lecture on Nashoba's "views on color, and on the sexual relation," created an additional furor. "Mentor" read the account in Lundy's paper and further inquired: "Is it possible that one of the trustees could shamelessly announce that he and one of the colored females had 'last night began to live together,' and this flagitiousness, announced to the community on Sunday evening, be solemnly entered on their records?" [15] Richardson replied to "Mentor's" inquiry, "I beg to inform you that the state of things at Nashoba is neither better nor worse than it is represented to be in the published records. They are correct." [16] Frances Wright defended miscegenation in her "Explanatory Notes:"

> The only question is, whether it shall take place in good taste and good feeling, & be made at once the means of sealing the tranquility & perpetuating the liberty of the country, and of peopling it with *a race more suited to its southern climate*, than the pure European,—or whether it shall proceed, as it does now, viciously and degrading, mingling hatred and fear with ties of blood-denial, indeed, but stamped by nature on the skin.[17]

The climate of Memphis proved unhealthy for Frances Wright and she was forced, in 1828, again to leave the Nashoba community to recuperate. Her sister, Camilla, who had always depended on Frances for counsel, married Richeson Whitby during Fanny's absence. Camilla, in spite of her sister's bitter statements regarding the servile position in monogamy, justified her marriage to Whitby on the ground that a lack of respect for the civil institutions of society would prejudice the public against Nashoba.[18] Robert Dale Owen, upon hearing of the marriage of Camilla, could only reply, "discouraging enough, certainly." [19] Soon after the birth of her baby Camilla left Nashoba and joined her sister in New York. The baby died shortly thereafter and Camilla never returned to her husband and Nashoba.

Conditions at Nashoba went from bad to worse and it is doubtful that the presence of Frances Wright would have staved off a collapse any longer. The community posed a financial drain on her resources and there were no immediate prospects that Nashoba would become self-supporting. In 1829 Fanny Wright decided to end the experiment. It is to her credit that she did not leave the Negroes stranded at Nashoba. On December 1, 1829, she chartered a ship and took them to Haiti. In November 1831 the property was returned to her by the trustees with the statement that she had emancipated her slaves and relocated them, and that "the individual circumstances of said trustees prevent them from carrying on any practical experiment for the benefit of the negro race on said property." [20]

Camilla and Frances Wright returned to France, where the former died in 1831. The following year, Frances countered her earlier pronouncements against matrimony and married Phiquepal d'Arusmont, who had conducted a small school at Owen's New Harmony community in Indiana. Robert Dale Owen described him as "a man well informed on many points, but withal a wrong-headed genius, whose extravagance, wilfulness, and inordinate self-conceit destroyed his usefulness." [21] Upon Fanny's marriage to d'Arusmont, she attempted to avoid being inconsistent with her earlier stated views on matrimony by insisting that her property remain in her name. The d'Arusmonts had two children, but only a daughter, Sylvia, survived infancy. Frances appeared reconciled to family life for the first four years of her marriage, but she afterward succumbed to the reformist urge and returned to America, leaving her husband and child in France. She championed women's rights and drew crowds on lecture tours and in a church building which she purchased in New York City and re-christened "The Hall of Science."

Married life was an anachronism for Fanny, and she asked her husband for a divorce. He wrote to her in response to her request,

> Your life was essentially an external life. You loved virtue deeply, but you loved also, and perhaps even more, grandeur and glory; and in your estimation . . . your husband and child ranked only as mere appendages to your personal existence . . . . You could not conceive that my daughter and myself should be anything but satellites revolving in your orbit. . . .[22]

Frances received a divorce in 1850 in the Circuit Court, Raleigh, Tennessee, the county seat of Shelby. She died the following year as a result of injuries sustained from a fall on the ice in Cincinnati, Ohio.

The Nashoba community failed in its initial objective to set a pattern for enlightened emancipation of Negro slaves. The ideas of Frances Wright on other reform issues which were injected into the community's operation after its establishment did nothing to assist the fulfillment of its original purpose. Attitudes toward marriage and complete freedom of thought and action only frustrated the Negroes at Nashoba, as they found themselves pushed further into the background. Although the concept of producing a more suitable race for the southern climate was a theoretical rationale for Richardson's relations with Josephine, Frances Wright never advanced a systemized plan for miscegenation at Nashoba. Such an arrangement would have been too slow and arduous for the impetuous Fanny Wright.

Josiah Warren, an associate of Frances Wright and Robert Owen at New Harmony, Indiana, was the most ardent advocate of free love in the utopian communal movement of the nineteenth century. Warren was responsible for the establishment of Equity, in Tuscarawas County, Ohio, in 1847, and Modern Times, on Long Island, New York, in 1851. After witnessing the collapse of the Owenite experiment in Indiana, Warren was convinced that a more fruitful attempt at communal living could be accomplished if the principles of "individual sovereignty" and "equitable commerce" were adopted. Warren interpreted "individual sovereignty" to mean peaceful anarchy without organizations, constitutions, laws, rules, or regulations, except what an individual made for himself and his own business. By "equitable commerce," Warren meant the issuance of labor notes in which one promised a certain amount of his labor in exchange for needed articles which he was not able to produce himself. At Modern Times these two principles found their fullest expression. "Every man and every woman," Warren told a visitor, "has a perfect and inalienable right to do and perform, all and singular, just exactly as he or she may choose, now and hereafter." [23] There was no exchange of money at Modern Times, but each was allowed to establish the rate of exchange for his own labor. Manufactured articles were sold outside the community to enable the members to purchase what the community was unable to produce.

The complete lack of rules within Modern Times attracted many people to it and gave the community a reputation as a den of iniquity. *The New York Tribune* ran an advertisement in 1853 which urged people to join the associationists at Modern Times and promised them that no pledges would be required and no one would be asked to submit to any regulations.[24] Adin Ballou wrote about two adulterers who were expelled from his Hopedale community and who went to Modern Times, "where they undoubtedly found congenial companionship, and unbridled liberty to carry their doctrines out to the farthest possible limit, with no one to question or reproach them, or say them nay." [25]

Warren asked no questions of the couples who took up residence at his settlement, as this would have been a violation of his revered principle of individual sovereignty. He explained:

> When two people—a man and a woman—come into the fold of Modern Times . . . no-body stops to inquire if aid has been solicited of those impertinent 'Laws' [of ordinary society] whereby they may be enabled to occupy the same domicile, and sleep under the same counterpane, without reproach or scandal to themselves or to those around them. A man may have two wives, or a woman two husbands, or a dozen each, for aught I care . . . everybody has a perfect right to do everything.[26]

Rumors of the practice of free love were freely spread and each official pronouncement by Warren and his associates confirmed the worst possible suspicions. Adin Ballou published the account of one who he claimed was unwittingly induced to move to Modern Times and live with those "peculiar people," which was typical of the tirades against Warren and his community. Ballou wrote:

> There is a lurking combination among the leaders to do away entirely with the name and essence of marriage and to introduce instead an open and respectful sanction of promiscuous co-habitation. They not only cut the bonds of legality and set at nought the proprieties of custom, but they also scout the idea of constancy in love, and ridicule the sensitiveness of one who refuses to barter connubialities. Wife with them is synonymous with slave and monogamy is denounced as a *vicious monopoly of affections*.[27]

Warren denied that the license at Modern Times gave anyone the right to take advantage deliberately of another and to spoil the peaceful arrangement between a husband and his wife. Unlike John Humphrey Noyes, he did not attempt to break up exclusive arrangements or to establish an organized system of pantagamy. "We don't steal *anything*," Warren asserted, "not our neighbor's ox . . . nor his wife, nor his niece, nor his daughter, nor his sister; that would be interfering with the sovereignty of the individual. But if we can make a fair compact—an amicable agreement, where all parties will be rendered more happy—who shall, or should complain?"[28] Wife swapping was perfectly legitimate at Modern Times, and a few took advantage of the opportunity.

The Modern Times community was dissipated in the panic of 1857, as their limited industries were unable to survive the economic distresses, which were particularly hard on northeastern manufacturing. But the idea of individual sovereignty, which permitted an assault on the sanctity of monogamy, did not die with the demise of the Long Island commune. Other communities afterward shared in the infamy of free love and each doing his own thing. In Benton County, Arkansas, a small group of anarchists, consisting of ten men and seven women, settled, in 1860, on a 500-acre tract and proclaimed themselves The Harmonial Vegetarian Society. They were dubbed by their neighbors as "the grass eaters," since they were strict vegetarians. Their diet would have caused little alarm, but their practice of free love was more than the ante-bellum Arkansans were willing to tolerate. Reports were circulated that members of the society had renounced all marriage ties and periodically chose partners by lot for cohabitation purposes.[29] J. E. Spencer, a self-styled physician and leader of the community, was attacked by angry neighbors in 1861 and was forced to flee for his life. The coming of the Civil War ended the community's life. Confederate soldiers entered the village and took possession of the crude buildings, which consisted of a community house, machine shop, saw and grist mills, a blacksmith shop, a general store, and a printing office, which housed the presses of their official organ, *The Theocrat*.

The economic cooperatives which came into vogue in the latter part of the nineteenth century were often charged with practicing free love, but the charges were usually nothing more than unfounded rumors spread by unsympathetic neighbors. Alexander Kent, in his investigation of the cooperatives on behalf of the United States Department of Labor, discovered that the Mutual Home community, founded in 1896 in the state of Washington, allowed the same type of individual sovereignty in sexual matters that was permitted at Josiah Warren's Modern Times. His report also revealed that two members had left the community at the time of his investigation because they did not approve of freedom in love which allegedly was advocated there.[30]

Some of the most unusual sexual practices associated with the utopian communities during the nineteenth century in America were almost wholly without sociological justification but stemmed from the fertile imaginations of religious fanatics. Sex was deified and orgies were periods of worship and adoration. Elaborate networks of esoteric theology were developed which gave sanction to the expression of physical passions outside of legal wedlock.

Thomas Lake Harris was the most notorious of the utopian architects who worshiped at the altar of sex. Harris was an ex-Universalist minister who found a kindred spirit in James L. Scott, an ex-Seventh Day Baptist preacher, and together they founded the Mountain Cove community in Fayette County, Virginia, in 1851. Mountain Cove was declared by Harris and Scott to be the actual site of the biblical Garden of Eden. About 100 individuals committed their lives and fortunes to the care and protection of the two, whom they regarded as God's mediums. They expected an imminent return of Jesus Christ and prepared themselves to reign with him eternally in the restored paradise. The project folded within a year; Harris moved to Dutchess County, New York, and took with him a remnant of the community, whom he organized into the Brotherhood of the New Life. In 1865 the brotherhood moved to Chautauqua County, New York, where Harris had purchased 1,600 acres of land and on which he had established the Brocton community, or Salem on Erie.

At Brocton Harris developed a strange theology, a mixture of Spiritualism, Swedenborgianism, and Oriental mysticism. He believed that God was not merely male or female, but the two in one.[31] The pivot of faith which supplied the directive force of the lives of the members of Brocton was "the doctrine of the Divine-human Two-in-One, in whose individual and social likeness, and in whose spiritual and physical likeness" they sought to be reborn.[32] Each mortal has a celestial counterpart, according to Harris, and in order to be as the gods, one must seek an affinity with his heavenly mate. It was through an entrance into conjugal love with his counterpart that one found ultimate bliss and confirmation of his status as being among the elect. It was also through the agency of the Lily Queen, the female counterpart of God, that nuptial arrangements were made.

Harris maintained that ordinary marriages in the world were not based on the counterpart theory, since no one could be certain that his counterpart dwelled within the body of his spouse.[33] Civil marriages were to be honored at Brocton until a member attained a spiritual status which would supersede all legal attachments in the world and introduce him into eternal, conjugal love. In attaining this state, one must then forgo the pleasures of sexual intercourse until it was made a sacrament of the Bridal World.[34] Harris insisted that those who continued to live together as husband and wife in the community must be purely platonic in their relationships.

There was no attempt to segregate the sexes at Brocton, as there had been in the celibate Shaker and German pietistic societies. Harris believed that those who were thoroughly converted to his doctrines would need no artificial barriers and restraints in order to compel them to live godly lives. For this reason he was very cautious about accepting new members, particularly attractive women. Harris explained that "Ladies whom we have every reason to esteem, as upright by intention and virtuous by conduct, ask to enter into closer association with our people; but we do not receive them: we know not what they are, in these last hours of an old race, when sorceresses walk the world." [35]

The world of Harris was one of fairies, which he called "fays." Mortal men are not able to see the fairies because God took away that potential of sight called "natural-aromal" when man fell from the Garden of Eden. But if the human body could become "demagnetized from the poisonous injections of the Infernal Demons," one could hear the melodious voices of the fays, "responding, with a faint, exquisite music, to the high and holy inspiration of the Divine Love." [36] The fairies were the children of the nuptial relations of the Lily Queen and they established tiny kingdoms within the bosoms of the women at Brocton. Harris claimed that within the feminine breasts the fairies

> become visible, and glide at will into and out from the interior planes of the spiritual form. They delight in the endearments of conjugal associates, and sometimes single out a married pair upon the orderly earths, and, like sportive, seriform children, they hive themselves within the wifely bosom, being found as well with her beloved counterpart. Those who inhabit the left feminine breast are called kings and queens, because they correspond to the truths of Divine Love, and live in a pure, ambrosial existence in the midst of sweet, blossoming affections of the inner life. Those in the right feminine breast are called priests and priestesses, because they are preeminently in

the good of Divine Truth. There are corresponding pairs in each bosom.[37]

The women of Brocton, who were attracted to Harris' strange theology, reported their discoveries of the miniature kingdom within them. One spinster declared:

> I heard the strange little noises in my breast, and everything there all day long has seemed to be in a flutter, as if little wings were moving, and something keeps singing to me, In your breast love will build his nest. I cannot even write this without the tears filling my eyes. Everytime I wake at night or in the morning, I always feel flowing into my body my counterpart. Wonderfully beautiful it all is, and beyond imagination to have someone inside of you. I scarcely know what to call it . . . Angel, husband, friend, or lover. 'Sweet my sweet, my own dear wife,' 'tis what he says, 'call me love and husband ever.' I kiss my hands for very joy when love's own life is in them.[38]

Although the members at Brocton were to refrain from having sexual intercourse, they feverishly sought to find the heavenly counterparts in the physical bodies of the members of the opposite sex. Harris spurred them forward in the search with his constant flow of erotic poetry. One of his poems, which described the community's search for counterparts, explained:

> Here shall Hymen have his court,
> And every priest & Cupid be,
> Till golden babes are born to sport,
> Where lift the waves of Mother-Glee.[39]

In order to assist members in their search, Harris instituted a "Luminous Year," at the beginning of which all former marriages were annulled and each member was demagnetized of all evil. New marriages were solemnized. The women were married first to Harris, and then to their hopeful counterpart. The men were married to the Lily Queen and then to their hopeful counterpart. Counterparts were elusive and skipped about from one human body to another, so that no one was certain in whose body his counterpart might reside at the moment. A man's female counterpart might inhabit his body and the body of a woman in the community. In such cases, individuals who were thus inhabited were at liberty to commune bodily, short of sexual intercourse, with one another. If at the same time the woman's counterpart had inhabited her body and the body of still another man in the community, she was also at liberty to seek a bodily communion with him. The result was an orgy which might set off a chain reaction and affect every member of the community, depending, of course, on the activity of the celestial counterparts. Hannah Whitall Smith was reportedly informed by Jane Waring, future wife of Thomas Lake Harris, about the procedure of bodily communion in seeking an affinity with the Lily Queen. She related the following account:

> The troubled soul was to go to Mr. Harris's room and get into bed with Lily Queen. 'But what becomes of Mr. Harris?' asked Miss X. 'Oh, Lily Queen is inside of the Father, and consequently he, of course, stays in bed, and by getting into his arms we get into her arms.' [40]

The exploitation and enjoyment of this type of contact with members of the opposite sex became an obsession with Harris. He was constantly surrounded by women; yet he repeatedly maintained that he was a celibate. He legally married three successive women but claimed that the last two relationships at Brocton were purely platonic.[41] Laurence Oliphant, one of Harris' converts at Brocton, affirmed that he slept with his arms around his beautiful wife, Alice, for twelve years without having intercourse with her.[42] Oliphant admitted that he later had a nervous breakdown, which his physician ascribed to his prolonged continence. He married Robert Dale Owen's daughter, Rosamond, after the death of Alice, and, although she was in sympathy with most of Harris' peculiar theories, she could not altogether restrain her normal sexual passions. Rosamond admitted that during the four months of their marriage, while Oliphant was slowly dying of lung cancer, they had sexual intercourse on several occasions, always as a sacred rite and with prayer.[43]

Rumors of sexual orgies at Brocton were spread, mainly by members who left the community and by hired hands and servants employed in the colony. The neighbors of Brocton were aroused and threatened to break up the community. Robert Martin, a former member and critic of Harris, came to Brocton's defense. He wrote that "If ever there was a strait-laced, God fearing band of men and women, it was that first handful of earnest souls who were led to believe that they, under the guidance of Harris, were to lead the world into the land where there was neither sin nor sorrow, neither suffering nor death." [44] But the neighbors believed otherwise and pressures mounted against the community. Harris, unwilling to become a martyr as had Joseph Smith at Nauvoo, chose to take the same course as did John Humphrey Noyes at Oneida, and flee for his life. In 1875 he and a few of his loyal followers went to California and established another colony after the order of Brocton, which they called Fountain Grove. His hegira was rationalized through his claim that the Lily Queen wanted a new home where she could enjoy the flowers year round.[45]

At Fountain Grove Harris thought it best to divide the sexes into separate living quarters. The men were placed in the "Commandery," and the women in the "Familistery." A few exceptions were made for those families who preferred to live separately, but always with the provision that husbands and wives would deny themselves the right of conjugal relations. Not all were able to observe strict continence and Harris was forced to admit in 1877 that five children had been born to the members of the brotherhood. Harris, as did John Humphrey Noyes, broke up exclusive attachments which interfered with the full development of the communal spirit. He sensed that Laurence Oliphant's attachment to his wife, Alice, was not in the best interest of the community, and he took her with him to Fountain Grove and left Oliphant behind at Brocton. In time this action precipitated a rupture between the two men which was never healed.

Regardless of the precautions taken by Harris to prevent a repetition of scandalous rumors which had forced his flight from Brocton, Fountain Grove was the target of righteous indignation from the California neighbors. He was accused of making improper advances toward some ot the young ladies. One man, who left the community in disgust, claimed Harris had molested his daughter. Alzire Chevailler, a Christian Scientist and a suffragette, joined Fountain Grove in 1891 and left after Harris allegedly made advances toward her. She related her story to the editor of *The San Francisco Chronicle*, and a lengthy article appeared in the paper on June 11, 1891, which revealed to the public the sexual irregularities at Fountain Grove. Harris abandoned the community in the midst of threats, married his secretary, Jane Waring, and left for Europe never to return. John Humphrey Noyes' assessment of Harris' esoteric sexual theory was not altogether without validity. Noyes claimed that a utopian community "is a worse place than ordinary society for working out the delicate problems of the negative theory of chastity." [46]

Fact or rumor, the strangest case on record associated with utopian community-building experiments involved one Cyrus Spragg, a religious fanatic who was expelled from the Mormon Church in the middle of the nineteenth century.[47] Spragg allegedly established a community at New Jerusalem, Illinois. He had earlier established a nudist colony in Michigan, which fell victim to cold weather and irate neighbors. Spragg and his followers next appeared at Cairo, Illinois, where he ordered the construction of an ark according to the dimensions of Noah's craft recorded in the Book of Genesis. He told them that there would be a deluge and the only means of survival would be the ark. The rains came, as predicted, and the Mississippi and Ohio rivers at Cairo overran their banks, but the water never reached the ark. Undaunted by having failed in his prediction, Spragg moved his colony north to New Jerusalem and ordered the construction of a temple and an ecclesiastical palace, as King Solomon had done during his reign over the Israelites. Upon completion of the edifice Spragg told his followers that he was going to enter the temple and there spend eternity in repose and meditation while he continued to direct them as "The Eternal and Invisible Presence."

Spragg allowed no one in the temple but virgins, who were to serve him and to carry forth his revelations to the community. One of his alleged revelations concerned the birth of a Messiah to a virgin of the community. Spragg did not designate the virgin, but ordered that a different one come to him each night with the promise that one of them would become the modern Madonna. He received the virgins in total darkness, as he claimed no one was permitted to look upon the face of the "Invisible Presence."

A postman from Kentucky, who delivered mail to the New Jerusalem community, fell in love with Eliza Weatherby, one of the virgins who had been summoned to the temple by Cyrus Spragg. In a jealous fit, the mailman broke into the temple, fired three shots, and fled. The report soon spread that "God is dead," but Spragg's loyal followers refused to believe it. None dared enter the temple. The following day, the virgin whose turn it was to go into the temple to serve the "Invisible Presence" entered while the community members waited breathlessly for her report. She emerged from the temple and reported that Spragg was very much alive. She carried a "revelation" from the "Invisible Presence," which read: "Fear not my people. Thy God is immortal." [48]

Several months passed until one day Spragg's daughter-in-law publicly accused her husband, Obadiah, and his brother, Jared Spragg, of taking turns sneaking into the temple and having intercourse with the virgins in the darkness of the sanctuary. "It took two of them to fill the place of the Prophet," she allegedly cried, "one wasn't good enough." [49] Four members of the community decided to settle the matter once and for all, and entered the temple amid the cries of "Sacrilege!" from Obadiah and Jared. After an hour they emerged from the temple with the news that it was empty, there was no "Invisible Presence." Obadiah claimed that his father had been taken to heaven in a chariot of fire, but no one would believe him. Without its charismatic leader, the community lost its purpose for being and collapsed. Fact or rumor, the case of Cyrus Spragg must take its place in the catalog of nineteenth-century utopian communities in America as the most bizarre.

Strange sexual practices in utopian communities were initiated by religious fanatics rather than by radical socialists, although the latter were generally charged with undermining the nation's morals. There were a few isolated cases where liberal communitarians advocated free love. Usually the free love practices were limited to but a few cases in the socialistic communities and involved only a few members. However, in the communities organized by fanatically religious cults, there was a concerted effort on the part of all members to engage in sexual variations conceived by their leaders and imposed as mandatory in order to conform to the communities' stated ideals. The religious communal architects expressed their own fears and urges in their dogmas and made them the dominant theme for all to accept. Once a sexual practice was shrouded in an esoteric theology, it was made a duty and a condition for salvation. The community leader was indispensable for at no time did a colony perpetuate a sexual practice more than a year or two after its leader departed. The psychological motive, often unrealized, which drew people to these communities, was more of an attraction to the man who headed the movement than to the prospects of satisfying unbridled passions with members of the opposite sex. Puritanical morals based on social orthodoxy had to be neutralized before one could conscientiously engage in the free range of sexual experiences afforded in community life, and intricate networks of theological systems gave community members the divine sanction which they needed to impel them to go counter to their former moral training.

XIV

Women's Rights in Utopian Communities

COMMUNAL EXPERIMENTS OF THE NINETEENTH CENTURY WERE FORCED to make concessions to women, as they could not long survive without the support of that vital segment of human society. Women, for the most part, were less inclined toward communism than were the men. The satisfying relationship, or even the prospect of it, between a wife and her husband and children was not easily sacrificed by women in favor of the communal system in which these ties were either weakened or altogether abolished. The literature of the period was filled with appeals to women to unite in a larger family relationship of communities where economic security and social equality were promised. Relief from the burdensome duties of endless housekeeping chores and perpetual care of children were incentives which were attractive to only a few independent feminine spirits. Usually the women in utopian communities were not there of their own volition, but were forced into the novel societies by the decisions of their husbands, who were unable to find happiness within the normal social order. Utopian communities for such couples were no more than hopeful rehabilitation centers for marriages gone awry.

Monogamous familism in ordinary society assigned the women a role which was more in keeping with their maternal instincts. American women were taught at an early age to be efficient wives and mothers, as this was God's intended will for womankind. Utopian communities which abolished familism countered their previous training and their adjustment to communal life was not easy to accept. The paltry benefits of uncertain equality were little recompense to women whose fulfillment in life appeared thwarted. The oppressive conditions of women in ordinary society were thoroughly exposed by zealots who were bent on a renovation of the world. In their rhetoric they often glossed over the contentment which most wives and mothers had found around their family firesides. Here they felt wanted and needed. The uncertainties of independence often created a vacuum in the lives of communal women which frustrations rushed in to fill.

Feminists generally found a measure of relief from their frustrations in those communities which gave them the liberty to fully express themselves. Margaret Fuller and Frances Wright discovered the communal settings perfectly adapted to bolster their egos. They were at the zenith of their mission when captive auditors patiently listened to them and nodded approval, and when the community organs were used to propagate their ideas. But both Margaret and Fanny were pathetic creatures in search of fulfillment in life and eventually bowed to the urge to marry and bear children, thereby contradicting by their actions their earlier tirades against marriage.

The rights of women in the celibate communities were usually in advance of those of their counterparts in ordinary society. In the Rappite communities, women had rights which Frances Wright and Robert Owen championed a quarter of a century later, and even some rights for which the current feminist movement is pleading. Women there, as early as 1807, had the right to vote in community affairs, to receive equal pay for equal work, and certainly the right, as well as the duty, to refuse to have intercourse with their husbands. Since the Harmonists guaranteed a livelihood for women in their communities, they were not bound by economic necessity to live with their husbands. Divorce was not only permissible among the Rappites, but sometimes encouraged.[1]

Women enjoyed equality in the Shaker villages, although the Society of Friends was by no means democratic. A basic tenet of Mother Ann Lee's theology was that with the coming of Christ in female form, i.e., in the person of Ann Lee, women were no longer subordinate to men, as the penalty for Eve's transgression had been removed.[2] In the government of each Shaker village an equal number of offices was held by both sexes. However, this was due more to necessity than to ideology, since women officeholders were needed to control the affairs of their own sex, which could not be entrusted to the men. Although women held equal rank with men in the government of the Shaker community, there were certain "manly" occupations from which they were barred. Elder Frederick W. Evans explained that "in general life the woman's work is in the house, the man's out of doors; and there is no reason to confuse the two." [3]

The sectarian utopias which maintained familism did not seek to elevate women to a position beyond that in ordinary society. At Amana, women were denied an opportunity to voice their opinions on any issue affecting the policy of the community, except on rare occasions when they were "inspired" of God and were thus regarded as belonging to the elite *Werkzeuge*. Otherwise they were to be in complete subjection to the men. They ate at separate tables and kept to themselves. They were not mistreated by any means. All work in which they engaged was carefully apportioned to their feminine strength. If they had children under two years of age, they were not required to engage in any work outside their homes and their meals were brought to them in a basket from the nearest kitchen.[4] When the children reached the age of two, they were cared for in a common nursery in order to give the mothers freedom to work outside the home.

The Mormons made no pretense of championing women's rights. Their system of polygyny was maintained partly because the women were under complete subjection to the men. The husband was both lord and master of his household. Brigham Young once stated that "If I did not consider myself competent to transact a certain business without taking my wife's or any woman's counsel with regard to it, I think I ought to let that business alone." [5] The outspoken Heber Kimball, in one of his sermons in the Salt Lake City Tabernacle, stated, "It is the duty of a woman to be obedient to her husband, and unless she is, I would not give a damn for all her queenly right or authority, nor for her either." [6] John D. Lee related how he treated his sixteen wives when they attempted to rebel against his authority:

> It is not a woman's place to council [*sic*] the Husband & the moment a man follows a woman he is led astray & will go down to

Hell unless he retracts his steps. I could have perfect Hell with my wives were I to listen to them, but when ever [*sic*] one begans [*sic*] to strut & lead out, I say go it & show your wisdom & soon she gets ashamed & curls down.[7]

In 1856 some of the polygynous wives revolted against their husbands' authority and Brigham Young was compelled to set them straight from the pulpit on their responsibilities. He told the women who complained over the hardships they had to bear in the polygynous households that he would give them two weeks to reflect on their state and to decide for themselves whether or not they wished to remain in Mormondom. If they decided they could no longer bear up under the strain of sharing their husbands, he promised to give them their freedom. If they chose to remain, he exhorted them to "round up your shoulders to endure the afflictions of this world and live your religion." [8] He vowed there would be no more "scratching and fighting," and that he would set all of them at liberty, whether they wanted it or not, if they did not stop it. He concluded the sermon by thundering: "Sisters, I am not joking!" The women evidently submitted to their husbands' rule, as there were no accounts of any of them leaving. But Young's sermon did not bring an end to the complaints of the women. Juanita Brooks, whose parents were children of polygynous households, claimed that her mother harbored ill feelings toward her father, not because he had more than one wife, but because she felt that he mistreated them.[9] Fanny Stenhouse, who shared her husband with other wives for a brief time, claimed that "Never, until new hearts and new natures are given to the women of Utah, and all that is womanly, and pure, and sacred, is crushed out from their souls, can one single woman be truly happy in Polygamy." [10]

The reformist utopians of the nineteenth century proposed to emancipate the women who joined their communities. They were promised economic independence from their husbands, and the right to share in the decision-making process of their communities. They were often promised relief from the household chores and the perpetual care and training of their children. They were guaranteed an equal education with the men, and in some communities no distinction of sex was to be made regarding occupations.

The Owenites promised women equality, and at New Harmony no distinction was made on the basis of sex in the enjoyment of rights and privileges. Frances Wright was attracted to New Harmony, where she founded the Woman's Social Society, in 1826, the first fully organized woman's club in America. Robert Owen was in full sympathy with the work of Fanny as regards sexual equality. In his debate with Alexander Campbell, in 1829, he outlined "a new state of existence," where "men and women will be equally well educated . . . will have the same rights and privileges and . . . will associate on terms of intimacy through their lives with those only for whom they cannot avoid feeling the most regard and greatest affection." [11] Owen attempted to shield the women at New Harmony in order to give them the fullest opportunity to express themselves in their newly-found freedoms. He insisted that "There must be . . . no anger . . . against the female members upon their aversion to the work of cooperation; or when they brawl, quarrel, or indulge in loud talk." [12]

Robert Dale Owen, son of New Harmony's founder, took up the cause of women's rights and carried it to the Indiana Constitutional Convention in 1850. Although he was an avowed believer in woman suffrage, he did not press that issue in the convention, for he realized that the delegates were not prepared to accept this bold measure at that early date. He passed over the issue by declaring that he did not wish to enter into the inquiry of whether or not women should vote.[13] His primary concern in the convention was to liberalize that state's laws regarding the property rights of women. In a very moving speech, which reportedly had a profound effect on the assembly of delegates, Robert Dale Owen set forth the plight of married women and widows under existing state laws. He mourned:

> Suppose she had laid by in her trunk,—the same trunk, perhaps, in which her mother had packed . . . on her daughter's marriage day, the little property she had given her,—suppose that the wife had laid by in that trunk a few dollars, hardly and bitterly earned, . . . to furnish clothing for her children against the inclemency of the winter. And suppose (alas! how often is the case a real one), suppose that drunken husband comes home in the evening; breaks open the trunk and carries off the money; is that larceny? Has he stolen? By no means. He broke into his own trunk; he took—so the law declares—his own money.[14]

He proceeded to call on the convention to incorporate into the new constitution a provision which would guarantee a woman the right to own and control property. The convention heeded the plea and inserted the provision:

> That women hereafter married in this state shall have the right to acquire and possess property to their sole use and disposal; and that laws shall be passed, securing to them, under equitable conditions, all property, real and personal, whether owned by them before marriage, or acquired afterwards, by purchase, gift, device or descent, and also providing for the registration of the wife's separate property.[15]

The principles which had been advocated in the utopian community at New Harmony, some twenty-five years before, were firmly affixed in the laws of the state of Indiana, and became a model for the other states to emulate. The women of Indiana, in appreciation of Robert Dale Owen's contribution to their welfare, presented him with an engraved silver pitcher and placed a bust of their benefactor in the entrance hall of the state capitol building in Indianapolis, which remains to this day.

The Fourierists also advocated emancipation and equality of women. Fourier, in fact, is credited with having coined the term "feminism." Charles Gide called him "the first 'feminist' in the sense of absolute equality of the sexes, not only before the law, but before morality." [16] Fourier claimed that in the initial stages of evolving humanity, there had been free love, equality of women, and the general happiness of all. But man embarked on a period of savagery and barbarism and made woman his servant. Monogamy was then instituted as a rationale for man's selfish desire to keep woman in bondage.[17] Fourier believed that the legal, social, and economic position of women in any country was an exact measure of that nation's true civilization, and that it was his mission to elevate Western civilization.

The Owenites had their Frances Wright, and the Fourierists had their Margaret Fuller, each of whom called for the abolition of every barrier that separated men and women in the exercise of the natural rights of the latter. Margaret Fuller, who wrote *Women in the Nineteenth Century*, in 1845, pointed up the inequities of the social arrangement which made women no more than men's handmaidens. The work was even bolder than Frances Wright had ever dared to be in her writings and speeches. Margaret Fuller blamed marriage and the relationship between the sexes as the prime cause for woman being the peculiar property of man, "instead of forming a whole with him." [18] Horace Greeley, Fourierism's greatest advertiser, published the book, which was intended to inspire American women to rise up *en masse* and demand their rights. Greeley did not altogether share Margaret Fuller's views regarding the emancipation of women. Although he did not dispute the mental capacity of women, he did insist that a wife ought to yield a general and cordial, though not servile, deference to her husband.[19] At that, he could tolerate Margaret Fuller more than he could Frances Wright. He referred to the latter's rhetoric as "the belchings of Fanny Wright." [20] All in all, the Fourierists were grateful to Margaret Fuller and her book, since the innermost thoughts of women were brought to the surface, and such gave credence to the issues to which the disciples of Fourier had addressed themselves.

The North American Phalanx took the lead among the Fourieristic settlements in providing women with equal rights. Not only were the women there permitted to participate in policy making, but they received equal pay with men for their work and all occupations were opened to them. Fredrika Bremer, on her visit to the phalanx in 1852, remarked that "All the women . . . have the right to speak in public assemblies, but none avail themselves of the right but they who have talent for it, or who have something good to say. Thoughtfulness and gentleness are the distinguishing features of these free women." [21]

The Sylvania Phalanx did not grant equal pay to women for equal work. For some unexplained reason, the pay scale differential was set so that the women received five-eighths of the wages paid to men for the same jobs.[22] Some additional compensations were made to the women; they were permitted to vote on issues affecting the community when they reached the age of eighteen. The men could not vote until they were twenty years of age.

Feminism was a popular topic at Brook Farm. Margaret Fuller visited the community frequently and captivated her audiences with talks on the elevation of womanhood. A group of women formed a small enterprise within the colony for the expressed purpose of "the elevation of woman to independence, and an acknowledged equality with the men." [23] They manufactured caps, capes, collars, and undersleeves, which they sent to the Hutchinson and Holmes Company in New York for distribution. The women at Brook Farm held no important offices in the organization of the community. Sophia and Marianne Ripley did share with Charles Dana the supervisory job over the children's education, but only men served as directors in all other facets of administration. Since the men greatly outnumbered the women at Brook Farm, it was not altogether from the principle of equality that they joined in the domestic chores of washing dishes and doing the laundry.

In the independent communities women enjoyed equal status with men. The Icarians particularly exalted the position of women. Cabet, in his imaginary utopia, placed women on a pedestal. Men were required to render special acts of homage to the women, but there is no evidence that this was ever carried out in the actual Icarian experiments in communal living. Females were given the same social rights as males. Cabet claimed that the Icarians at Nauvoo regarded it their primary interest and duty to insure the happiness of women.[24] Men deferred to women in sharing foods that were scarce. The scanty supply of milk was poured into coffee pots and served only to the women. Women were not required to work more than four hours per day during the winter months, while their husbands worked seven. The women also retired from communal labors at the age of fifty, while their husbands were not permitted to retire until they were sixty-five. Unlike most of the independent communities, there were no nurseries in the Icarian village to care for the children of working mothers.

The economic cooperatives championed women's rights. William Weitling, at Communia in Iowa, called for women to be given all the rights to which they were naturally entitled and capable. He was cautious about giving them the opportunity to take part in the policy-making decisions for the community, but he was unwilling to risk having his reform program altered or restrained by the whims of women, since he believed they were more individualistic than men and not naturally disposed toward communism.[25]

The Kaweah colony in California did not share Communia's fear that women would thwart the aims of communal living. The community's bylaws gave males and females alike the right to vote on all issues, and guaranteed them equal pay for equal work. In order to assure complete independence of the women, the sexes were financially independent of each other.[26]

Women at Modern Times, in addition to enjoying sexual freedoms without censure, had rights and privileges which were not accorded their counterparts in ordinary society. They had the same right as men to set a price on their labor which was equal to, or even above, that which was set by the men.[27]

Women's rights were of particular concern to John Humphrey Noyes at Oneida. Monogamy and excessive childbearing, according to him, had made slaves of American women and they were as much entitled to emancipation in the ante-bellum years as the Negro slaves on Southern plantations. He did not regard women as equal to men in all matters, like some feminists of his day, but he did see to it that women served on all of the committees at Oneida. However, he asserted that in the fellowship between the sexes, "man is naturally the superior." [28] Charles Nordhoff, during his visit to Oneida, observed that, as far as he could tell, the women were inferior to the men.[29] Noyes believed that women should be given equal opportunities and he made few distinctions between women's work and men's work at Oneida. Women were emancipated from the responsibility of perpetual housekeeping and child care, and were permitted to labor alongside the men in the community enterprises. One female member at Oneida declared:

> Communism gives woman, without a claim from her, the place which every true woman most desires, as the free and honored companion of man. Communism emancipates her from the slavery and corroding cares of a mere wife and mother; stimulates her to seek the improvement of mind and heart that will make her worthy of a higher place than ordinary society can give her. Freed from forced maternity, a true and holy desire for children grows in her heart. Here no woman's hand is red with the blood of innocents, as is whispered so often of many of her sisters in bondage. Gradually, as by natural growth, the Community women have risen to a position where, in labors, in mind, and in heart, they have all and more than all that is claimed by the women who are so loudly asserting their rights. And through it all they have not ceased to love and honor the truth that 'the man is the head of the woman,' and that woman's highest, God-given right is to be 'the glory of the man.' [30]

Women also had economic independence at Oneida, as they did not have to depend for their well-being on one man's uncertain fortunes. Their bodies belonged to them and they exercised the fullest liberty in the choice of sexual experiences without fear of scandal or resignation to prostitution. Oneida women who joined the community with their husbands had two rights which were fully sanctioned by the community and which were generally denied to women in ordinary society: they could refuse to honor their husband's request for sexual relations; and they could join in a mutual criticism session and tell them of their faults, which they may have longed to do for many years.

Women's dress in several utopian communities was a symbol of newly-found freedoms. Robert Owen attempted to impose a uniform of black and white striped cotton on the women at New Harmony, but without success.[31] His purpose was to establish equality among the women, and not to conceal their feminine features. Women in the Fourieristic communities frequently adopted the bloomer costume, which was the current style of the feminists. Macdonald observed at the North American Phalanx that the costume was no more than a shortened dress, about the same length as Scottish kilts, beneath which the women wore men's trousers.[32] French gowns, laces, and diamonds were taboo in the Fourieristic communities. They were regarded as useless trappings of the society which they wished to reform. The vanity of the women at Brook Farm was not altogether subdued by the adoption of Fourierism. In keeping with their philosophy regarding the natural man, the women selected wild vines and berries from the woods and entwined them in their hair.[33] Some of the women at Modern Times chose to wear the bloomer costume. Josiah Warren claimed that they had the privilege of wearing breeches if they wanted to.[34]

The dress of Oneida women was in keeping with their ideas regarding feminine liberation. Noyes was opposed to the current fashions, which made them appear like churns moving about on casters, and which covered up their most comely parts, that is, their legs. The Oneida costume, trousers and a short, tight fitting dress, was designed mainly for convenience and to allow freedom of exercise. William Hepworth Dixon admitted that "a plain woman escapes notice, and a pretty girl looks bewitching" while wearing the costume.[35] Nordhoff did not particularly care for the outfit, as it was, in his words, "totally lacking in grace and beauty," and so scant that it forbade the "graceful arrangement of drapery." [36] The Oneida women cut their hair short and parted it like the men, mainly as a time-saving measure and to avoid the appearance of vanity. Extravagant hats were forbidden, and if a woman wore a hat at all, it was usually of simple straw construction and served the purpose of protecting her from the rays of the sun. Dress adornment was equally simple, usually no more than a breast pin. The women made no effort to outdo one another in fashions, as that would have been contrary to the principle of equality in all things, on which the Oneida community was founded. If a woman spent too much time on her personal appearance, she was censured in a mutual criticism session. One young lady was severely reprimanded because she spent too much time before the mirror primping to attract the men.[37]

Most feminists of the nineteenth century preferred to move within the circles of ordinary society rather than confine their activities to the limits of a utopian community. Susan B. Anthony, Elizabeth Cady Stanton, and Lucretia Mott, three of the century's most ardent protagonists for feminine equality, had no affiliation, except through casual acquaintances, with communal projects.

Epilogue

AMERICAN UTOPIAN COMMUNITIES IN THE NINETEENTH CENTURY failed, for the most part, in their objectives, although they attracted some of the best minds and energies of Europe and America. It appeared that America was ideally suited for social experimentation; this appraisal accounted for the proliferation of communal experiments, which occurred nowhere else in the world on the scale that it did in this country. An infant state in the midst of raw nature offered unlimited possibilities to both the reformers who were certain that they could renovate the world, and the religionists who wished to withdraw from the evils of organized society that they might work out their own salvation. In America there was legendary freedom for those who wished to experiment. Vast expanses of unsettled land, far removed from the evils of the Old World, provided an unusual laboratory for experimenting with social systems which before existed only on paper or in men's fertile imaginations.

The American frontier was not altogether removed from the mainstream of social traditions; there were no vacuums completely untouched by Western civilization. Total isolation, so fundamental for successful social experimentation, was never attained by any of the utopian communities of the nineteenth century in America. The established social institutions, laws, mores, customs, and prejudices of organized society posed constant threats to the survival of communities which denied all or some part of the old social order. Conducting an experiment under these conditions was like trying to gather feathers in a windstorm. No utopian community was able to attain a state of total self-sufficiency. Each was forced to depend upon its neighbors, near and far, in order to survive economically. This type of dependence subjected the communities, as both producers and consumers, to the laws of competitive society from which they had withdrawn.

Several factors contributed to the collapse of the communal experiments. A prime cause of failure was the loss of leadership. Rarely did a community survive the departure of its original leader. Few community founders took the trouble to groom successors and there was no assurance that the members would follow the direction of any but the founders of their society. It was a serious offense to question the authority of a founder, for to do so was to question the justification for the community's existence.

Another cause of community failure involved economics. Poor management by those who had never managed anything larger than their own purses brought many of the communities into bankruptcy. Nathaniel Hawthorne, as a case in point, was the head of the Finance Committee at Brook Farm, and admitted his ineptness in this department.[1] At Fruitlands Bronson Alcott, who was the recipient of numerous handouts, could hardly be trusted to create a thriving enterprise. The Ruskinites transferred from the fertile lands and friendly neighbors of Tennessee to the Okefenokee Swamps and xenophobic neighbors of southern Georgia, a move hardly indicative of sound economic planning. Poor lands for farming, malaria-infested lowlands, remoteness from markets, and other such unlikely circumstances proved fatal to many communities.

Outside opposition was a third factor which caused several communities to disband. Although communitarians were content to limit their unorthodox practices to the confines of their own villages, neighbors often feared that if the communities were too successful in their ventures, they might exceed their property limits and threaten the social order outside. They also feared that their sons and daughters might be attracted to the communities, particularly if they were notoriously immoral, which would undermine parental authority. If communities were able to produce at a profit and undercut their neighbors in the market place, the latter feared the loss of economic status. It was often out of fear, rather than righteous indignation, that neighbors formed vigilante committees or resorted to the courts to rid their vicinity of the communitarians. Conservatives who opposed the ideals of social-reform utopians were not altogether negative in their opposition. Happiness was also their goal and they counted on the institutions of constitutional democracy, capitalism, and the Christian religion in pursuit of that goal. The spokesmen of Jacksonian democracy accepted the genius of Americans working within the framework of these institutions to make all material, social, and political dreams come true. If the existing institutions were at fault, there were legitimately established channels to effect the necessary changes without resorting to the radical schemes of the utopian reformers, who wished to uproot American society before it was given the opportunity to blossom and bear fruit.

The collapse of utopian communities was not always attributable to external pressures. Many were destroyed from within. Social reform communities and economic cooperatives assumed the natural goodness of man and opened their doors to all comers. These communities attracted practically every type and temperament of humankind, including, as Horace Greeley aptly observed, "the conceited, the crotchety, the selfish, the headstrong, the pugnacious, the unappreciated, the played out, the idle, the good-for-nothing, generally, who finding themselves utterly out of place and at discount in the world as it is, rashly concluded that they were exactly fitted for the world as it should be." [2] Every community, except those devoutly religious communities which made a severe test of fellowship, had its share of eccentrics, many of whom traveled from one colony to another and left discord in their wake. Gossip was a dignified pastime among the community deadbeats. The astute Ralph Waldo Emerson observed: "American social communities . . . were whispering galleries in which the adored Saxon privacy was lost." [3] The disenchanted Robert Dale Owen, when surveying the collapse of New Harmony, moaned, "Liberty, equality, and fraternity, in downright earnest! It found favor with that heterogeneous collection of radicals, enthusiastic devotees to principles, honest latitudinarians, and lazy theorists, with a sprinkling of unprincipled sharpers thrown in." [4] In assuming the natural goodness of man, the utopians failed to reckon with man's potential for evil and thereby oversimplified human behavior.

A primary cause for the failure of utopian communities was the inability of the members to subordinate their own selfish interests to the interests of the community at large. The two bulwarks of individual interests were the institutions of private property and the nuclear family. Communitarians were generally aware of the threat that these two institutions posed to harmonious communal life and attempted either to modify them or to exclude them altogether in their social arrangements. Some attempted to effect a balance between individualism and communalism. The economic cooperatives and a few of the Owenite and Fourieristic associations were able to offer a modified system of socialism which permitted a limited holding of private property and allowed the monogamous family to remain intact while affording some benefits of the associative life. These communities paid the price for their allowance of individualism, as they were victimized by internal dissension which brought about their demise within a relatively short period. The Owenite communities survived on an average of two years, the Fourieristic associations three and one-half years, and the economic cooperatives five years.

There appears to be a correlation between the length of time which the utopian communities survived and the degree to which private property and familism were either abolished or greatly modified. Those communities which abolished private property and nuclear families survived longer than those which retained these two institutions. The Ephrataites survived 166 years; the Shakers more than a century and a half; the Harmonists nearly a century; the Zoarites eighty-one years; and the Perfectionists at Putney and Oneida thirty-five years. Two utopian groups, the Mormons and the Hutterites, survived the nineteenth century and are still extant, although the former no longer practice communal living. The Mormons modified marriage when they adopted polygyny, and they modified property rights when they adopted the United Order of Enoch, in which all property was committed to the Church and each Mormon was made a steward. The Hutterites have a loosely-knit social structure, without unitary housing or common dining halls, two characteristic features of most nineteenth-century utopian communities. Their social individualism compares to village life in ordinary frontier society. They have an other-worldly view and regard all property as belonging to God, but committed to their stewardship. The Hutterites permit a controlled familism and have proved that a modified form of communalism can exist indefinitely without abandoning monogamous marriages.

Those communities which adopted pure communism and strict celibacy survived longer in the nineteenth century than those which permitted their members to retain a portion of their property and to live in separate houses as private families. None but the religious utopian communities experimented with a social system which abolished both private property and all sexual relations. Secular ideologies developed by Robert Owen and Charles Fourier called for eventual dissolution of private property and monogamous marriages, but these ideologies never received any more than lip service as the Owenites and Fourierists never attempted to put them into practice. The Owenite Frances Wright claimed monogamous marriage was not a feature of Nashoba, but her sister married Richeson Whitby while there. The cessation of monogamous marriage in no wise implied the abolition of sexual intercourse in the ideologies of Owen and Fourier; the common charge of free love was leveled against the associationists who professed to follow their teachings. The charges stemmed from a reading of Owen's and Fourier's works and not from the actual practices of those communities which bore their names, with the possible exception of Nashoba and Modern Times. Both Owen and Fourier envisioned a day when private property and monogamous marriage would be abolished. But society, as constituted in their time, was unprepared to accept such radical views and threatened to destroy any community which dared to employ them. Therefore Owen and Fourier advised patience until society could be educated, by their example of the merits of communal living, to accept the principles of the associative life before moving toward the more radical phases of their ideologies.

Religious communities which abolished monogamy in favor of celibacy managed to replace one socially acceptable institution with another which was equally acceptable. Although ordinary society regarded celibacy as unorthodox, it did not regard it as an evil or as a threat. It was only when socially unacceptable institutions were substituted for monogamy that society at large became alarmed and attacked the communities which adopted them. Polygamy, polygyny, polyandry, and free love drew the wrath of a culture which had been educated to believe that sexual relations outside of monogamy were evil. The Mormons and the Perfectionists, although both were devoutly religious, felt the fury of an enraged society and were forced to abandon their practices. Ordinary society, even within the framework of religious orthodoxy, had accepted divorce and remarriage, which was tantamount to tandem polygamy, but was unwilling to accept any deviation in sexual practices outside the limits of its own laws. Monogamous marriages were deemed the best of all possible social arrangements to ensure the protection of the mothers and the socialization of their children. When monogamy was threatened, the whole social structure was equally threatened. Again, it was fear which prodded Americans to chase down the Mormon polygynists and the free-loving Perfectionists like common criminals.

The institution of celibacy needed strong theological backing before it became a feature of utopian communities in the nineteenth century. All communities which adopted celibacy attempted to justify its adoption on theological grounds. The Jansonists, Ephrataites, and Zoarites instituted the practice out of social expediency but attempted to give it some theological underpinning. But in every other case, celibacy was adopted from deep religious convictions. Celibate theology usually found its roots in a belief in a bisexual deity and the creation of a bisexual man. The fall of man from his first estate was associated with sexual intercourse. If a man were to regain his paradise, he must begin by a denial of the sexual urge. Celibate theology also posited a belief in an imminent return of Jesus Christ and a millennium. These features were perfect complements to communalism and help to account for the fact that all celibate communities were communistic. Private property held no incentive, nor was propagation a concern, for those who were convinced that the end of the world was near.

Religious conviction, although a powerful motivator, could not alone be relied upon to keep the minds of community members free from sex. Monasteries and convents were able to provide a monosexual environment and temptations were only in the form of mental images or rare encounters with members of the opposite sex. Celibate utopian communities were every whit as strict as the cloisters regarding mastery over physical passions, but they had the additional temptation occasioned by daily association of the sexes. Safeguards were generally erected in celibate communities to shield the members against sexual temptations: (1) all social intercourse was strictly regulated to prevent intimacy between the sexes; (2) living quarters were segregated; (3) men and women rarely did the same chores simultaneously; (4) women's dress codes were regulated so as to conceal the curvatures of the feminine form; and (5) a system of catharsis was established to enable one to confess his psychological guilt and to cleanse his mind of lustful thoughts. These rules assured a conformity to the basic ideals of the society and served to reduce the tensions which otherwise might develop and threaten the community. Celibate communities required the greatest sacrifices of personal and selfish ideas. Mere ideology was not sufficient to elicit this type of sacrifice and may account for the fact that no social reform communities or economic cooperatives attempted to impose the practice on their members, although there were living testimonials all around them in the Shaker, Rappite, Zoarite, and Ephrataite communities that celibacy was the most effective institution in subordinating individual interests to communal interests. Charles Lane, impressed with these testimonials, attempted to convert the Transcendentalists, in his articles in *The Dial*, to the merits of celibacy in communal life, and even tried to pressure Bronson Alcott to leave his wife and daughters at Fruitlands and join him in living a celibate life.

Dictatorships within utopian communities proved more effective than democracies in perpetuating the original ideals of the societies. Democractic institutions gave occasion for the expression of unbridled individualism. Robert Dale Owen complained that at New Harmony "One form of government was first adopted, and when that appeared unsuitable another was tried, until it appeared that the members were too various in their feelings and too dissimilar in their habits to govern themselves harmoniously as one community . . . . New Harmony, therefore, is not now a community." [5] Communal dictators avoided the collision of personal ideas which threatened to alter the original aims of their societies. Two elements were essential in a community dictatorship: (1) the dictator had to possess extraordinary powers which were revered by the community; and (2) the members had to be of below average intelligence or to be kept in ignorance. The religious communities were more adaptable to dictatorships, since their leaders were regarded as spiritual shepherds who were in communication with God, and with but few exceptions the members of the religious communities were of the lower socioeconomic classes who had been deprived of formal education. The source of the extraordinary powers of the religious communal dictators resided within the divine will of the Deity and to question the dictators was to question none other than God himself. Dictators could easily effect changes in community institutions by a simple declaration of a revelation which was not subject to argument or to a vote by the members. The social reform communities and economic cooperatives, some of which were diametrically opposed to organized religion, were deprived of this type of dictatorship, and discovered that their democratic individualism and collectivism could find no common ground for harmony. One old gentleman, Millard Rice, who spent eighty-nine years in a commune, exclaimed: "The only way in which collectivism can be practiced is as a religious ideal or a dictatorship." [6] The history of nineteenth-century collectivism in America appears to support his thesis.

Exclusive attachments between couples and between mother and children were constant threats to the social order of communistic communities and were strongly discouraged or punished. The fact that such attachments occurred indicated that indoctrination was too weak or that prior training was too thoroughly ingrained in the members to cause them to place the welfare of the community above their own selfish interests. Possessiveness is a trait of human nature which manifests itself in the crib of the very young. Utopians who abolished family ties blamed the familial arrangement for aiding and abetting possessiveness in children. But adult education in socialistic ideologies could not be trusted to eradicate the curse of possessiveness. Utopian communities sought to completely submerge the ego in the group, a task of such gargantuan proportions as to defy imagination. While they promised to provide freedom for their members, they made them slaves. Individualism, that vital corollary of freedom, was denied to all but the dictators who engineered the projects. For if individualism were allowed to express itself, collectivism was impossible. The Owenite and Fourieristic societies attempted to maintain that uneasy balance between collectivism and individualism, but were unable to do so. Private interests were too powerful to be indefinitely sublimated to communal interests. Men, for a brief period, sacrificed personal desires and ambitions for what they deemed a worthy cause, but human nature manifested itself too soon for communalism to fix firmly itself on the social patterns of American life. Only those communes with intensely religious orientation were able to succeed in mastering the human ego and individual possessiveness. But even here their ego was bolstered by promises of eternal life, enthronement as gods, and a heavenly inheritance. These future prospects were worth a brief lifetime of deprivation and submissiveness.

Epilogue

Utopian communities of the nineteenth century in America were faced with what appeared to be an irreconcilable problem: the release of the sexual urge in a socially acceptable arrangement which would not militate against a total dedication to a collective idea. Free love, complex marriage, polygyny, and orgies wherein utopians searched for celestial counterparts afforded a release for the sexual urge, but they were not socially acceptable, as the wrath of organized society was vented against them. Those communities which adopted these practices were forced to drop them or face certain annihilation. Monogamy, the only socially acceptable arrangement for the release of the sexual urge, militated against collectivism as monogamic familism placed individual interests above the interests of the community at large. The only alternative which remained for communalism to succeed was the adoption of celibacy, a practice which would place each community but a generation away from extinction, and which would deny man fulfillment in one of his strongest biological urges. Unless there were sufficient religious commitment to an other-worldly prospect, celibacy was an unlikely alternative, as none but the religious communities ever adopted it. These were the ones which survived the longest. Mere sociological ideologies did not have the power of attraction to mortals to cause them to deny the pleasures of sex for the cause of collectivism.

NOTES

PROLOGUE

1. Horace Greeley lauded the Fourier plan and claimed that "While it will ensure independence and comfort to the Poor, it increases rather than diminishes the wealth and enjoyments of the Rich." *The New York Tribune*, April 20, 1842.

2. The observation of William Faux, an Englishman who visited George Rapp's community in Indiana in 1819, is typical. He wrote: "The spell, or secret, by which these people are held in voluntary slavery, is not to be known or fathomed by inquiry." William Faux, *Memorable Days in America: Being a Journal of a Tour to the United States, November 27, 1818, July 21, 1820*, Vol. XI of *Early Western Travels, 1784–1846*, ed. Reuben Gold Thwaites (Cleveland: Arthur H. Clark, 1905), p. 249.

3. Sectarian communities were not totally without hope of reforming society. George Rapp remarked to Robert Owen that the Harmonists had "set mankind an example of the advantages of union in creating abundance with easy labor." Unpublished manuscript collection of A. J. Macdonald; microfilm 2116, Yale University Library, New Haven, Connecticut, p. 228.

4. Oliver Carlson, *Brisbane: A Candid Biography* (New York: Stackpole Sons, 1937), p. 55.

5. Entry, August 2, 1840, John Quincy Adams, *The Diary of John Quincy Adams, 1794–1845*, ed. Allan Nevins (New York: Scribner's, 1951), pp. 510–511.

6. Ralph Waldo Emerson, *The Letters of Ralph Waldo Emerson*, Vol. II, ed. Ralph L. Rush (New York: Columbia University Press, 1939), p. 353.

7. Nicholas V. Riasanovsky, *The Teachings of Charles Fourier* (Berkeley: University of California Press, 1969), p. 43.

8. Orestes Brownson, "The Laboring Classes," *Boston Quarterly Review* (1840), quoted in *Social Theories of Jacksonian Democracy: Representative Writings of the Period, 1825–1850*, ed. J. L. Blau (New York: Liberal Arts Press, 1947), p. 308.

9. Richard T. Ely, *Recent American Socialism*, Vol. IV of *Johns Hopkins University Studies in Historical and Political Science*, ed. Herbert B. Adams (Baltimore: Johns Hopkins University Press, 1885), p. 14.

10. Entry, October 17, 1840, Ralph Waldo Emerson, *Journals of Ralph Waldo Emerson*, Vol. V, eds. E. W. Emerson and W. E. Forbes (Boston: Houghton Mifflin, 1911), pp. 473–474.

11. Entry, September 26, 1840, ibid., p. 465.

12. Charles Dana, *Association in Its Connection with Education and Religion* (Boston: Benjamin H. Greene, 1844), pp. 25–26.

13. Karl Marx and Frederick Engels, *Manifesto of the Communist Party* (Moscow: Progress Publishers, 1967), pp. 89–93.

I. Germs of New Institutions and New Modes of Action

1. Jean-Jacques Rousseau, *The Social Contract or Principles of Political Right*, in *The World's Great Thinkers* series (New York: Carlton House, 1953), p. 14.

2. Unpublished manuscript collection of A. J. Macdonald; microfilm 2116, Yale University Library, New Haven, Connecticut, p. 50.

3. "Constitution of the Brook Farm Association, for Industry and Education, West Roxbury, Massachusetts. With an Introductory Statement," in Henry W. Sams, ed., *Autobiography of Brook Farm* (Englewood Cliffs, N.J.: Prentice-Hall, 1958), p. 95.

4. Webster's *New World Dictionary* (1966) defines polygyny as: "The state or practice of having two or more wives or concubines at the same time."

5. Joseph Smith, Jr., *The Doctrine and Covenants of the Church of Jesus Christ of Latter-day Saints, Containing the Revelations Given to Joseph Smith, Jr., The Prophet for the Building of the Kingdom of God in the Last Days* (Salt Lake City: Deseret News, 1914), p. 473.

6. United Society of Believers, *A Holy, Sacred, and Divine Roll and Book; from the Lord God of Heaven, to the Inhabitants of the Earth: Revealed in the United Society of New Lebanon, County of Columbia, State of New York, United States of America*, Part I (Canterbury, N.H.: United Society, 1843), p. 30.

7. Flavius Josephus, *The Works of Flavius Josephus*, Vol. II, ed. William Whiston (Philadelphia: J. Griggs, 1829), p. 41.

8. Thomas More, *Utopia*, ed. Paul Turner (Middlesex: Penguin, 1965), p. 82.

9. Margaret Fuller, *Women in the Nineteenth Century, and Kindred*

Papers Relating to the Sphere, Conditions and Duties of Women (Boston: Roberts, 1884), p. 218.

10. John Hyde Preston, "Collective Living," *Harper's Monthly Magazine*, CLXXVI (May 1938): 611.

11. Henrik Infield, *Utopia and Experiment: Essays in the Sociology of Cooperation* (New York: Frederick A. Praeger, 1956), p. 200.

12. Frank Cox, *American Marriage: A Changing Scene?* (Dubuque: Wm. C. Brown, 1972), p. 240.

13. Little Rock *Arkansas Gazette*, April 24, 1971.

14. David French, "After the Fall: What this Country Needs is a Good Counter Culture," *New York Times Magazine* (October 3, 1971), 24.

15. Herbert Otto, "Communes: The Alternative Life-Style," *Saturday Review* (April 24, 1971), 17.

16. Ibid., 20.

17. John Humphrey Noyes, *History of American Socialisms* (Philadelphia: J. B. Lippincott, 1870), p. 139.

18. J. F. C. Harrison, *Quest for the New Moral World: Robert Owen and the Owenites in Britain and America* (New York: Scribner's, 1969), p. 59.

19. Charles Lane, "Brook Farm," *The Dial*, IV (January 1844): 355–356.

20. Ralph Waldo Emerson, *Complete Works of Ralph Waldo Emerson*, Vol. X, ed. E. W. Emerson (Boston: Houghton Mifflin, 1904), p. 365.

II. They Neither Marry Nor Are Given in Marriage

1. I Corinthians 7:32–33.

2. Edward Deming Andrews, *The People Called Shakers: A Search for the Perfect Society* (New York: Oxford University Press, 1953), p. 8.

3. Charles Edson Robinson, *A Concise History of the United Society of Believers Called Shakers* (East Canterbury, N.H.: United Society, 1893), p. 15.

4. Ann Lee regarded her marriage bed as a "bed of embers" which she strove to avoid lest she "wake up in hell." Andrews, *The People Called Shakers*, p. 8.

5. Ibid., p. 9.

6. Unpublished manuscript collection of A. J. Macdonald; microfilm 2116, Yale University Library, New Haven, Connecticut, p. 640.

7. Robinson, *A Concise History*, p. 19.

8. Marguerite Fellows Melcher, *The Shaker Adventure* (Princeton: Princeton University Press, 1941), p. 114.

9. The United Society of Believers, *A Summary View of the Millennial Church, or United Society of Believers, Comprising the Rise, Progress, and Practical Order of the Society, Together with the General*

Principles of their Faith and Testimony (Albany, N.Y.: C. Van Benthuysen, 1848), p. 107.

10. Genesis 6:5.

11. Statement prepared by "A Prominent Member" of the Shaker Society, reprinted in William Alfred Hinds, *American Communities* (New York: Corinth Books, 1961), p. 89.

12. Andrews, *The People Called Shakers*, p. 12.

13. Ibid., p. 22.

14. United Society of Believers, *A Holy, Sacred, and Divine Roll and Book; from the Lord God of Heaven, to the Inhabitants of the Earth: Revealed in the United Society of New Lebanon, County of Columbia, State of New York, United States of America*, Part I (Canterbury, N.H.: United Society, 1843), p. 30.

15. Andrews, *The People Called Shakers*, p. 23.

16. United Society of Believers, *A Summary View of the Millennial Church*, p. 145.

17. Albert Thomas, *Plain Talks upon Practical Religion: Being Candid Answers to Earnest Inquirers* (Watervliet, N.Y.: United Society, 1873), p. 27.

18. Robinson, *A Concise History*, p. 33.

19. United Society of Believers, *A Holy, Sacred, and Divine Roll and Book*, p. 31.

20. Matthew 22:30.

21. Macdonald MSS, p. 640.

22. Melcher, *The Shaker Adventure*, p. 51.

23. D. E. Nevin, "The Late George Rapp and the Harmonists," *Scribner's Monthly*, XVII (March 1879): 703.

24. Robert Dale Owen, *Threading My Way: Twenty-seven Years of Autobiography* (New York: G. W. Carleton, 1874), p. 243.

25. William Faux, *Memorable Days In America: Being a Journal of a Tour to the United States, November 27, 1818, July 21, 1820*, Vol. XI of *Early Western Travels, 1784–1846*, ed. Reuben Gold Thwaites (Cleveland: Arthur H. Clark, 1905), p. 251.

26. Thomas Hulme, *Hulme's Journal of a Tour in the Western Countries of America, September 30, 1818 to August 8, 1819*, Vol. X of *Early Western Travels, 1784–1846*, ed. Reuben Gold Thwaites (Cleveland: Arthur H. Clark, 1905), p. 10.

27. Faux, *Memorable Days in America*, p. 191.

28. Robert Dale Owen, "The Social Experiment at New Harmony: A Chapter of Autobiography," *Atlantic Monthly*, XXXII (Agusut 1873): 224.

29. Hinds, *American Communities*, pp. 12–13.

30. George Gordon, *The Poetical Works of Lord Byron* (London: Oxford University Press, 1904), p. 836.

31. Karl J. R. Arndt, *George Rapp's Harmony Society, 1785–1847* (Philadelphia: University of Pennsylvania Press, 1965), p. 610.

32. From a statement made by R. L. Baker, a Trustee of the Economy Community, January 19, 1857, quoted in ibid., p. 583.

33. Nevin, "The Late George Rapp," p. 707.

34. Charles Nordhoff, *The Communistic Societies of the United States, from Personal Visit and Observation* (New York: Hillary House, 1961), p. 73.

35. Ibid., p. 74.

36. Adlard Welby, *A Visit to North America*, Vol. XII of *Early Western Travels, 1784–1846*, ed. Reuben Gold Thwaites (Cleveland: Arthur H. Clark, 1905), p. 262.

37. Arndt, *George Rapp's Harmony*, p. 201.

38. John Wood, *Two Years' Residence in the Settlement on the English Prairie in the Illinois Country*, Vol. X of *Early Western Travels, 1784–1846*, ed. Reuben Gold Thwaites (Cleveland: Arthur H. Clark, 1905), p. 251.

39. Hulme, *Hulme's Journal of a Tour*, p. 34.

40. Faux, *Memorable Days in America*, p. 249.

41. Harmonist Society, *Verzeichnis der Copulations*, quoted in Arndt, *George Rapp's Harmony Society*, p. 610. Lockwood was certain there were no marriages among the Harmonists after 1807, except those who eloped. George Lockwood, *The New Harmony Movement* (New York: D. Appleton and Co., 1905), p. 13.

42. William E. Wilson, *The Angel and the Serpent: The Story of New Harmony* (Bloomington: Indiana University Press, 1964), p. 25.

43. Hulme, *Hulme's Journal of a Tour*, p. 60.

44. Sidney Ditzion, *Marriage, Morals and Sex in America: A History of Ideas* (New York: Nelson, 1961), p. 208.

45. Karl J. R. Arndt, "The Harmonists and the Mormons," *The American German Review*, X (June 1944): 6.

46. Nevin, "The Late George Rapp," p. 707.

47. Victor Francis Calverton, *Where Angels Dared to Tread* (Indianapolis: Bobbs-Merrill, 1941), p. 77.

48. May 1, 1853.

49. Hinds, *American Communities*, pp. 34–35.

50. May 1, 1853.

51. Hinds, *American Communities*, p. 33.

52. Calverton, *Where Angels Dared to Tread*, p. 63.

53. Howard Pyle, "A Peculiar People," *Harper's New Monthly Magazine*, LXXIX (October 1889): 784.

54. Oswald W. Seidensticker, "A Colonial Monastery," *Century Magazine*, XXIII (December 1881): 219.

55. Alice Felt Tyler, *Freedom's Ferment: Phases of American Social History to 1860* (Minneapolis: University of Minnesota Press, 1944), p. 136.

56. Fredrika Bremer, *The Homes of the New World: Impressions of America* (New York: Harper and Brothers, 1854), pp. 68–69.

57. Calverton, *Where Angels Dared to Tread*, p. 118.

58. Sivert Erdahl, "Eric Janson and the Bishop Hill Colony," Illinois State Historical Society *Journal*, XVIII (October 1925): 561.

59. Michael Mikkelsen, "The Bishop Hill Colony: A Religious Communistic Settlement in Henry County, Illinois," *Church and State, Columbus and America*, Vol. X of *Johns Hopkins University Studies in Historical and Political Science*, ed. Herbert B. Adams (Baltimore: Johns Hopkins University Press, 1892), p. 43.

60. Macdonald MSS, p. 447.

61. Everett Webber, *Escape to Utopia: The Communal Movement in America*, in *The American Procession* series, ed. Henry G. Alsbert (New York: Hastings House, 1959), p. 79.

62. Ralph Albertson, "A Survey of Mutualistic Communities in America," *The Iowa Journal of History and Politics*, XXXIV (October 1936): 393.

63. *The New York Tribune*, June 18, 1853.

64. R. Bruce Taylor, "Communistic Communities," *Encyclopaedia of Religion and Ethics*, Vol. III, ed. James Hastings (New York: Scribner's, 1925), p. 787.

III. It is Good for a Man Not to Touch a Woman

1. I Corinthians 7:1.

2. Philos-Harmoniae, *A Selection of Hymns and Poems for the Use of Believers: Collected from Sundry Authors* (Watervliet, N.Y., 1833), quoted in Charles Nordhoff, *The Communistic Societies of the United States, from Personal Visit and Observation* (New York: Hillary House, 1961), p. 125.

3. Unpublished manuscript collection of A. J. Macdonald; microfilm 2116, Yale University Library, New Haven, Connecticut, pp. 721–722.

4. United Society of Believers, *A Brief Exposition of the Established Principles and Regulations of the United Society of Believers Called Shakers* (Canterbury, N.H.: United Society, 1843), p. 7.

5. Macdonald MSS, p. 713.

6. Frederick Rapp's answer to Edward Page of New York, who had written to him, January 5, 1822, and inquired about the society. Reprinted in Karl J. R. Arndt, *George Rapp's Harmony Society, 1785–1847* (Philadelphia: University of Pennsylvania Press, 1965), p. 235.

7. D. E. Nevin noted later at Economy, Pennsylvania, that the practice of husband and wife sleeping in the same bed had ceased. At that time, around 1850, the husband slept upstairs and the wife down below. D. E. Nevin, "The Late George Rapp and the Harmonists," *Scribner's Monthly*, XVII (March 1879): 707–708.

8. Adlard Welby, *A Visit to North America*, Vol. XII of *Early Western Travels, 1784–1846*, ed. Reuben Gold Thwaites (Cleveland: Arthur H. Clark, 1905), p. 261.

9. Howard Pyle, "A Peculiar People," *Harper's New Monthly Magazine*, LXXIX (October 1889): 777.

10. Brother Lamech, *Chronicoan Ephratense*, p. 88, quoted in Victor Francis Calverton, *Where Angels Dared to Tread* (Indianapolis: Bobbs-Merrill, 1941), p. 63.

11. Pyle, "A Peculiar People," 777.

12. Macdonald MSS, p. 651.

13. William Hepworth Dixon, *New America* (Philadelphia: J. B. Lippincott, 1867), p. 311.

14. Nordhoff, *Communistic Societies*, p. 186. Everett Webber believes that this rule was not always adhered to. He observed cards in the guest rooms which asked that the marital privileges be forgone under the Shaker roof and he assumed they would be allowed to occupy the same bed. However, it is likely that such cards were nothing more than subtle reminders that the husband should seek another room. Everett Webber, *Escape to Utopia: The Communal Movement in America*, in *The American Procession* series, ed. Henry G. Alsbert (New York: Hastings House, 1959), p. 58.

15. Charles Edson Robinson, *A Concise History of the United Society of Believers Called Shakers* (East Canterbury, N.H.: United Society, 1893), p. 115.

16. Webber, *Escape to Utopia*, p. 57.

17. B. J. Lossing, "The Shakers," *Harper's New Monthly Magazine*, XV (July 1857): 169.

18. Hervy Elkins, *Sixteen Years in the Senior Order of the Shakers*, quoted in Nordhoff, *Communistic Societies*, pp. 175–176.

19. Thomas Hamilton, *Men and Manners in America* (Philadelphia: Carey and Lee, 1833), p. 355.

20. Dixon, *New America*, p. 305.

21. William Wilson, "Pioneers in Paradise," *Holiday*, XXV (June 1959): 44.

22. William Faux, *Memorable Days in America: Being a Journal of a Tour to the United States, November 27, 1818, July 21, 1820*, Vol. XI of *Early Western Travels, 1784–1846*, ed. Reuben Gold Thwaites (Cleveland: Arthur H. Clark, 1905), p. 249.

23. John Wood, *Two Years' Residence in the Settlement on the English Prairie in the Illinois Country*, Vol. X of *Early Western Travels, 1784–1846*, ed. Reuben Gold Thwaites (Cleveland: Arthur H. Clark, 1905), p. 316. Some of the Rappites' contemporaries on the frontier did not find the dress particularly distasteful. An Englishman, Morris Birbeck, who settled in Illinois, near Harmony, Indiana, outfitted his family with clothing manufactured by and purchased from the Harmonists. Faux, *Memorable Days in America*, p. 192.

24. Ibid., p. 250.

25. Welby, *A Visit to North America*, p. 266.

26. Macdonald MSS, p. 492.

27. Michael Mikkelsen, "The Bishop Hill Colony: A Religious Communistic Settlement in Henry County, Illinois," *Church and State, Columbus and America*, Vol. X of *Johns Hopkins University Studies in*

Historical and Political Science, ed. Herbert B. Adams (Baltimore: Johns Hopkins University Press, 1892), p. 55.

28. Nordhoff, *Communistic Societies*, p. 177.

29. Webber, *Escape to Utopia*, p. 79.

30. Mikkelsen, "Bishop Hill Colony," pp. 63–64.

31. John Duss, *The Harmonists: A Personal History* (Harrisburg: Pennsylvania Book Service, 1943), p. 30.

32. Arndt, *George Rapp's Harmony*, p. 612.

33. Nevin, "The Late George Rapp," pp. 708–709.

34. Arndt, *George Rapp's Harmony*, pp. 429–431.

35. Letter from George Kurtz to George Rapp, October 12, 1830, reprinted in John Andressohn, "Three Additional Rappite Letters," *The Indiana Magazine of History*, XLV (June 1949): 184.

36. Nevin, "The Late George Rapp," p. 710.

37. Macdonald MSS, p. 657.

38. Thomas Brown, *Account of the People Called Shakers: Their Faith, Doctrines and Practices* (Troy, N.Y.: Parker and Bliss, 1812), p. 32.

39. David Lamsen, *Two Years' Experience Among the Shakers*, quoted in Sidney Ditzion, *Marriage, Morals and Sex in America: A History of Ideas* (New York: Nelson, 1961), p. 214.

40. Marguerite Fellows Melcher, *The Shaker Adventure* (Princeton: Princeton University Press, 1941), p. 242.

41. James Flint, *Letters from America Containing Observations on the Climate and Agriculture of the Western States, the Manners of the People, the Prospects of Emigrants, Etc., Etc.*, ed. W. & C. Tait, Vol. IX of *Early Western Travels, 1784–1846*, ed. Reuben Gold Thwaites (Cleveland: Arthur H. Clark, 1905), p. 300.

42. Melcher, *The Shaker Adventure*, p. 128.

43. Nordhoff, *Communistic Societies*, p. 166.

44. William Alfred Hinds, *American Communities* (New York: Corinth Books, 1961), p. 32.

45. Macdonald MSS, p. 663.

46. Nordhoff, *Communistic Societies*, pp. 192–193.

47. J. P. MacLean, "The Shaker Community of Warren County," *Ohio Archaeological and Historical Quarterly*, X (January 1902): 304.

48. Thomas Hulme, *Hulme's Journal of a Tour in the Western Countries of America, September 30, 1818, to August 8, 1819*, Vol. X of *Early Western Travels, 1784–1846*, ed. Reuben Gold Thwaites (Cleveland: Arthur H. Clark, 1905), p. 64.

49. Donald Macdonald, *The Diaries of Donald Macdonald, 1824–1826* (Indianapolis: Indiana Historical Society, 1942), p. 249.

50. It is also to be noted here that in 1807, at the time they adopted celibacy, they also outlawed the use of tobacco among their members. Nordhoff, *Communistic Societies*, p. 74.

51. Ibid., p. 160.

IV. Separate Firesides: The Owenites

1. Charles Lane, "Brook Farm," *The Dial*, IV (January 1844): 356.

2. Robert Owen, *A New Society & Other Writings by Robert Owen*, ed. Ernest Rhys (New York: E. P. Dutton, 1927), p. 110. In his sixth address during his debate with Alexander Campbell in Cincinnati, April 1829, Owen said: "The whole system of the world is, therefore, bad from its foundation." Robert Owen, *The Evidences of Christianity: A Debate Between Robert Owen, of New Lanark, Scotland, and Alexander Campbell, President of Bethany College Virginia; Containing an Examination of the "Social System," and all the Systems of Skepticism of Ancient and Modern Times* (St. Louis: Christian Board of Publication, 1829), p. 83.

3. Owen, *A New Soiety*, p. 113.

4. Rapp gave the unhealthy climate in Indiana as a cause for his decision to remove the colony to Pennsylvania. It is true that the Harmonists had suffered from fevers in the initial stages of their communal life, but they drained the area and eliminated an unhealthy environment. In 1824 only two deaths were recorded in the community, out of a population of about 1,200, a testimony in the behalf of the health of the place. George B. Lockwood, *The New Harmony Movement* (New York: D. Appleton and Co., 1905), p. 71.

5. *The New Harmony Gazette*, October 1, 1825.

6. Ibid., October 29, 1825.

7. Ibid., December 28, 1825.

8. Ibid., January 25, 1826.

9. Katharine Dos Passos and Edith Shay, "New Harmony, Indiana," *The Atlantic Monthly*, CLXVI (November 1940): 606.

10. Lockwood, *The New Harmony Movement*, p. 101.

11. "The pursuit of happiness" was at the basis of Owen's philosophy, and hardly a document of any merit composed by Owen omits a reference to this as the ultimate purpose of human life.

12. *New Harmony Gazette*, September 10, 1828.

13. Ibid., October 1, 1825.

14. Ibid., September 10, 1828.

15. Ibid., July 12, 1826.

16. Robert Owen, *Lectures on the Marriages of the Priesthood of the Old Immoral World, Delivered in the Year 1835, before the Passing of the New Marriage Acts* (Leeds: Author, 1835), pp. 7–8.

17. Ibid., p. 68.

18. Ibid., p. 162.

19. Arthur John Booth, *Robert Owen, the Founder of Socialism in England* (London: Trubner, 1869), pp. 219–220.

20. William Maclure, letter, August 21, 1826, to Madame Fretageot, reprinted in *Education and Reform at New Harmony: Correspondence*

of William Maclure and Marie Duclos Fretageot, 1820–1830, ed. Arthur E. Bestor (Indianapolis: Indiana Historical Society, 1948), p. 355.

21. William Maclure, *Opinions on Various Subjects; Dedicated to the Industrious Producers*, Vol. I (New Harmony, Ind.: Author, 1831–1838), p. 355.

22. Everett Webber, *Escape to Utopia: The Communal Movement in America*, in *The American Procession* series, ed. Henry G. Alsbert (New York: Hastings House, 1959), p. 124.

23. Sarah Pears, *New Harmony, An Adventure in Happiness: Papers of Thomas and Sarah Pears*, ed. Thomas Clinton Pears, Jr. (Indianapolis: Indiana Historical Society, 1933), p. 73.

24. Arthur Eugene Bestor, Jr., *Backwoods Utopias: The Sectarian and Owenite Phases of Communitarian Socialism in America, 1663–1829* (Philadelphia: University of Pennsylvania Press, 1950), p. 223.

25. Owen, *Lectures on Marriages*, p. 88.

26. *New Harmony Gazette*, October 27, 1825.

27. Ibid., April 4, 1826.

28. Ibid.

29. Pears, *New Harmony*, p. 70.

30. *The New Harmony Free Enquirer*, June 2, 1832.

31. Elizabeth Cady Stanton, Susan B. Anthony, and M. J. Cage, *The History of Women Suffrage*, Vol. I (Rochester, N.Y.: Charles Manor, 1887), p. 295.

32. Robert Dale Owen, *Threading My Way: Twenty-seven Years of Autobiography* (New York: G. W. Carleton, 1874), p. 281.

33. Robert Owen, *The Book of the New Moral World, Containing the Rational System of Society Founded on Demonstrable Facts, Developing the Constitution and Laws of Human Nature and of Society* (New York: G. Vale, 1845), p. 174.

34. Ibid., p. 204.

35. Unpublished manuscript collection of A. J. Macdonald; microfilm 2116, Yale University Library, New Haven, Connecticut, p. 520.

36. *New Harmony Gazette*, October 1, 1825.

37. Owen, *Lectures on Marriages*, p. 36.

38. Owen, *Book of the New Moral World*, pp. 28, 210.

39. Pears, *New Harmony*, pp. 72–73.

40. Lockwood, *The New Harmony Movement*, p. 268.

41. Ibid., p. 246.

42. Margaret Cole, *Robert Owen of New Lanark* (New York: Oxford University Press, 1953), p. 159.

43. Kenneth William McKinley, "A Guide to the Communistic Communities of Ohio," *Ohio Archaeological and Historical Quarterly*, XLVI (January 1937): 9.

44. Wendall P. Fox, "The Kendall Community," *Ohio Archaeological and Historical Quarterly*, XX (January 1911): 194.

45. James McKnight, *A Discourse Exposing Robert Owen's System*,

as Practiced by the Franklin Community at Haverstraw (New York: N. P., 1826), p. 59.

46. Macdonald MSS, p. 30.

47. Morris Hillquit, *History of Socialism in the United States* (New York: Russell and Russell, 1965), p. 65.

V. Family Life in a Phalanx: The Fourierists

1. Unpublished manuscript collection of A. J. Macdonald; microfilm 2116, Yale University Library, New Haven, Connecticut, p. 429.

2. Nicholas V. Riasanovsky, *The Teaching of Charles Fourier* (Berkeley: University of California Press, 1969), p. 43.

3. *The New York Tribune*, March 30, 1843.

4. *The New York Daily Tribune*, May 6, 1843.

5. *The New York Tribune*, April 20, 1842.

6. Julian Hawthorne, *Nathaniel Hawthorne and His Wife, A Biography* (Boston: James R. Osgood, 1885), pp. 268–269.

7. Elizabeth Peabody, "Fourierism," *The Dial*, IV (April 1844): 478.

8. Ralph Waldo Emerson, *The Works of Ralph Waldo Emerson* (Roslyn, N.Y.: Black's Readers Service, 1960), p. 99.

9. Macdonald MSS, p. 429.

10. Oliver Carlson, *Brisbane: A Candid Biography* (New York: Stackpole, 1937), p. 46.

11. *The New York Daily Tribune*, March 1, 1842.

12. McElrath, Greeley's business partner, claimed no payment was ever made by Brisbane. W. E. Hale, *Horace Greeley: Voice of the People* (New York: Harper, 1950), p. 99.

13. Victor Francis Calverton, *Where Angels Dared to Tread* (Indianapolis: Bobbs-Merrill, 1941), p. 60.

14. *The New York Tribune*, April 20, 1842.

15. Charles Fourier, *Selections from the Works of Fourier*, trans. Julia Franklin (London: Sonnenschein, 1901), p. 142.

16. Riasanovsky, *The Teaching of Charles Fourier*, p. 238.

17. Madame Gatti de Gammon, *Fourier et son Système* (1839), quoted in Richard T. Ely, *French and German Socialism in Modern Times* (New York: Harper, 1903), p. 99.

18. Riasanovsky, *Teaching of Charles Fourier*, p. 240.

19. Charles Fourier, *Manuscrits, Années, 1857–1858* (Paris, 1858), p. 108, quoted in Riasanovsky, *Teaching of Charles Fourier*, p. 149.

20. Fourier, *Selections from the Works of Fourier*, p. 80.

21. Riasanovsky, *Teaching of Charles Fourier*, p. 216.

22. Hawthorne, *Nathaniel Hawthorne and His Wife*, Vol. I, p. 267.

23. *The New York Daily Tribune*, May 6, 1843.

24. Horace Greeley, *Recollections of a Busy Life* (New York: Treat, 1868), p. 579.

25. *The New York Tribune*, November 20, 1846.

26. Ibid., December 4, 1846.
27. Ibid., March 3, 1847.
28. Ibid., March 12, 1847.
29. Ibid.
30. *The New York Daily Tribune*, October 19, 1855.
31. Francis N. Zabriskie, *Horace Greeley, The Editor* (New York: Funk and Wagnalls, 1890), p. 183.
32. Hale, *Horace Greeley*, p. 100.
33. *The New York Tribune*, November 3, 1866.
34. Macdonald MSS, p. 50.
35. Fredrika Bremer, *The Homes of the New World: Impressions of America* (New York: Harper and Brothers, 1854), p. 612.
36. N. C. Meeker, "Post Mortem and Requiem, by an Old Fourierist," *The New York Tribune*, November 3, 1866.
37. Macdonald MSS, p. 61.
38. *The New York Tribune*, November 3, 1866.
39. Victor Considerant, *Au Texas* (Paris: Au Bureau du Populaire, 1854), pp. 83–85.
40. Macdonald MSS, p. 375.
41. John Humphrey Noyes, *History of American Socialisms* (Philadelphia: J. B. Lippincott, 1870), p. 235.
42. Macdonald MSS, p. 377.
43. "Constitution of the Sylvania Association, Adopted in 1842," Macdonald MSS, p. 371.
44. Noyes, *History of American Socialisms*, p. 414.
45. Ibid., p. 416.
46. Warren Chase, "The Wisconsin Phalanx," *The Harbinger*, January 8, 1848.
47. Noyes, *History of American Socialisms*, p. 444.
48. Macdonald MSS, p. 205.
49. Ibid., p. 231.
50. Ibid., p. 237.
51. Ibid., p. 239.
52. Noyes, *History of American Socialisms*, p. 348.
53. *The New York Tribune*, October 20, 1845.
54. Ibid.
55. Ibid.
56. Ibid., July 4, 1846.

VI. And Fools Rush In

1. O. B. Frothingham, *George Ripley* (Boston: Houghton Mifflin, 1882), pp. 307–308.
2. Margaret Fuller Ossoli, *Memoirs of Margaret Fuller Ossoli*, Vol. II (Boston: Phillips, Sampson and Co., 1852), p. 268.
3. Ibid., p. 74.

4. Lindsay Swift, *Brook Farm, Its Members, Scholars and Visitors* (New York: Macmillan, 1900), p. 219.

5. Ralph Waldo Emerson, *Journals of Ralph Waldo Emerson*, ed. E. W. Emerson and W. E. Forbes (Boston: Houghton Mifflin, 1911), Vol. V, p. 474.

6. Ibid., Vol. VI, p. 491.

7. Charles Lane, "Brook Farm," *The Dial*, IV (January 1844): 353.

8. Arthur Sumner, "A Boy's Recollections of Brook Farm," *New England Magazine*, X (March–August 1894): 239.

9. Amelia Russell, "Home Life of the Brook Farm Association," *Atlantic Monthly*, LX (November 1878): 561.

10. "The Community at West Roxbury, Massachusetts," *The Monthly Miscellany of Religion and Letters* (August 1841), 116.

11. Sophia Eastman, letter, July 25, 1843, to Mehitable Eastman, reprinted in Henry W. Sams, ed., *Autobiography of Brook Farm* (Englewood Cliffs, N.J.: Prentice-Hall, 1958), p. 82.

12. Lane, "Brook Farm," 355.

13. Henry L. Stoddard, *Horace Greeley, Printer, Editor, Crusader*, (New York: G. P. Putnam's Sons, 1946), p. 103.

14. Ora Sedgwick, "Girl of Sixteen at Brook Farm," *Atlantic Monthly* LXXXV (March 1900): 402.

15. Amelia Russell, "Home Life of the Brook Farm Association," p. 559.

16. Robert Carter, "The Newness," *The Pioneer* (1843), quoted in Clara Endicott Sears, *Bronson Alcott's Fruitlands* (Boston: Houghton Mifflin, 1915), p. 37.

17. Marianne Dwight, letter, April 27, 1844, to Anna Parsons, reprinted in *Letters from Brook Farm, 1844–1847*, ed. Amy L. Reed (Poughkeepsie, N.Y.: Vassar College, 1928), pp. 12–13.

18. Marianne Dwight, letter, March 2, 1845, to Anna Parsons, ibid., p. 83.

19. Emerson, *Journals*, Vol. VI, p. 391.

20. Ibid.

21. Swift, *Brook Farm*, p. 192.

22. Edith R. Curtis, *A Season in Utopia: The Story of Brook Farm* (New York: Thomas Nelson and Sons, 1961), p. 64.

23. Sedgwick, "Girl of Sixteen," 402.

24. Georgianna Bruce, letter, undated, to Sarah Edes Allen, reprinted in Swift, *Brook Farm*, p. 80.

25. Ossoli, *Memoirs*, Vol. II, p. 76.

26. Stoddard, *Horace Greeley*, p. 103.

27. Elizabeth Peabody, "Fourierism," *The Dial*, IV (April 1844): 483.

28. "Constitution of the Brook Farm Association, for Industry and Education, West Roxbury, Massachusetts, with an Introductory Statement," reprinted in Sams, *Autobiography of Brook Farm*, p. 95.

29. Unpublished manuscript collection of A. J. Macdonald; microfilm 2116, Yale University Library, New Haven, Connecticut, p. 12.

30. Charles Dana, *Association in its Connection with Education and Religion* (Boston: Benjamin H. Greene, 1844), p. 26.

31. Sams, *Autobiography of Brook Farm*, p. 96.

32. John Finch, *The Communist*, II (April 1844), pamphlet in the Macdonald MSS, p. 18.

33. Sedgwick, "Girl of Sixteen," p. 398.

34. Swift, *Brook Farm*, p. 281.

35. Victor Francis Calverton, *Where Angels Dared to Tread* (Indianapolis: Bobbs-Merrill, 1941), p. 220.

36. Marianne Dwight, letter, March 9, 1845, to Anna Parsons, reprinted in *Letters from Brook Farm, 1844–1847*, pp. 86–87.

37. Marianne Dwight, letter, April 27, 1844, to Anna Parsons, ibid., pp. 13–14.

38. Swift, *Brook Farm*, pp. 66.

39. Marianne Dwight, letter, August 31, 1845, to Anna Parsons, reprinted in *Letters from Brook Farm, 1844–1847*, p. 116.

40. Charles Dana, letter, March 12, 1846, to John S. Dwight, quoted in Zoltan Haraszti, *The Idyll of Brook Farm* (Boston: Public Library, 1937), p. 31.

41. George Ripley, letter, March 19, 1846, to John S. Dwight, ibid., p. 38.

42. Swift, *Brook Farm*, p. 117.

43. Ibid., p. 161.

44. Sears, *Bronson Alcott's Fruitlands*, p. 11.

45. Bronson Alcott, *Journals of Bronson Alcott*, ed. Odell Shepard (Boston: Little, Brown and Co., 1938), p. 152.

46. Charles Lane and Bronson Alcott, "Bronson Alcott's Fruitlands," (1843), unidentified article reprinted in Henry Steele Commager, ed., *Era of Reform, 1830–1860* (Princeton, N.J.: D. Van Nostrand, 1960), p. 42.

47. Ibid.

48. Robert Carter, "The Newness," *The Pioneer*, I (November 1843): 3.

49. Charles Lane, "A Day with the Shakers," *The Dial*, IV (October 1843): 165–173.

50. Sears, *Bronson Alcott's Fruitlands*, pp. 44–45.

51. Lane is reported to have had an unhappy marriage, which may, in part, account for his aversion to the institution of marriage. Ernest Sutherland Bates, *American Faith: Its Religious, Political and Economic Foundations* (New York: W. W. Norton, 1940), p. 383. Calverton suggested that Lane may have also been a homosexual. Calverton, *Where Angels Dared to Tread*, p. 251.

52. Alcott, *Journals*, p. 157.

53. Louisa May Alcott, *Transcendental Wild Oats, A Chapter from an Unwritten Romance* (Boston: Houghton Mifflin, 1915), p. 171.

54. F. B. Sanborn, *Bronson Alcott at Alcott House, England, and Fruitlands, New England, 1842–1844* (Cedar Rapids, Iowa: Torch Press, 1908), pp. 66–67.

55. Charles Lane, letter, June 7, 1843, to Henry David Thoreau, quoted in Sears, *Bronson Alcott's Fruitlands*, p. 72.
56. Sanborn, *Bronson Alcott*, p. 65.
57. Alcott, *Journals*, p. 155.
58. Sanborn, *Bronson Alcott*, p. 65.
59. Ibid., p. 66.
60. Odell Shepard, *Pedlar's Progress: The Life of Bronson Alcott* (Boston: Little, Brown and Co., 1937), p. 389.
61. Ibid., p. 418.
62. Alcott, *Journals*, p. 158.
63. Ibid., p. 157.
64. Shepard, *Pedlar's Progress*, p. 389.
65. Lane, "Brook Farm," pp. 351–357.
66. Alcott, *Transcendental Wild Oats*, p. 168.

VII. Godly Communes and Saintly Families

1. John Humphrey Noyes, *History of American Socialisms* (Philadelphia: J. B. Lippincott, 1870), p. 123.
2. *The New York Daily Tribune*, July 16, 1853.
3. Adin Ballou, *History of the Hopedale Community from Its Inception to Its Virtual Submergence in the Hopedale Parish*, ed. W. S. Heywood (Lowell, Mass.: Thompson and Hill, 1897), p. 339.
4. Adin Ballou, *Concise Exposition of the Hopedale Community: Descriptive, Statistical, Historical and Constitutional* (1851), pamphlet in the unpublished manuscript collection of A. J. Macdonald; microfilm 2116, Yale University Library, New Haven, Connecticut, p. 64.
5. Ibid.
6. Bronson Alcott, *Journals of Bronson Alcott*, ed. Odell Shepard (Boston: Little, Brown and Co., 1938), p. 157.
7. "Constitution of the Practical Christian Republic," reprinted in Ballou, *History of the Hopedale Community*, p. 406.
8. Adin Ballou, "Community Affairs," *The Practical Christian*, I (June 11, 1842): 2.
9. Ballou, *History of the Hopedale Community*, p. 89.
10. Ibid., p. 106.
11. Ibid., p. 362.
12. Ibid., p. 247.
13. Ibid., p. 248.
14. Ibid., pp. 248–249.
15. Noyes, *History of American Socialisms*, p. 131.
16. Bertha M. Horack Shambaugh, *Amana: The Community of True Inspiration* (Iowa City, Iowa: State Historical Society, 1908), p. 132.
17. Richard T. Ely, "Amana: A Study of Religious Communism," *Harper's Monthly Magazine*, CV (October 1902): 668.
18. Nelson A. Crawford, "Communism Goes Broke in Iowa," *American Magazine*, CXLII (November 1946): 44.

19. Shambaugh, *Amana*, p. 155.

20. Charles Nordhoff, *The Communistic Societies of the United States, From Personal Visit and Observation* (New York: Hillary House, 1961), p. 59.

21. Ibid., p. 35.

22. Bertha M. Horack Shambaugh, "Amana Society," *Encyclopaedia of Religion and Ethics*, I, ed. James Hastings (New York: Scribners, 1924), p. 364.

23. M. L. Bach, "Amana—The Glory Has Departed," *Christian Century*, LII (August 28, 1935): 1084.

24. James 5:16.

25. Acts 2:44–45.

26. William Albert Allard, "The Hutterites, Plain People of the West," *National Geographic*, CXXXVIII (July 1970): 107.

27. Peter Riedemann, *Account of Our Religion, Doctrine and Faith, Given by Peter Riedemann of the Brothers Whom Men Call Hutterites*, trans. Kathleen E. Hasenberg (London: Hodder and Stroughton, 1950), p. 100.

28. Robert Friedmann, "Marriage, Hutterite Practice," *Mennonite Encyclopedia*, III, eds. Harold S. Bender and Henry Smith (Scottsdale, Pa.: Mennonite Publishing House, 1956), pp. 510–511.

29. Paul Kay Conkin, *Two Paths to Utopia, the Hutterites and the Llano Colony* (Lincoln: University of Nebraska Press, 1964), p. 89.

30. Robert J. Weil, *Culture and Mental Disorders: A Comparative Study of the Hutterites and Other Populations* (Glencoe, Ill.: Free Press, 1955), p. 143.

31. Allard, "The Hutterites," 117.

32. John E. Simon, "William Kiel and Communistic Colonies," *The Oregon Historical Quarterly*, XXXVI (Winter 1935): 147.

33. Robert J. Hendricks, *Bethel and Aurora, An Experiment in Communism as Practical Christianity with some Account of Past and Present Ventures in Collective Living* (New York: The Press of the Pioneers, 1933), p. 17.

34. Nordhoff, *Communistic Societies*, p. 394.

35. Victor Calverton, *Where Angels Dared to Tread* (Indianapolis: Bobbs-Merrill, 1941), p. 94.

36. Nordhoff, *Communistic Societies*, p. 314.

VIII. A Better Tomorrow

1. Etienne Cabet, *Voyage en Icarie* (Paris: Au Bureau du Populaire, 1848), p. 33.

2. Katherine Holland Brown, "Icarian Community," *Harper's Monthly Magazine*, CX (December 1904): 142.

3. M. Prevost, "Etienne Cabet," *Dictionnaire de Biographie Française*, Vol. VII (Paris: Letorizey, 1933): 763.

4. Unpublished manuscript collection of A. J. Macdonald; microfilm 2116, Yale University Library, New Haven, Connecticut, p. 187.

5. I. G. Miller, "The Icarian Community of Nauvoo, Illinois," Illinois State Historical Society *Transactions*, I (1906): 104.

6. William Alfred Hinds, *American Communities*, in *The American Experience* Series, ed. Henry Bamford Parkes (New York: Corinth Books, 1961), p. 73.

7. "Constitution of the Icarian Community," Macdonald MSS, p. 181.

8. Ibid., p. 153.

9. Etienne Cabet, *Colony or Republic of Icaria in the United States of America, Its History* (Nauvoo, Ill.: Icarian Printing Office, 1852), p. 26.

10. Ibid., p. 5.

11. Etienne Cabet, *Icarian Community: Conditions of Admission* (Nauvoo, Ill.: Icarian Printing Office, 1854), p. 7.

12. "Constitution of the Icarian Community," Macdonald MSS, p. 182.

13. Ibid., p. 153.

14. Ibid., p. 154.

15. Albert Shaw, "Cooperation in the Northwest," *History of Cooperation in the United States*, Vol. VI in *Johns Hopkins University Studies in Historical and Political Science*, ed. Herbert B. Adams (Baltimore: Johns Hopkins University Press, 1888), p. 356.

16. "The Constitution of the Northampton Association," Macdonald MSS, p. 71.

17. Ibid.

18. Bronson Alcott, *Journals of Bronson Alcott*, ed. Odell Shepard (Boston: Little, Brown and Co., 1938), p. 157.

19. Macdonald MSS, p. 70.

20. Ibid., p. 68.

21. John A. Collins, "Articles of Belief and Disbelief, and Creed," *The Skaneateles Columbian*, November 19, 1843.

22. Macdonald MSS, p. 112.

23. John Humphrey Noyes, *History of American Socialisms* (Philadelphia: J. B. Lippincott, 1870), p. 165.

24. Ibid., p. 167.

25. Ibid., p. 179.

26. Sarah Vanvelzer, "Recollections of Sarah Vanvelzer," quoted in Noyes, *History of American Socialisms*, p. 179.

27. Ibid., p. 180.

28. John Collins, *The Harbinger*, Vol. I, quoted in Whitney R. Cross, *The Burned-Over District: The Social and Intellectual History of Enthusiastic Religion in Western New York, 1800–1850* (Ithaca: Cornell University Press, 1950), p. 253.

29. Carl Wittke, *The Utopian Communist: A Biography of Wilhelm Weitling, Nineteenth-Century Reformer* (Baton Rouge: Louisiana State University Press, 1950), p. 247.

30. "The Constitution of Communia," Macdonald MSS, p. 422.

31. Wittke, *The Utopian Communist*, p. 248.

32. Ibid., p. 275.

33. Ibid., p. 273.

34. Francelia Butler, "The Ruskin Commonwealth: A Unique Experiment in Marxian Socialism," *The Tennessee Historical Quarterly*, XXIII (December 1964): 336. Earl Miller, a member of the Ruskin Community, later complained that the fee of $500 per family was unfair, since it was the same for a single person. He advocated that a more equitable arrangement would have been to charge $1,000 per husband and wife, and an additional amount for each child who was too young to do productive work. Earl Miller, "Recollections of the Ruskin Cooperative Association," ed. Charles H. Kegel, *The Tennessee Historical Quarterly*, XVII (March 1958): 51.

35. Butler, "The Ruskin Commonwealth," p. 338.

36. H. C. McDill, "Why Ruskin Colony Failed," *Gunton's Magazine*, XXII (May 1902): 441.

37. Miller, "Recollections," p. 57.

38. J. W. Braam, "Ruskin Cooperative Colony," *The American Journal of Sociology*, VIII (March 1903): 668.

39. Miller, "Recollections," p. 69.

40. Ralph Albertson, "The Christian Commonwealth," *The Social Gospel*, III (February 1898): 132.

41. Charles Howard Shinn, "Cooperation on the Pacific Coast," *History of Cooperation in the United States*, Vol. VI of *Johns Hopkins University Studies in Historical and Political Science*, ed. Herbert B. Adams (Baltimore: Johns Hopkins University Press, 1888), p. 464.

42. U.S. Congress, *Senate Reports*, 52nd Congress, 2nd Sess., Vol. I, No. 1248 (Washington: U.S. Govt. Printing Office, 1893), p. 70.

43. U.S. Congress, *Congressional Record*, 52nd Congress, 2nd Sess., Vol. XXIV, Part II (Washington: Govt. Printing Office, 1893), p. 1475.

44. Shinn, "Cooperation on the Pacific Coast," p. 472.

45. Ibid., p. 471.

IX. Celestial Marriage: An Experiment in Polygyny

1. The Blackfoot Indians of Utah practiced polygyny. Oscar Lewis, *The Effects of White Contact upon Blackfoot Culture with Special Reference to the Role of the Fur Trade*, Monograph 6 (Washington, D.C.: American Ethnological Society, 1942), pp. 38–40.

2. William Hepworth Dixon, *New America* (Philadelphia: J. B. Lippincott, 1867), p. 214.

3. T. D. Woolsey, *Communism and Socialism* (New York: Scribner's, 1880), p. 49.

4. Brigham Young, et. al., *Journal of Discourses*, Vol. XIII (Salt Lake City: Deseret Press, 1903), p. 3.

5. *The Book of Mormon*, Chapter 4 (Salt Lake City: C. J. C. L.-D. S., 1920), p. 144.

6. Alexander Campbell, "Sidney Rigdon," *The Millennial Harbinger*, II (February 7, 1831): 100.

7. Karl J. R. Arndt, "The Harmonists and the Mormons," *The American German Review*, X (June 1944): 6.

8. Hamilton Gardner, "Communism Among the Mormons," *Quarterly Journal of Economics*, XXXVII (November 1922): 139.

9. J. N. Beadle and O. J. Hollister, *Polygamy, or, The Mysteries and Crimes of Mormonism, being a Full Authentic History of this Strange Sect from its Origin to the Present Time, with a Thrilling Account of the Inner Life and Teachings of the Mormons and an Exposé of the Secret Rites and Ceremonies of the deluded Followers of Brigham Young* (Salt Lake City: National Publishers, 1884), p. 78.

10. Brigham Young, *Discourses of Brigham Young*, ed. John A. Widtsoe (Salt Lake City: Deseret Book Co., 1951), p. 288.

11. Amos Warner, "Cooperation among the Mormons," American Economic Association *Publications*, Vol. II, Number 1 (1888): 115–117.

12. *The Book of Mormon*, Jacob 2:23–28, p. 111.

13. Joseph Smith and Brigham Henry Roberts, *History of the Church of Jesus Christ of Latter-day Saints*, Vol. II (Salt Lake City: Deseret News, 1902), p. 247.

14. Ibid., Vol. I, pp. 569–570.

15. Joseph Smith, Jr., *The Doctrine and Covenants of the Church of Jesus Christ of Latter-day Saints, Containing the Revelations Given to Joseph Smith, Junior, the Prophet for the Building Up of the Kingdom of God in the Last Days* (Salt Lake City: Deseret Press, 1914), p. 469.

16. Smith and Roberts, *History of the Church*, Vol. V, pp. 36–37.

17. Fawn M. Brodie, *No Man Knows My History: The Life of Joseph Smith, the Mormon Prophet* (New York: Alfred A. Knopf, 1945), p. 311.

18. Smith and Roberts, *History of the Church*, Vol. V. pp. 18–19.

19. Smith, *The Doctrine and Covenants*, pp. 463–473.

20. Ibid., p. 474.

21. Dixon, *New America*, p. 225.

22. William Mulder and A. R. Mortensen, *Among the Mormons: Historic Accounts by Contemporary Observers* (New York: Alfred A. Knopf, 1958), pp. 118–119.

23. Smith and Roberts, *History of the Church*, Vol. II, p. 731.

24. Ibid., p. 733.

25. Robert B. Flanders, *Nauvoo: Kingdom on the Mississippi* (Urbana: University of Illinois Press, 1965), p. 276.

26. William Marks, *Zion's Harbinger and Baneemy's Organ*, XXX (July 1853): 52–53.

27. Wallace Stegner, *The Gathering of Zion: The Story of the Mormon Trail* (New York: McGraw-Hill, 1964), p. 26. When the text of Smith's revelation on polygyny was read before the High Council of the

Twelve Apostles, August 12, 1843, Austin Cowles and Leonard Soby joined Law in vigorously opposing it. The hierarchy of the Church was divided into polygynist and antipolygynist factions. Brodie, *No Man Knows My History*, p. 343.

28. Dixon, *New America*, p. 218.

29. Richard F. Burton, *The City of the Saints*, ed. Fawn M. Brodie (New York: Alfred A. Knopf, 1963), p. 493.

30. Ibid., p. 481.

31. *Journal of Discourses*, Vol. IV, p. 55.

32. Jules Remy and Julius Brenchley, *A Journey to Great-Salt-Lake-City*, Vol. II (London: W. Jeffs, 1861), p. 60.

33. Burton, *The City of the Saints*, p. 488.

34. *Journal of Discourses*, Vol. IV, p. 57.

35. Ibid.

36. Ibid., Vol. IX, p. 37.

37. Juanita Brooks, "A Close-up of Polygamy," *Harpers' Magazine*, CLXVIII (February 1934): 301.

38. Remy and Brenchley, *A Journey*, Vol. II, p. 202.

39. *The New York Times*, September 9, 1877.

40. Kimball Young, *Isn't One Wife Enough?* (New York: Henry Holt, 1954), p. 43.

41. Burton, *The City of the Saints*, p. 488.

42. Ibid., p. 487.

43. *The New York Daily Tribune*, September 3, 1859.

44. Benjamin Ferris, *Utah and the Mormons: The History, Government, Doctrines, Customs and Prospects of the Latter-day Saints from Personal Observation During a Six Months' Residence at Great Salt Lake City* (New York: Harper and Brothers, 1856), p. 249.

45. *Journal of Discourses*, Vol. V, p. 22.

46. *Deseret News*, September 14, 1852.

47. *The New York Tribune*, August 20, 1859.

48. Burton, *The City of the Saints*, p. 482.

49. Dixon, *New America*, p. 218.

50. Ibid., p. 217.

51. Joseph Smith, Jr., *Joseph Smith's Teachings: A Classified Arrangement of the Doctrinal Sermons and Writings of the Great Latter-day Prophet*, ed. Edwin F. Parry (Salt Lake City: Deseret News, 1912), p. 104.

52. *Journal of Discourses*, Vol. V, p. 90.

53. Ibid., Vol. XXX, p. 264.

54. Ibid., Vol. XV, p. 56.

55. Ibid.

56. Smith and Roberts, *History of the Church*, Vol. V, pp. 391–392.

57. Frances B. H. Stenhouse, *Tell It All: The Story of a Life's Experience in Mormonism* (Hartford, Conn.: Worthington, 1874), p. 298.

58. *Deseret News*, September 14, 1852.

59. James E. Talmage, *A Study of the Articles of Faith, Being a Consideration of the Principal Doctrines of the Church of Jesus Christ of Latter-day Saints* (Salt Lake City: C. J. C. L.–D. S., 1942), pp. 445–446.

60. William A. Linn, *The Story of the Mormons, from the Date of their Origin to the Year 1901* (New York: Macmillan, 1902), p. 587.

61. *The New York Tribune*, August 20, 1859.

62. Burton, *The City of the Saints*, p. 486.

63. Apostle Taylor accused Colonel Hooper, Utah's representative in the U. S. Congress, with being "only half a Mormon," because he had not consented to take additional wives. Dixon, *New America*, p. 203.

64. *The New York Tribune*, August 19, 1869.

65. Burton, *The City of the Saints*, p. 426.

66. *Journal of Discourses*, Vol. IV, p. 259.

67. Ibid., p. 260.

68. Sarah Comstock, "The Mormon Woman," *Colliers*, XLIV (October 2, 1909): 433.

69. Mulder and Mortensen, *Among the Mormons*, p. 385.

70. Ibid.

71. Dixon, *New America*, pp. 236–237.

72. Orson Pratt, *The Seer*, Vol. I, p. 41, quoted in Linn, *The Story of the Mormons*, p. 586.

73. Brooks, "A Close-up of Polygamy," 307.

74. Ibid.

75. Burton, *The City of the Saints*, p. 483.

76. Stenhouse, *Tell It All*, pp. 320–321.

77. *The New York Times*, May 29, 1857.

78. John D. Lee, *A Mormon Chronicle: The Diaries of John D. Lee, 1848–1876*, eds. Robert G. Cleland and Juanita Brooks (San Marino, Calif.: Huntington Library, 1955), pp. 75–76.

79. Dixon, *New America*, p. 201.

80. *Journal of Discourses*, Vol. XII, p. 97.

81. Stenhouse, *Tell It All*, p. 322.

82. *The New York Tribune*, May 15, 1860.

83. Ibid.

84. Remy and Brenchley, *A Journey*, Vol. II, p. 169.

85. Stanley Ivins, "Notes on Mormon Polygamy," *Western Humanities Review*, X (Summer 1956): 230, 233, 234.

86. Young, *Isn't One Wife Enough?*, p. 444.

87. Dixon, *New America*, p. 204.

88. Young, *Isn't One Wife Enough?*, p. 56.

89. *The New York Times*, May 1, 1858.

90. Ibid., April 17, 1860.

91. Ibid., May 19, 1856.

92. Dixon, *New America*, p. 216.

93. *The New York Times*, May 28, 1873.

94. *The New York Tribune*, January 3, 1859.

95. Lee, *A Mormon Chronicle*, Vol. I, p. 191.
96. Young, *Isn't One Wife Enough?*, p. 45.
97. Ibid.

X. No Cross, No Crown

1. J. N. Beadle and O. J. Hollister, *Polygamy, or, The Mysteries and Crimes of Mormonism, being a Full Authentic History of this Strange Sect from its Origin to the Present Time, with a Thrilling Account of the Inner Life and Teachings of the Mormons and an Exposé of the Secret Rites and Ceremonies of the Deluded Followers of Brigham Young* (Salt Lake City: National Publishers, 1884), p. 78.

2. Richard F. Burton, *The City of the Saints*, ed. Fawn M. Brodie (New York: Alfred A. Knopf, 1963), p. 482.

3. Kimball Young, *Isn't One Wife Enough?* (New York: Henry Holt, 1954), p. 45.

4. Beadle and Hollister, *Polygamy*, pp. 221–222.

5. Susan Young Gates, *The Life Story of Brigham Young* (New York: Macmillan, 1930), pp. 340–341. There is evidence that dissension arose in the Young household as he was once sued for divorce. In a sermon delivered September 21, 1856, he included his own wives among the "whiners" who were asked to reform or get out. He said, "I will go into heaven alone, rather than having scratching and fighting around me." Brigham Young, et. al., *Journal of Discourses*, Vol. IV (Salt Lake City: Deseret Press, 1903), p. 57.

6. Sylvester Mowery, letter, April 27, 1855, to Edward Bickness, reprinted in William Mulder and A. R. Mortensen, *Among the Mormons: Historic Accounts by Contemporary Observers* (New York: Alfred A. Knopf, 1958), p. 278.

7. Fawn M. Brodie, *No Man Knows My History: The Life of Joseph Smith the Mormon Prophet* (New York: Alfred A. Knopf, 1945), p. 447.

8. John M. Coyner, *Handbook on Mormonism* (Salt Lake City: Deseret Press, 1882), p. 37.

9. Benjamin Ferris, *Utah and the Mormons: The History, Government, Doctrines, Customs and Prospects of the Latter-day Saints from Personal Observation During a Six Month's Residence at Great Salt Lake City* (New York: Harper and Brothers, 1856), pp. 307–308.

10. Frances B. H. Stenhouse, *Tell It All: The Story of a Life's Experience in Mormonism* (Hartford, Conn.: A. D. Worthington, 1874), p. 262.

11. Juanita Brooks, "A Close-up of Polygamy," *Harper's Magazine*, CLXVIII (February, 1934): 302.

12. John D. Lee, *A Mormon Chronicle: The Diaries of John D. Lee, 1848–1876*, ed. Robert G. Cleland and Juanita Brooks, Vol. II (San Marino, Calif.: Huntington Library, 1955), p. 27.

13. Ferris, *Utah and the Mormons*, p. 249.

14. William Hepworth Dixon, *New America* (Philadelphia: J. B. Lippincott, 1867), p. 211.

15. Udney Hay Jacobs, *An Israelite, and a Shepherd of Israel, an Extract from a Manuscript Entitled The Peacemaker, or the Doctrine of the Millennium, being a Treatise on Religion and Jurisprudence, or a New System of Religion and Politics* (Nauvoo, Ill.: J. Smith, Printer, 1842), pp. 15–16.

16. Stanley Hirshon, *The Lion of the Lord: A Biography of Brigham Young* (New York: Alfred A. Knopf, 1969), p. 133.

17. *The New York Tribune*, August 20, 1859.

18. Joseph Smith, Jr., *The Doctrine and Covenants of the Church of Jesus Christ of Latter-day Saints, Containing the Revelations Given to Joseph Smith, Junior, the Prophet for the Building up of the Kingdom of God in the Last Days* (Salt Lake City: Deseret Press, 1914), p. 234.

19. Dixon, *New America*, p. 234.

20. Samuel L. Clemens, *Roughing It*, Vol. I (New York: Harpers, 1903) pp. 121–122.

21. Brigham Young, *Mormon Expositor*, Vol. I (1875), quoted in Morris Werner, *Brigham Young* (New York: Harcourt, Brace and Co., 1925), p. 314.

22. *Journal of Discourses*, Vol. XV, p. 39.

23. Ibid., Vol. XIX, p. 75.

24. Kimball believed the tight-fitting trousers worn by the men would cause their children to be impotent and imbecile. *Journal of Discourses*, Vol. VI, p. 191.

25. Mulder and Mortensen, *Among the Mormons*, pp. 121–122.

26. Ernest Sutherland Bates, *American Faith: Its Religious, Political and Economic Foundations* (New York: W. W. Norton, 1940), p. 358.

27. Howard Stansbury, *Exploration and Survey of the Valley of the Great Salt Lake Utah* (Philadelphia, 1852), quoted in Mulder and Mortensen, *Among the Mormons*, p. 248.

28. Brodie, *No Man Knows My History*, p. 399.

29. Zenos Gurley, William Marks, and William Blair, "Polygamy Contrary to the Revelations of God," *The True Latter-day Saints Herald*, I (January 1860): 8.

30. William Marks, "Opposition to Polygamy," ibid., p. 22.

31. Isaac Sheen, "The Mormons Again," ibid., p. 34.

32. David Whitmer, *An Address to all Believers in Christ by a Witness to the Divine Authenticity of the Book of Mormon* (Richmond, Mo.: Author, 1887), p. 41.

33. Beadle and Hollister, *Polygamy*, p. 500.

34. Werner, *Brigham Young*, p. 196.

35. Beadle and Hollister, *Polygamy*, p. 501.

36. Milo M. Quaife, *The Kingdom of Saint James: A Narrative of the Mormons* (New Haven, Conn.: Yale University Press, 1930), p. 238.

37. Ibid., p. 165.

38. Werner, *Brigham Young*, p. 198.
39. *The Northern Islander*, Vol. I, April 3, 1856.
40. *The Voree Herald*, September 1846.
41. Ibid., October 1847.
42. Ibid., August 1847.
43. Joseph Smith, Jr., and Brigham Henry Roberts, *History of the Church of Jesus Christ of Latter-day Saints*, Vol. IV (Salt Lake City: Deseret News, 1902–1959), p. 39.
44. O. W. Riegel, *Crown of Glory: The Life of James J. Strang, Moses of the Mormons* (New Haven, Conn.: Yale University Press, 1935), pp. 168–169.
45. Smith and Roberts, *The History of the Church*, Vol. IV, p. 39.
46. Russell B. Nye, *A Baker's Dozen* (East Lansing: Michigan State University Press, 1956), pp. 170–171.
47. Quaife, *The Kingdom of Saint James*, p. 183.
48. Werner, *Brigham Young*, p. 198.
49. Ferris, *Utah and the Mormons*, pp. 368–369.
50. *Deseret News*, September 14, 1852.
51. Letter written by Perry E. Brocchus, Associate Justice of the Supreme Court of the U. S. for the Utah Territory, September 20, 1851. U. S. Congress, *Congressional Globe*, 32nd Congress, 1st Sess., Appendix XXV (Washington: John C. Rives, 1852), p. 151.
52. Ulysses S. Grant, "Annual Message to the Congress of the United States" (December 4, 1871), *A Compilation of the Messages and Papers of the Presidents, 1789–1908*, Vol. VII, ed. James D. Richardson (Washington: Bureau of National Literature and Art, 1909), p. 151.
53. Rutherford B. Hayes, "Annual Message to the Congress of the United States" (December 2, 1879), ibid., p. 560.
54. Ibid. (December 6, 1880), p. 606.
55. James A. Garfield, "Inaugural Address" (March 1881), ibid., Vol. VIII, p. 11.
56. Chester A. Arthur, "Annual Message to the Congress of the United States" (December 1, 1884), ibid., p. 250.
57. Grover Cleveland, "Annual Message to the Congress of the United States" (December 8, 1885), ibid., p. 361.
58. Ibid. (December 3, 1888), p. 794.
59. Thomas O'Dea, *The Mormons* (Chicago: University of Chicago Press, 1957), p. 111.
60. *Reynolds vs U. S.*, cited in *Cases Argued and Decided in the Supreme Court of the United States*, October Term, 1878, Book 25, Lawyers' Edition (Rochester, N.Y.: Lawyers Co-operative Publishing Co., 1926), p. 250.
61. Smith, *Doctrine and Covenants*, pp. 493–494.
62. Austin and Alta Fife, *Saints of Sage and Saddle: Folklore Among the Mormons* (Bloomington: Indiana University Press, 1956), pp. 162–179.
63. Ibid., p. 171.

64. William Chandless, *A Visit to Salt Lake* (London: Smith, Elder, and Co., 1857), p. 191.

65. Burton, *The City of the Saints*, p. 479.

66. Coyner, *Handbook on Mormonism*, p. 40.

XI. Complex Marriage at Oneida

1. *The New York Herald*, January 9, 1848.

2. John Humphrey Noyes, *History of American Socialisms* (Philadelphia: J. B. Lippincott, 1870), p. 615.

3. Charles Nordhoff, *The Communistic Societies of the United States, From Personal Visit and Observation* (New York: Hillary House, 1961), p. 269.

4. Unpublished manuscript collection of A. J. Macdonald; microfilm 2116, Yale University Library, New Haven, Connecticut, p. 77.

5. Noyes, *History of American Socialisms*, p. 148.

6. Oneida Community, *Handbook of the Oneida Community* (Wallingford, Conn.: *Circular* Office, 1871), p. 29.

7. John Humphrey Noyes, *The Putney Community*, ed. G. W. Noyes (Oneida, N.Y.: Oneida Community, 1931), p. 193.

8. John Humphrey Noyes, *The Witness*, I (September 1839): 78.

9. Everett Webber, *Escape to Utopia: The Communal Movement in America*, in *The American Procession* series, ed. Henry G. Alsbert (New York: Hastings House, 1959), p. 379.

10. Erik Achorn, "Mary Cragin, Perfectionist Saint: Noyes' Theory and Experiments," *The New England Quarterly*, XXVIII (December 1955): 499.

11. R. A. Parker, *A Yankee Saint: John Humphrey Noyes and the Oneida Community* (New York: Putnam, 1935), p. 87.

12. William Alfred Hinds, *American Communities*, in *The American Experience* series, ed. H. B. Parkes (New York: Corinth Books, 1961), p. 127.

13. Noyes, *The Putney Community*, p. 201.

14. Ibid.

15. Parker, *A Yankee Saint*, p. 122.

16. Morris Bishop, "The Great Oneida Love-in," *American Heritage*, XX (February 1969): 86.

17. Noyes, *The Putney Community*, p. 122.

18. Bishop, "The Great Oneida Love-in," p. 87.

19. John B. Ellis, *Free Love and its Votaries; American Socialism Unmasked* (San Francisco: Bancroft, 1870), pp. 66–67.

20. John Humphrey Noyes, *The Witness*, I (November 1838): 26.

21. Macdonald MSS, p. 79.

22. *The Oneida Circular*, February 2, 1874.

23. Bishop, "The Great Oneida Love-in," p. 87.

24. Noyes, *The Putney Community*, p. 302.

25. Macdonald MSS, p. 93.

26. Nordhoff, *Communistic Societies*, p. 389.

27. John Humphrey Noyes, letter, March 27, 1881, to Mrs. Yoder, quoted in Maren Lockwood Carden, *Oneida: Utopian Community to Modern Corporation* (Baltimore: Johns Hopkins University Press, 1968), p. 26.

28. Oneida Community, *Handbook of the Oneida Community* (1871), p. 3.

29. Noyes, *History of American Socialisms*, pp. 630–631.

30. Stow Persons, "Christian Communitarianism in America," *Socialism and American Life*, Vol. I, eds. Donald D. Egbert and Stow Persons (Princeton: Princeton University Press, 1952), p. 145.

31. Aldous Huxley, *Tomorrow and Tomorrow and Tomorrow, and Other Essays* (New York: Harper and Brothers, 1952), p. 292.

32. Noyes, *The Putney Community*, pp. 17–18.

33. Bishop, "The Great Oneida Love-in," p. 90.

34. Ibid.

35. Noyes, *History of American Socialisms*, p. 633.

36. Oneida Association, *Bible Communism* (Oneida, N.Y.: *Circular* Office, 1853), p. 54.

37. Parker, *A Yankee Saint*, p. 183.

38. Noyes, *The Putney Community*, p. 120.

39. Bishop, "The Great Oneida Love-in," p. 88.

40. Noyes, *History of American Socialisms*, p. 625.

41. I Corinthians 7:29–31.

42. John 17:21.

43. Noyes, *History of American Socialisms*, p. 626.

44. Ibid., p. 627.

45. Ibid.

46. Colossians 2:14.

47. Noyes, *History of American Socialisms*, p. 628.

48. Ibid., p. 629.

49. Ibid., p. 630.

50. Ibid., p. 636.

51. Macdonald MSS, p. 82.

52. *The Oneida Circular*, February 2, 1874.

53. Nordhoff, *Communistic Societies*, pp. 300–301.

54. Noyes, *History of American Socialisms*, p. 640.

55. C. C. Church, "Communism in Marriage: Human Relationships at the Oneida Community," *The Nation*, CXIII (August 11, 1926): 125.

56. Before the adoption of the practice of having an intermediary to keep a record of requests for his services, the individuals themselves were asked to report all sexual relations between them. Dr. Ely Van de Warker found the records of sexual encounters valuable in his basic conclusions regarding complex marriage in 1877. Ely Van de Warker, "A Gynecological Study of the Oneida Community," *American Journal of Obstetrics and Diseases of Women and Children*, XVII (August 1884): 792.

57. Pierrepont Burt Noyes, *My Father's House, an Oneida Boyhood* (New York: Farrar and Rinehart, 1937), p. 131.

58. Worth Tuttle Hedden, "Communism in New York, 1848–1879," *The American Scholar*, XIV (Summer 1945): 287.

59. Allan Estlake, *The Oneida Community; a Record of an Attempt to Carry Out the Principles of Christian Unselfishness and Scientific Race Improvement* (London: George Redway, 1900), p. 46.

60. Maren Lockwood, "Experimental Utopia in America," *Daedalus*, XCIV (Spring 1965): 409.

61. Carden, *Oneida*, p. 70.

62. P. B. Noyes, *My Father's House*, p. 65.

63. Ibid., p. 66.

64. Nordhoff, *Communistic Societies*, p. 281.

65. Corinna Ackley Noyes, *The Days of My Youth* (Kenwood, N.Y.: Author, 1960), p. 73.

66. John Humphrey Noyes, *Home Talks by John Humphrey Noyes*, Vol. I, eds. Alfred Barron and George Miller (Oneida, N.Y.: Oneida Community, 1875), p. 96.

67. P. B. Noyes, *My Father's House*, p. 131.

68. Oneida "Record," October 29, 1863, quoted in Carden, *Oneida*, p. 59.

69. Van de Warker, "A Gynecological Study," p. 789.

70. P. B. Noyes, *My Father's House*, p. 39.

71. Hilda Herrick Noyes MSS, quoted in Carden, *Oneida*, p. 53.

72. Russell B. Nye, *A Baker's Dozen* (East Lansing: Michigan State University Press, 1956), p. 157.

73. William Hepworth Dixon, *New America* (Philadelphia: J. B. Lippincott, 1867), p. 423.

74. Macdonald MSS, p. 93.

75. Van de Warker, "A Gynecological Study," p. 795.

76. Havelock Ellis, *Sex in Relation to Society*, Vol. VI of *Studies in the Psychology of Sex* (Philadelphia: F. A. Davis, 1911), pp. 553–554.

XII. On To Perfection

1. John Humphrey Noyes, *Dixon and His Copyists* (Wallingford, Conn.: *Circular* Office, 1874), p. 34.

2. Genesis 38:8–9.

3. Aldous Huxley, *Tomorrow and Tomorrow and Tomorrow, and Other Essays* (New York: Harper and Brothers, 1952), p. 291.

4. John 17:21.

5. Stow Persons, "Christian Communitarianism in America," *Socialism and American Life*, Vol. I, eds. Donald D. Egbert and Stow Persons (Princeton: Princeton University Press, 1952), pp. 144–145.

6. John Humphrey Noyes, *History of American Socialisms* (Philadelphia: J. B. Lippincott, 1870), p. 631.

7. Genesis 3:16.

8. John Humphrey Noyes, *Male Continence* (Oneida: Oneida Community, 1872), p. 13.

9. Ibid.

10. Noyes, *Dixon and His Copyists*, p. 34.

11. Whitney R. Cross, *The Burned-Over District: The Social and Intellectual History of Enthusiastic Religion in Western New York, 1800–1850* (Ithaca, N.Y.: Cornell University Press, 1950), p. 340.

12. Noyes, *Male Continence*, p. 7.

13. Ibid., p. 10.

14. Ibid., p. 8.

15. Alfred C. Kinsey, Wardell Pomeroy, and Clyde Martin, *Sexual Behavior in the Human Male* (Philadelphia: W. B. Saunders, 1948), pp. 158–159.

16. Havelock Ellis, *Sex in Relation to Society*, Vol. VI of *Studies in the Psychology of Sex* (Philadelphia: F. A. Davis, 1911), p. 553.

17. Worth Tuttle Hedden, "Communism in New York, 1848–1879," *The American Scholar*, XIV (Summer 1945): 287–288.

18. Aldous Huxley, *Island* (New York: Harper, 1962), pp. 86–87.

19. Noyes, *History of American Socialisms*, p. 632.

20. William Alfred Hinds, *American Communities*, in *The American Experience* series, ed. H. B. Parkes (New York: Corinth Books, 1961), p. 134.

21. Unpublished manuscript collection of A. J. Macdonald; microfilm 2116, Yale University Library, New Haven, Connecticut, p. 96.

22. Ibid.

23. Harriett M. Worden, *Old Mansion House Memories* (Kenwood, N.Y.: Author, 1909), p. 15.

24. Allan Estlake, *The Oneida Community; a Record of an Attempt to Carry Out the Principles of Christian Unselfishness and Scientific Race Improvement* (London: George Redway, 1900), p. 68.

25. Oneida Association, *Mutual Criticism* (Oneida, N.Y.: Office of *The American Socialist*, 1876), pp. 53–54.

26. Charles Nordhoff, *The Communistic Societies of the United States, From Personal Visit and Observation* (New York: Hillary House, 1961), p. 292.

27. Manuscript Record of the Daily Events at the Oneida Community, from January 1, 1863, to September 15, 1864, quoted in Maren Lockwood Carden, *Oneida: Utopian Community to Modern Corporation* (Baltimore: Johns Hopkins University Press, 1968), p. 72.

28. John Humphrey Noyes, *Essay on Scientific Propagation*, quoted in Ellis, *Sex in Relation to Society*, Vol. VI, p. 619.

29. Stewart H. Holbrook, *Dreamers of the American Dream* (Garden City, N.Y.: Doubleday, 1957), p. 21.

30. Oneida Association, *Bible Communism* (Oneida, N.Y.: *Circular* Office, 1853), p. 17.

31. Ellis, *Sex in Relation to Society*, Vol. VI, p. 618.

32. Hilda Herrick Noyes and George Wallingford Noyes, "The

Oneida Community, Experiment in Stirpiculture," *Scientific Papers of the Second International Congress of Eugenics*, Vol. I, *Eugenics, Genetics and the Family* (Baltimore: Williams and Wilkins, 1923), p. 376.

33. Ibid.

34. John Humphrey Noyes, *Home Talks by John Humphrey Noyes*, Vol. I, eds. Alfred Barron and George Miller (Oneida, N.Y.: Oneida Community, 1875), p. 141.

35. Sidney Ditzion, *Marriage, Morals, and Sex in America: A History of Ideas* (New York: Thomas Nelson and Sons, 1961), p. 225.

36. Nordhoff, *Communistic Societies*, p. 276.

37. Noyes and Noyes, "The Oneida Community Experiment," p. 273.

38. P. B. Noyes, *My Father's House, an Oneida Boyhood* (New York: Farrar and Rinehart, 1937), p. 10.

39. Ibid.

40. William M. Kephart, "Experimental Family Organization: An Historico-Cultural Report on the Oneida Community," *Marriage and Family Living*, XXV (August 1963): 268.

41. Anita Newcomb McGee, "An Experiment in American Stirpiculture," *The American Anthropologist*, IV (October 1891): 324–325.

42. Russell B. Nye, *A Baker's Dozen* (East Lansing: Michigan State University Press, 1956), p. 157.

43. Hinds, *American Communities*, p. 132.

44. Ely Van de Warker, "A Gynecological Study of the Oneida Community," *American Journal of Obstetrics and Diseases of Women and Children*, XVII (August 1884): 795.

45. P. B. Noyes, *My Father's House*, p. 158.

46. T. D. Woolsey, *Communism and Socialism* (New York: Scribner's, 1880), p. 73.

47. P. B. Noyes, *My Father's House*, p. 164.

48. Ibid., p. 170.

49. R. A. Parker, *A Yankee Saint: John Humphrey Noyes and the Oneida Community* (New York: Putnam, 1935), p. 288.

50. Kephart, "Experimental Family Organization," p. 266.

51. Macdonald MSS, p. 97.

XIII. Unusual Sexual Practices, Fact and Rumor

1. *New Harmony Gazette*, January 30, 1828.

2. Frances Wright, letter, September 13, 1827, to Charles Wilkes, reprinted in William Randall Waterman, *Frances Wright*, Vol. CXV in *Studies in History, Economics and Public Law*, eds. the faculty of Political Science of Columbia University (New York: A. M. S. Press, 1967), pp. 118–119.

3. Frances Wright, *Views of Society and Manners in America*, ed. Paul Baker (Cambridge, Mass.: Belknap Press of the Harvard University Press, 1963), p. 69.

4. New Harmony *Free Enquirer*, April 29, 1829.

5. Karl J. R. Arndt, *George Rapp's Harmony Society, 1785–1847* (Philadelphia: University of Pennsylvania Press, 1965), p. 334.

6. Shields McIlwaine, *Memphis Down in Dixie* (New York: E. P. Dutton, 1948), p. 70.

7. *New Harmony Gazette*, February 21, 1827.

8. Unpublished manuscript collection of A. J. Macdonald; microfilm 2116, Yale University Library, New Haven, Connecticut, p. 635.

9. *New Harmony Gazette*, October 1, 1825.

10. Frances Trollope, *Domestic Manners of the Americans* (New York: Alfred A. Knopf, 1949), p. 29.

11. James Richardson, "Nashoba Book," *The Genius of Universal Emancipation*, July 28, 1827.

12. Ibid., August 18, 1827.

13. *New Harmony Gazette*, January 20, 1828.

14. *The Genius of Universal Emancipation*, July 28, 1827.

15. Ibid., August 18, 1827.

16. Ibid., September 1, 1827.

17. *New Harmony Gazette*, February 13, 1828.

18. Trollope, *Domestic Manners of the Americans*, p. 29.

19. Robert Dale Owen, *Threading My Way: Twenty-seven Years of Autobiography* (New York: G. W. Carleton, 1874), p. 272.

20. Book E, Register's Office of Shelby County, Tennessee, p. 228.

21. George B. Lockwood, *The New Harmony Movement* (New York: D. Appleton and Co., 1905), p. 247.

22. A. J. G. Perkins and Theresa Wolfson, *Frances Wright: Free Enquirer* (New York: Harper and Brothers, 1939), pp. 378–379.

23. "A Peep into Modern Times," Macdonald MSS, pp. 139–140.

24. *The New York Tribune*, April 4, 1853.

25. Adin Ballou, *History of the Hopedale Community from its Inception to its Virtual Submergence in the Hopedale Parish* (Lowell, Mass.: Thompson and Hill, 1897), p. 248.

26. "A Peep into Modern Times," Macdonald MSS, pp. 139–140.

27. Ballou, *History of the Hopedale Community*, p. 248.

28. "A Peep into Modern Times," Macdonald MSS, pp. 139–140.

29. *The New York Evening Post*, December 1, 1860.

30. Alexander Kent, "Cooperative Communities in the United States," U.S. Department of Labor *Bulletin*, VI (July 1901): 637.

31. Thomas Lake Harris, letter, August 22, 1877, to William A. Hinds, reprinted in William A. Hinds, *American Communities*, in *The American Experience* series, ed. Henry B. Parkes (New York: Corinth Books, 1961), p. 147.

32. Ibid.

33. Thomas Lake Harris, *First Book of the Christian Religion* (New York: New Church, 1858), p. 10.

34. Thomas Lake Harris, "The Annunciation of the Son of Mary," an unpublished manuscript, p. 71, quoted in Herbert W. Schneider and

George Lawton, *A Prophet and a Pilgrim: Being the Incredible History of Thomas Lake Harris and Laurence Oliphant; The Sexual Mysticism and Utopian Communities Amply Documented to Confound the Skeptic* (New York: Columbia University Press, 1942), p. 302.

35. Thomas Lake Harris, *The Golden Child*, Vol. IV (Fountain Grove, Calif., 1878), p. 14.

36. Thomas Lake Harris, *The Arcana of Christianity: An Unfolding of the Celestial Sense of the Divine Word Through Thomas Lake Harris*, Vol. I (New York: New Church, 1858), p. 193.

37. Ibid., p. 192.

38. Everett Webber, *Escape to Utopia: The Communal Movement in America*, in *The American Procession* series, ed. Henry G. Alsbert (New York: Hastings House Publishers, 1959), p. 327.

39. Thomas Lake Harris, *Star-Flowers*, Vol. III (Fountain Grove, Calif., 1879), p. 6, quoted in Robert V. Hine, *California's Utopian Colonies* (San Marino, Calif.: Huntington Library, 1953), p. 25.

40. Hannah Whitall Smith, *Religious Fanaticism, Extracts from the Papers of Hannah Whitall Smith*, ed. Ray Starchy (London, 1928), p. 229.

41. Thomas Lake Harris, letter, August 22, 1877, to William A. Hinds, reprinted in Hinds, *American Communities*, p. 142.

42. Rosamond Dale Owen, *My Perilous Life in Palestine* (London: Blackwood, 1928), p. 23.

43. Ibid., p. 250.

44. Schneider and Lawton, *A Pilgrim and a Prophet*, p. 180.

45. Webber, *Escape to Utopia*, p. 334.

46. John Humphrey Noyes, *History of American Socialisms* (Philadelphia: J. B. Lippincott, 1870), p. 593.

47. Information on the New Jerusalem community and Cyrus Spragg is limited as Spragg left nothing in writing. Louis Bromfield related the story in *The Strange Case of Miss Annie Spragg* (New York: Frederick A. Stokes Co., 1928). Bromfield does not give the sources of his material, other than to say that he had access to the writings of Amelia Bossert, who was once a member of the community. He claimed that she had three children by Spragg, and that one of them became a U.S. Senator from Nebraska. P. 61.

48. Ibid., p. 63.

49. Ibid., p. 64.

XIV. Women's Rights in Utopian Communities

1. Christina F. Knoedler, *The Harmony Society: A Nineteenth-Century American Utopia* (New York: Vantage Press, 1954), pp. 76–78.

2. Charles Edson Robinson, *A Concise History of the United Society of Believers Called Shakers* (East Canterbury, N.H.: United Society, 1893), p. 16.

3. Charles Nordhoff, *The Communistic Societies of the United States, From Personal Visit and Observation* (New York: Hillary House, 1961), p. 116.

4. Bertha M. Horack Shambaugh, *Amana: The Community of True Inspiration* (Iowa City: State Historical Society of Iowa, 1908), p. 176.

5. *The New York Tribune*, August 20, 1859.

6. *Deseret News*, Vol. VI, p. 291, quoted in William Alexander Linn, *The Story of the Mormons from the Date of their Origin to the Year 1901* (New York: Macmillan, 1902), p. 585.

7. John D. Lee, *A Mormon Chronicle: The Diaries of John D. Lee, 1848–1876*, eds. Robert Cleland and Juanita Brooks, Vol. I (San Marino, Calif.: Huntington Library, 1955), p. 7.

8. Brigham Young, et. al., *Journal of Discourses, 1854–1885*, ed. Joseph Geddes, Vol. IV (Liverpool: C. J. C. L.–D. S., 1854–1886), pp. 55–56.

9. Juanita Brooks, "A Close-up of Polygamy," *Harper's Magazine*, CLXVIII (February 1934): 299.

10. Frances B. H. Stenhouse, *Tell it All: The Story of a Life's Experience in Mormonism* (Hartford, Conn.: A. D. Worthington, 1874), p. 622.

11. Robert Owen, *The Evidences of Christianity: A Debate between Robert Owen, of New Lanark, Scotland, and Alexander Campbell, President of Bethany College, Virginia, Containing an Examination of the "Social System," and all the Systems of Skepticism of Ancient and Modern Times* (St. Louis: Christian Board of Publications, 1829), p. 124.

12. George M. Lockwood, *The New Harmony Communities* (Marion, Ind.: The Chronicle Co., 1902), p. 137.

13. Oliver H. Smith, *Early Indiana Trials and Sketches* (Cincinnati: Moore, Wilstach, Keys and Co., 1858), p. 371.

14. Ibid.

15. "Constitution of the State of Indiana," adopted in 1851, reprinted in Charles Kettleborough, *Constitution Making in Indiana: A Source Book of Constitutional Documents with Historical Introduction and Critical Notes, 1780–1851*, Vol. I (Indianapolis: Indiana Historical Commission, 1916), pp. 234–235.

16. Nicholas V. Riasanovsky, *The Teaching of Charles Fourier* (Berkeley: University of California Press, 1969), p. 208.

17. Ibid., p. 144.

18. Margaret Fuller, *Women in the Nineteenth Century, and Kindred Papers Relating to the Sphere, Conditions and Duties of Women* (Boston: Roberts, 1884), p. 36.

19. William Harlan Hale, *Horace Greeley: Voice of the People* (New York: Harper and Brothers, 1950), p. 101.

20. Glyndon Garlock Van Deusen, *Horace Greeley, Nineteenth-Century Crusader* (Philadelphia: University of Pennsylvania Press, 1953), p. 73.

21. Fredrika Bremer, *The Homes of the New World: Impressions of America* (New York: Harpers and Brothers, 1854), p. 616.

22. "Sylvania Constitution," Article 10, in the unpublished manuscript collection of A. J. Macdonald; microfilm 2116, Yale University Library, New Haven, Connecticut, p. 371.

23. Marianne Dwight, letter, August 30, 1844, to Anna Parsons, reprinted in *Letters from Brook Farm, 1844–1847*, ed. Amy L. Reed (Poughkeepsie, N.Y.: Vassar College, 1928), p. 32.

24. Etienne Cabet, *Colony of Republic of Icaria in the United States of America, Its History* (Nauvoo, Ill.: Icarian Printing Office, 1852), p. 13.

25. William Weitling, *Die Republik der Arbeiter*, August 28, 1852, quoted in Carl Wittke, *The Utopian Communist: A Biography of Wilhelm Weitling, Nineteenth Century Reformer* (Baton Rouge: Louisiana State University Press, 1950), p. 159.

26. Charles H. Shinn, "Cooperation on the Pacific Coast," *History of Cooperation in the United States, Vol. VI* in *Johns Hopkins University Studies in Historical and Political Science*, ed. Herbert B. Adams (Baltimore: Johns Hopkins University Press, 1888), p. 471.

27. *The New York Tribune*, April 4, 1853.

28. John Humphrey Noyes, *Home Talks by John Humphrey Noyes*, Vol. I, eds. Alfred Barron and George Noyes Miller (Oneida, N.Y.: Oneida Community, 1875), p. 205.

29. Nordhoff, *Communistic Societies*, p. 288.

30. William Alfred Hinds, *American Communities*, in *The American Experience* series, ed. Henry B. Parkes (New York: Corinth Books, 1961), p. 122.

31. Thomas Clinton Pears, *New Harmony: An Adventure in Happiness, Papers of Thomas and Sarah Pears* (Indianapolis: Indiana Historical Society, 1933), p. 84.

32. Macdonald MSS, p. 27.

33. Lindsay Swift, *Brook Farm, Its Members, Scholars and Visitors* (New York: Macmillan, 1900), p. 64.

34. John B. Ellis, *Free Love and its Votaries; American Socialism Unmasked* (San Francisco: Bancroft, 1870), p. 388.

35. William Hepworth Dixon, *New America* (Philadelphia: J. B. Lippincott, 1867), p. 391.

36. Nordhoff, *Communistic Societies*, p. 283.

37. Maren Lockwood Carden, *Oneida: Utopian Community to Modern Corporation* (Baltimore: Johns Hopkins University Press, 1968), p. 72.

Epilogue

1. Nathaniel Hawthorne, letter, May 25, 1842, to David Mack, reprinted in Manning Hawthorne, "Hawthorne and Utopian Socialism," *The New England Quarterly*, XII (October 1939): 730.

2. *The New York Tribune*, October 20, 1845.

3. Ralph Waldo Emerson, *Complete Works of Ralph Waldo Emer-*

son, ed. E. W. Emerson, Vol. X (Boston: Houghton Mifflin, 1904), p. 365.

4. Robert Dale Owen, *Threading My Way: Twenty-seven Years of Autobiography* (New York: G. W. Carleton, 1874), p. 286.

5. Ibid., p. 286.

6. Millard Rice, "Eighty-Nine Years of Collective Living," *Harpers' Monthly Magazine*, CLXXVI (October 1938): 526.

INDEX

Some other books published by Penguin
are described on the following pages.

BEYOND WORDS

The Story of Sensitivity Training and the Encounter Movement

Kurt W. Back

Kurt W. Back traces the sensitivity-encounter movement from its fortuitous beginnings through its growth across the country, its many new centers (especially in California), and its transformation into an all but religious exercise. He goes on to examine its conflicting goals of self-expression and of change and to show how these contradictions have affected it. Finally, *Beyond Words* assesses the movement's overall impact and its meaning as a symptom of the state of society. Kurt W. Back is Professor of Sociology and Psychiatry at Duke University.

THE SUBORDINATE SEX
A History of Attitudes toward Women

Vern L. Bullough,
with a final chapter by Bonnie Bullough

This is a candid survey of attitudes toward women, from the most remote periods to the present day. Ancient Egypt and ancient Greece, early Judaism and early Christianity, the Middle Ages and the Victorian era, as well as the concept of romantic love, the teachings of the prophet Muhammad, and the Hindu theory of female eroticism, are all considered. The authors' many sources range from ancient law codes to a modern study of ideas about women in Soviet fiction. "Taken all together, the evidence overwhelmingly supports Bonnie Bullough's contention that the 'historical barriers' to women's equality will be harder to overcome than any biological, political, or economic impediments. Fascinating and an excellent source book"—*Publishers Weekly*. Vern L. Bullough is Professor of History at California State University, Northridge.

WOMAN'S CONSCIOUSNESS, MAN'S WORLD

Sheila Rowbotham

Here is a new voice in the cause of women's liberation. In *Woman's Consciousness, Man's World*, Sheila Rowbotham traces the development of the new feminine consciousness and examines the social changes that lie behind it. She looks at the role of women within the capitalist state and shows how family life is threatened by existing social norms. For her, the cultural and economic liberation of women is inseparable from the creation of a new society totally free of subordination by sex, race, or class. Active in the socialist movement for ten years, Sheila Rowbotham is now teaching in the Workers' Education Association, in England.

SEX IN LATER LIFE

Ivor Felstein

To what age is sexual activity likely to continue? Can it or should it be prolonged indefinitely? How does the "change of life" affect sexual activity in the male as well as in the female? Do conventional ideas about youth and age inhibit married love among the elderly? Answering such questions in simple, nonmedical terms, Dr. Felstein provides facts, disperses nonsense, and offers practical suggestions. His humane and often entertaining discussion of sexual behavior in the light of today's longer average life can contribute greatly to human enlightenment and happiness.

HUMAN SEXUALITY AND THE MENTALLY RETARDED

Edited by Felix F. de la Cruz and Gerald D. LaVeck

Experts in medicine, law, education, social work, and other fields explore the sexuality of the mentally retarded. The topics covered in this book include the physical and psychological factors in retardates' sexual activity, the role of sex education, the effects of institutionalization on sexuality, and the arguments over contraception, sterilization, marriage, and parenthood. Difficult questions regarding the rights of the retarded are also considered as well as how retardates will be affected by society's evolving sexual concepts. Felix F. de la Cruz is Special Assistant for Pediatrics in the Mental Retardation Program of the National Institute of Child Health and Human Development. Gerald D. LaVeck is Visiting Professor in the School of Public Health and Community Medicine at the University of Washington.